Young Children's Personal, Social and Emotional Development

Second Edition

Marion Dowling was involved in the pre-school playgroup movement and was headteacher of a state nursery school. She was an educational adviser and a member of Her Majesty's Inspectorate, and now works as a trainer and consultant in the UK and overseas.

Marion is an experienced author and is President of Early Education, a national charity.

Young Children's Personal, Social and Emotional Development

SECOND EDITION

MARION DOWLING

London: Paul Chapman, 2005   1412906911

P·C·P
Paul Chapman
Publishing

© Marion Dowling 2005

First published 2000 by Paul Chapman Publishing
Second Edition published in 2005 by Paul Chapman Publishing

Reprinted 2006, 2007

Paul Chapman Publishing
A SAGE Publications Company
1 Oliver's Yard
55 City Road
London EC1Y 1SP

SAGE Publications Inc
2455 Teller Road
Thousand Oaks, California 91320

SAGE Publications India Pvt Ltd
B-42, Panchsheel Enclave
Post Box 4109
New Delhi 110 017

Library of Congress Control Number: 2004116715

A catalogue record for this book is available from the British Library

ISBN: 978-1-4129-0691-3 (pbk)
ISBN: 978-0-4129-0690-6 (hbk)

Typeset by Dorwyn Ltd, Wells, Somerset
Printed in Great Britain by Athenaeum Press, Gateshead, Tyne and Wear

Contents

Foreword by Lillian Katz

In the five years since the publication of the first edition of this very welcome book, the importance of getting children's personal, social and emotional development off to the right start has been even further supported by long-term follow-up research (1). However, alongside this growing awareness for the importance of these aspects of development, a clear trend has emerged in both our countries to emphasise academic instruction and early formal testing of its effects. While there is general agreement that all of our children should acquire basic literacy and numeracy skills, the assumption that 'the earlier the better' is not supported by a body of evidence. On the contrary, as Marion Dowling reminds us so well, when we consider the potential anguish and frustration pre-school-age children can feel when subjected to premature formal instruction we are wise to provide, instead, rich intellectual engagement and to capitalise on opportunities to support children's personal and socio-emotional development as they arise during such experiences.

The now well established term Foundation Stage, characterising the beginning years of education, invites exploration of the analogy from which it derives. We can explore the many educational challenges during the early years in much the same way that architects, engineers, and builders approach the work of constructing the foundation of a building. At the outset, three basic principles must be applied to the design of a building's foundation. The first is to *take into account comprehensive information concerning the nature of the soil* the building will be resting upon; for example, the structure would have to be designed differently depending on whether the soil is rocky, or muddy or sandy. All available detailed information about the soil must be carefully considered during the design process. In a similar way, as we can see in her case studies, Dowling encourages teachers and others who work with young children to observe each child closely, thereby gathering as much information as possible about the kinds of experiences that each child in the group has or has not already had, and what each child has or has not already learned. A teacher uses this information as a basis for deciding which experiences to offer them next. In order to do this effectively, the teacher gives time and effort not just to knowing *about* each child, but also to *knowing* each child. Dowling provides many practical suggestions teachers can use to follow up on her observations and the insights they provide.

The second principle of foundation design *is to focus on the characteristics of the structure* that is to be placed on the soil. Thus information about the building's attributes such as its height, area, horizontal expanse and so forth, are taken into account by designers. Similarly, teachers and others who work with young children plan experiences for them in terms of their broad aims and goals as well as their more immediate specific objectives. A good foundation in the early years, then, takes into account all domains of development: social, emotional, cognitive, dispositional, physical, aesthetic, cultural and other fundamental aspects of growth, development and learning; it is not simply limited to learning letters of the alphabet and to the mastery of a few discrete skills practised on worksheets. Rather, the experiences we plan for the children are based on how they can be expected to contribute to a foundation for future learning, based on the best available knowledge of the relationships between early experience and mature functioning. Dowling's choice of topics and practical suggestions reflect a comprehensive view of the ultimate desired structure, that is, the long-term goals of early education and how best to address them early on.

Finally, in the design of buildings, the third basic principle is to *anticipate the possible stresses* the structure is likely to be subjected to in the future (e.g. hurricanes, earthquakes, floods, etc.). In a similar way, parents and teachers are urged to strive to lay foundations that can support the long-term goals explored in this book. All Dowling's chapter topics address the important personal, social and emotional capacities that will support the fully grown persons as they ultimately cope with the kinds of complex societies in which they are likely to be living as adults.

Parents and educators might also keep in mind what builders know only too well: if the foundations of a building are not properly laid at the outset, it can be difficult and expensive to repair later on; indeed, some kinds of early errors may even be the cause of significant injuries in the future.

As in the first edition of this important book, Dowling takes up all the main issues confronting those who work with young children in a wide variety of settings. The explanations, case studies and suggestions provide an invaluable resource for all of us who aim to build solid foundations right from the start.

REFERENCE
■

1. See for example Zins, J.E., Weissberg, R.P., Wang, M.C. and Walberg, H.H. (2004) *Building Academic Success on Social and Emotional Learning*. New York: Teachers College Press.

Preface

Those of us working in the world of early childhood sometimes get so immersed in it that we neglect to look at what happens beyond.

My oldest grandchild Chloe who was two and a half when I started the first edition of this book is now seven. Her early years experiences are in the past in terms of time but the legacy remains. Early independence fostered so well initially now emerges in clear decision-making, ability to make choices in daily life and certainly an aptitude to pursue and argue her case! The early love of fantasy play has developed into a passion for dancing and drama. Friendship skills learnt early in life have strengthened and she enjoys, and is at ease with, a wide social circle. Volatile and sometimes hasty behaviour is tempered by sensitive intuition to the responses of others. Now emerging into middle childhood, Chloe's strong personality and confidence have remained intact. It is early days but she already appears to be a going concern, growing up in an ever changing and challenging world.

Whatever our views on the nature/nurture debate, Chloe's personality must be at least partly attributed to her early experiences at home and in her nursery as it has to others like her. Parents and early years practitioners have the privilege and responsibility of helping to shape the lives of young children. This book calls attention to the need to respect all that makes each child a unique person and to nurture the positive aspects of their personal development.

This is not to suggest that this is the only task in early years work; clearly there is a need to scaffold children's learning and progress in all areas. But first things first. Sir Christopher Ball stressed in the influential Start Right report that 'the art of learning is concerned with the "super skills and attitudes" of learning, of which motivation, socialisation and confidence are the most important. These are the fruits of early learning' (1). If we take this message seriously, attention to young children's personal, social and emotional development becomes the priority.

Some of this book remains the same with updated references. I have also included new chapters on young children's behaviour, their spiritual development and learning outside. Once again I am tremendously grateful to all the staff and children with whom I have been fortunate enough to work and who have provided the material for the pen portraits included. For the sake of simplicity I use the following general terms and phrases

- Parent is used for any person who assumes parental responsibility for a child. The term can apply to birth parents or other relatives, foster or adoptive parent, childminders or other carers who are deemed responsible for the child.

- Setting/early years setting is used to cover any provision that offers education and care for children and support for parents.

- Practitioner/early year's practitioner/staff are used as general terms to cover any person who works in an early years setting. Occasionally when referring to a particular circumstance, I specify a particular professional.

However, in using these umbrella terms to describe the provision and the staff, I do not wish to boil everything down to a common denominator. There continue to be massive differences in early years provision and across the country children and their families still receive very dissimilar services. Moreover, it is not helpful to pretend that by calling everyone and everything by the same name this makes them the same. Nevertheless, the messages in this book are intended for all who work with children in their earliest years; indeed, most of the messages can apply to those who work with other age groups. Some readers will be experienced and highly qualified, others just starting out on their careers and training. I firmly believe that, whatever the stage of their professional development, successful practitioners need to understand what lies behind young children's behaviour and be equipped to help them to grow into worthwhile people.

Once again my thanks to all the numerous friends and colleagues who encouraged me to complete this second edition. I particularly appreciate the generosity of Lillian Katz in writing the Foreword. A special thank you to Charlotte for sharing her reception class with me and to Barry for his constant patience and support.

REFERENCE

1. Ball, C. (1994) *Start Right: The Importance of Early Learning*. London: RSE, para 2.17.

Acknowledgements

The author and publishers would like to thank the following for permission to reproduce items in this book:

Chloe Dowling for the illustration on the front cover.

Anne Knight for the extract taken from Knight, A. (1992) Starting school – a painful process, in *T.A.L.K The Journal of the National Oracy Project*, No. 5, Autumn '92, pp. 3–5; Bridgwater College Early Excellence Centre for photographs of their Forest School on p. 159.

Stay and Play Session, Sure Start Links 4, Links 4 Children's Centre, Huddersfield, for the photograph on p. 64.

Introduction: The Significance of Young Children's Personal, Social and Emotional Development

Since I wrote the first edition to this book, young children and their families continue to be at the top of the political agenda and new initiatives are both multiple and far-reaching. In this introduction, some of the major developments will be examined briefly in so far that they impinge on children's personal development.

One big concern confronting the government is the welfare and safety of young children. Lord Laming's report on the tragic death of eight-year-old Victoria Climbié prompted the Green Paper *Every Child Matters* (1) and, subsequently, the Children Bill (2). These two documents are impressive in principle: they place young children and their families at the heart of policy; different agencies will be required to work together to ensure a fully co-ordinated and swift approach to dealing with concerns; and the proposed appointment of a Children's Commissioner signals a single person to overview issues of child abuse.

Moves to further reduce the divide between care and education and to strengthen joint working were marked in 2003 by the first ever appointment of a Minister for Children and giving responsibility for services to young children to the newly branded Sure Start Unit in the Department for Education and Skills (DfES). These developments are intended to bring children's Services under one umbrella and so secure a more holistic approach to children's issues.

Ten years ago childcare barely featured on the government's agenda; now it is at the centre of scrutiny by the Treasury. There continues to be substantial financial investment in early years. Spending on under-fives increased overall from £2 billion in 1997–98 to £3.6 billion in 2002–03. These monies have been spent in support of the national Childcare Strategy and a number of other government initiatives designed to increase the accessibility, affordability and quality of childcare and early education (3).

The amount of early years provision has increased dramatically across the country and provision is varied. At present there are 524 Sure Start local programmes for nought to three-year-olds, 1,139 Neighbourhood nurseries, 107 early excellence centres and 67 children's centres in place (4).

The Foundation Stage of education introduced in 2000 importantly established the nursery years (three to five) as a discrete and important stage of education. The status of the phase, slow to be accepted in some schools, was crystallised when, two years later, the Foundation Stage was made statutory and a part of the National Curriculum (5). The significance of the Foundation Stage is also acknowledged in the new proposals for primary schools by the appointment of the first National Director and a team of regional directors for the Foundation Stage. Initial misgivings about the Early Learning Goals implying hard-edged outcomes for young children have now been laid to rest, and most reception teachers and assistants are now beginning to feel that they are supported in providing a play-based and active curriculum. One very helpful and necessary message now emphasised to practitioners in reception classes is that the edicts that came from the Primary Literacy and Numeracy Strategies are now superseded by the Foundation Stage Guidance.

Early years practitioners now have national guidance to steer their practice. The two National Frameworks, *Curriculum Guidance for the Foundation Stage* and *Birth to Three Matters* provide signposts in the stages of development for babies and young children and pointers for helping them to flourish and progress (6, 7). Both documents place as a priority personal, social and emotional development. In *Birth to Three Matters* this development is woven into each of the four aspects which highlight the skill and competence of babies and toddlers. The Foundation Stage Framework intentionally places personal, social and emotional development as the first of the six areas of learning.

There have, and continue to be improvements to the quality of what is available both at local authority level and centrally. Early Years Partnerships and local authorities have introduced quality assurance schemes which are monitored. The national regulation of provision undertaken by the Office for Standards in Education (OfSTED) inspects private and voluntary early years settings against National Minimal Standards. Proposals have been put forward to change the approach to inspection as from April 2005; judgements will show how the National Standards are linked to outcomes for children, and the new framework will integrate more closely care and education of young children There are also proposals to inspect settings giving little or no notice (8).

This impressive range of developments should be fully and warmly acknowledged. The government has shown unprecedented commitment to invest in children's services and this has produced some very good outcomes for young families. Nevertheless there is no room for complacency. The investment is not enough, the new initiatives are often not well thought out and, indeed, those same early years workers who recognise the benefits of government intervention share concern that some of the developments have worrying consequences for the personal development of young children.

The proposals in *Every Child Matters* and subsequently in the government's ten-year strategy are unquestionably exciting but hugely ambitious. Although one cannot argue with the intentions, translating them into effective practice is another matter. The implementation of co-ordinated practice is still far off in many local authorities; it will require both new structures in local authorities and extensive training for a shift to take place and professionals at all levels to share a common perspective. The good news of the appointment of a Children's Commissioner is tempered by the reality of the post carrying restricted powers; the person appointed cannot investigate individual cases of child abuse and has no power to take or support legal action on children's behalf. An important amendment to the Children's Bill to abolish smacking was rejected outright in a three-hour debate by the House of Lords who voted to allow parents to only be permitted to 'moderately' smack their children (9). This decision clearly raises the question of what 'moderate' smacking involves and how this can be clarified. The decision is also in contrast to what happens in other European countries. For example, in Sweden, Finland, Denmark, Norway, Austria, Cyprus, Croatia and Latvia any physical assault on a child is expressly forbidden; the decision is based on affording children the same rights as adults (10). The refusal of the Lords to go down this road only contributes to the larger query about whether recent measures proposed by the government are sufficiently strong to protect children.

The additional financial resources made available by the government has enabled a great deal to happen but also caused much frustration. A classic example is the development of early excellence centres, many of which have received considerable capital and revenue funding in recent years. The investment has paid off. In these centres, as in other good quality early years establishments, confident practitioners interpret the areas of learning in a creative way and children are being helped to progress towards the goals through a well planned, imaginative and play-based curriculum. The Office for Standards in Education praised the quality of early excellence centres in their evaluation of 23 centres and two early years networks. Children's personal, social and emotional development was reported to be particularly well fostered. Chief Inspector, David Bell, described the centres as 'ahead of the game' when it comes to providing services in some of the poorest areas of the country (11). But, this quality has been achieved at a cost. The diverse and short-term grants made available through a huge range of different funding streams have only been accessed as a result of detailed and repetitive applications. This has required a tremendous amount of time on the part of local officials and heads of centres. The limited time span of the grants has also meant that many staff appointments have had to be temporary, which is a stress on the workforce. Accountability is essential, particularly where public money is used on new initiatives; however, although staff recognised the need to be accountable, evaluation frameworks were cumbersome and sometimes confusing. These constraints understandably sometimes etched away the energy of senior staff in their central work of caring for staff and children and parents in the centres.

Great play is made of the financial support given to allow free nursery placements to all three and four-year-olds but this support is only for two and a half hours, five sessions a week during term time. Where early years settings charge fees that exceed the grant, parents are faced with paying the excess.

The increase in provision is evident with a net growth of 325,000 places by 2003. But the Public Accounts Committee found that provision was patchy; there are still many parents who cannot get or afford pre-school places for their children, particularly in London and in pockets of deprivation that fall outside those areas which are targeted by the DfES (12).

Although the Foundation Stage of education is now more secure, it is still very new. Initial national training for practitioners on the Foundation Stage was very limited, based on one day of training for the trainers and reliant on a cascade model of training to reach a hugely diverse group of practitioners ranging from well qualified and experienced early years teachers to childminders (13). This minimal and inadequate support was in stark contrast to the massive investment in training and guidance offered to schools for the Literacy and Numeracy Strategies which often permeated to nursery and reception classes. Little wonder then that, without the good support of early years officers and senior managers, reception and nursery teachers felt unsure about their practice. The culture of a top-down curriculum for young children is slow to change and the promised refocusing of practice which builds on the Foundation Stage has not had sufficient impact as yet. Anecdotal evidence from school practitioners shows that there are still primary headteachers, literacy and numeracy co-ordinators and governors who are not familiar with the requirements of the Curriculum Guidance for the

Foundation Stage and who consequently are not able to support those staff who are implementing it. Some reception teachers are still not empowered to organise sensitive transition procedures to school, still have inadequate outside provision and feel under pressure from senior staff to use inappropriate teaching methods and to ensure that young children demonstrate reading and writing skills as soon as possible. These restrictions and dictates go against all that early years staff know to be right for children's well-being.

The quality of provision remains a concern across the range of settings. Both the Qualifications and Curriculum Authority (QCA) *Curriculum Guidance for the Foundation Stage* and *Birth to Three Matters* require substantial reading. Despite opportunities for training, for those working in full-time daycare there is little opportunity to come to grips with the important messages in the frameworks and really understand how they can be applied in practice. Despite the considerable progress made in all the different provisions, there remain huge gaps between the excellent practice which nurtures young children and poor practice where they suffer. A recent BBC television programme on standards in daycare provided stark examples of the latter. Hidden cameras were used to film staff mistreating toddlers, poor and inadequate hygiene and under-staffing at three private nurseries, in Stoke-on-Trent, Greater Manchester and Teddington, West London. An undercover reporter spent four months working in the nurseries and found under-qualified and overworked staff. All the nurseries had previously passed OfSTED inspections. As a result of screening the programme, four members of staff were dismissed (14). Shortly after this, OfSTED's annual early years report revealed that the provision observed in these three nurseries is not exceptional. Although the majority of 6,250 reported concerns about daycare providers and nurseries were deemed to be minor, 1,100 of the complaints dealt with during 2003–04 had a child protection element (15). The BBC programme showed only too clearly that quality placements for children is closely linked to the quality of the staff employed to work with children. Too often private providers of childcare, working on tight budgets and to required staffing ratios, employ the cheapest staff possible – young, inexperienced staff who have few other options and often have little interest in pursuing a career with young children. These young adults often do not have the skills to relate or model desirable behaviour to impressionable children. Moreover fatigue and poor wages lead to staff feeling unsupported and undervalued; in these circumstances they have little to offer young children.

Apart from the concerns about poor practice, it is important to recognise that the National Standards used by OfSTED inspectors only set down a minimum requirement for settings; a judgement of satisfactory, therefore, which indicates that these standards are only just achieved, should surely not be regarded as sufficient to fully meet the needs of our youngest children. Mediocrity is not good enough.

At the other end of the quality spectrum there is the worrying demise of nursery schools in some local authorities. Findings from the major longitudinal EPPE study make clear that the best quality of pre-school provision was observed in nursery schools and integrated centres (16). This is not surprising, as the provision is costly and staffed by expert early years practitioners. However, while many nursery schools are rightly expanding into children's centres, over the last three years around forty schools have closed in the interests of rationalisation and economy and this number is increasing. This is a short-sighted measure given the need to protect what early years expertise and quality provision we have in order to offer a model to others.

In fairness to the government, it openly recognises some of the limitations in current policies and appears determined to continue to maintain and indeed increase its programme for children's services. Government targets for the next five years and forthcoming plans for a ten-year strategy are extremely ambitious, with a strong emphasis on more accessible and affordable provision for parents. At a National Policy Conference in September 2004, the Education Secretary spoke of his intention to provide a 'wrap around' childcare package for children under five in children's centres. By March 2008, 2,500 children's centres will provide wrap around care from 8 a.m. to 6 p.m. for forty-eight weeks of the year for all under-fives in the 30 per cent of the most deprived wards in England; ultimately the aim is for this to be made available to every community across the country (17). We know, that there are schools and children's centres which already successfully provide this service in needy areas; it is another matter for the government to make it the norm. Undoubtedly such comprehensive provision is helpful in encouraging mothers into work which, the government has recognised, is the best way of reducing child poverty. The question remains though whether such long hours in group care are right for three- and four-year-olds.

Certainly the social gains of some hours of early education and care for three and four year olds are well documented in research notably in the EPPE study (18). By contrast, research studies now demonstrate that group care is not so beneficial for the social development of babies up to two years of age. Penelope Leach, co-director of the largest ever UK study of childcare from birth to school age, Families, Children and Child Care (FCCC) states that initial findings from her research fit in with messages from other projects. 'It is fairly clear from data from different parts of the world that the less time children spend in group care before three years the better.' Leach suggests that even twelve hours in a day nursery on a weekly basis had negative outcomes for these youngest children. They 'showed slightly lower levels of social development and emotional regulation (less enthusiastic co-operation, concentration, social engagement and initiative as toddlers)' (19). *Birth to Three Matters* emphasises the huge importance of this age group needing to establish a secure attachment with one adult (20). Leach agrees with this and points out that it is easier for infants to catch up on cognitive skills later on, but they cannot catch up on insecure attachment (21).

Despite these findings (of which many parents will not be aware) daycare for very young children continues to be very well used and has increased tremendously. In the last ten years private nursery places have quadrupled. Of course there are examples of good practice which employ a high ratio of well-trained staff – these are in the minority and too often they are reserved for wealthy parents. What are the alternatives? Respected experts such as Penelope Leach and Professor Ted Melhuish suggest that rather than group care, childminders are likely to be more responsive to babies and toddlers. The main message that emerges is the government must invest more in care and education, particularly for the under-twos. Melhuish suggests that the cost of subsidising high-quality childcare for this age group will be as costly as offering generous parental leave. It appears that the government is listening as the Education Secretary has hinted that the five-year plan includes a commitment to allow parents more opportunities to stay at home with their children from birth to two years if they wish to (22). However the government has also promised to provide nursery education to 12,000 two-year-olds to operate in 500 areas (23). In the light of research it will be interesting to see how well this provision is tailored to the needs of the age group. At present Britain spends only 0.3 per cent of gross domestic product on childcare, as compared with Sweden which spends 2 per cent. These figures sit uncomfortably aside the Secretary of State's recent passionate statement. 'Children are our most precious asset. How we nurture, care and support them in their early years is a fundamental test of whether a society values individuals and believes in opportunity for all' (24).

Against this background early years practitioners continue their work. In the following chapters the adult is seen as the key to helping children develop sound qualities and attitudes. Regardless of background, the early years practitioner stands as a model for the child. Leo Tolstoy describes this very powerfully in his account of the experimental primary school he set up on his estate:

> If we come to understand that we can educate others only through ourselves, the question of education is made void, and only the question of life is left. 'How must I live myself?' I do not know a single act in the education of children which is not included in the education of oneself (25).

A headteacher of a nursery school once told me that the main aim in her school was to 'help to get the person right'. I agree with her wholeheartedly. People might think differently as to what constitutes 'getting right' – however, most of us would agree with the idea of an 'adequate person'. We all appreciate and admire people who have good interpersonal skills, live their lives by a clear moral code, and are able to show their own feelings and have empathy with the feelings of others. These individuals are usually confident when they take decisions in life and are brave in facing up to difficult situations; they are enthusiastic and show sticking power in seeing things through both at work and in their personal lives. Regardless of their intellectual abilities, these individuals appear equipped both to get the most out of life and to deal with problems. These are rough and ready definitions of 'adequacy' but it is surely these qualities that we want to encourage and promote in our young children. The type of person we become colours all else we do in life.

There is clearly ground for optimism. In this country there is now a strong and established political searchlight on children aged under five. What is more, there is a pervasive acknowledgement from research, which is being carried into practice, that we are educating and caring for more than a child's intellect. If early years settings foster children's personal, social and emotional qualities they are surely opening doors for them to live a life of personal fulfilment whatever their other achievements. However, it is unrealistic and unfair to place this requirement on settings alone. Society as a whole must take ultimate responsibility for children's personal development. When we see examples of child exploitation and abuse, and some of the negative models of adult behaviour to which they are exposed personally and through the media, it is difficult to see that this responsibility is being regarded. In the conclusion to her book *Children First*, Penelope Leach argues powerfully for every one of us to face up to the fact that the responsibility is ours:

> Neither 'society' nor 'social attitudes' can ultimately let individuals off their own moral obligations, because there is no society that is separate from us. The whole complicated, conservative, consumerist collective is nothing but the children we were, the children we have had, the children we have now and those they will have in the future. The people who work, care and are cared for are the same people. There is nobody else to turn the social tide (26).

REFERENCES

1. HM Treasury (2003) *Every Child Matters*. London: The Stationery Office.
2. DfES (2004) *The Children Bill*. http://www.publications.parliament
3. Leigh, E. MP (2004) *Report to the House of Commons on the Thirty-Fifth Report of the Public Accounts Committee: Early Years: Progress in Developing High Quality Childcare and Early Education Accessible to All*. House of Commons, 7 September.
4. DfES (2004) *Children Now: Education and Childcare Targets for 2008*. London: DfES.
5. House of Commons (2003) *The Education (National Curriculum) (Foundation Stage Early Learning Goals)*. England Order 2003, Statutory Instrument 2003, No. 391.
6. QCA (2000) *Curriculum Guidance for the Foundation Stage*. London: QCA/DfEE.
7. Sure Start (2003) *Birth to Three Matters: A Framework to Support Children in their Earliest Years*. London: DfES.
8. OfSTED (2004) *The Future of Early Years Inspection Consultation*. London: OfSTED Publications.
9. BBC News, World Edition (2004) *Report on the Decision of the House of Lords to Reject an Amendment to the Children Bill on Smacking*, 6 July.
10. BBC News, World Edition (2004) op. cit. (note. 9).
11. Viewers, S. (2004) Stamp of approval for early excellence, *Nursery World*, 17 June. p. 7.
12. Leigh, E. MP (2004) op. cit. (note 3).
13. DfEE (2000) *A Training Support Framework for the Foundation Stage*. London: DfEE.
14. BBC 1 (2004) *Real Story: Nurseries Undercovered*. BBC Network Current Affairs, Manchester.
15. OfSTED (2004) *Protection through Regulation*. London: OfSTED Publications, 1 September.
16. Sylva, K., Melhuish, E., Sammons, P. and Siraj-Blatchford, I. (2000) The Effective provision of Pre-School Education (EPPE) Project. Briefing information prepared for the House of Commons Education Committee Enquiry into Early Years Education.
17. Clarke, C. (2004) More childcare, early education and family support: report of the Government's five-year-plan presented to the National Policy Conference, *Every Childhood Matters*. London: DfES, 8 September.
18. Sylva, K. et al. (2004) op. cit. (note 16).
19. Leach, P. (2004) quoted in Nursery Tales, *Guardian*, G2, pp. 7–8. 8 July.

20. Sure Start (2003) op cit. (note 7).
21. Leach, P. (2004) op. cit. (note 19).
22. Clarke, C (2004) op. cit. (note 17).
23. Rumbelow, H. (2004) Brown wants to be father of universal nursery childcare, *The Times*, 13 July. p. 13.
24. Clarke, C. (2004) op. cit. (note 17).
25. Quoted in McAllister, W.J. (1931) *The Growth of Freedom in Education*. London: Constable, p. 399.
26. Leach, P. (1994) *Children First*. London: Michael Joseph, p. 265.

CHAPTER ONE

Confident Children

Confidence is a characteristic valued by all and one that parents most want for their children. We may hear of parents who deliberately send their children to certain schools or arrange for them to join clubs 'in order to give them confidence'. Many parents see that the prime role of early education is to help children to acquire social skills and become confident before entering mainstream school. The confident person is well equipped to deal with life, whether in school or work or in social situations. Conversely under-confident people find coping with these aspects of life often difficult and painful. Above all, truly confident people are comfortable with themselves and have insights into their own strengths and weaknesses. This distinguishes them from over-confident people, who although they think well of themselves may lack self-insight and have a false sense of optimism of what they can achieve. In a world that demands so much of them, children do need to become confident from an early age. It is necessary for their early success in life and also for the future. In a sixty-year study of more than a thousand men and women of high intelligence followed through from childhood to retirement, those most confident in their early years were most successful as their careers unfolded (1). What then is required to achieve this precious personal attribute, and how can we help young children to develop it?

An interesting question is whether confidence is an inherited trait and whether some babies are blessed with it at birth. To some extent this might be true: very small babies show clear signs of personality traits, for example, sociable and shy behaviours. However, being outgoing does not necessarily link with a good level of confidence, while low key, seemingly unassuming persons can be quietly sure of themselves. So as Lillian Katz suggests, perhaps it is not what we are born with that counts so much but what we are allowed to do and who we are encouraged to be (2). Thus young children's levels of confidence are coloured by their early experiences, successes and failures, the thoughts they have about themselves and other people's reactions to them. Most people would admit that their confidence ebbs and flows according to the people they are with and the situations demanded of them. However, a person's confidence is linked closely to three factors. These are: becoming aware of oneself (self-concept); developing a view of oneself, either positive or negative (self-esteem); and getting to know about one's strengths and weaknesses (self-knowledge). Children become aware of the first two at a very early stage of their lives; their experiences in the nursery will influence powerfully all three factors.

BECOMING AWARE OF ONESELF

Birth to Three Matters states that 'At the core of "A Strong child" lies the development of the baby's and young child's sense of personal and group identity and the ways this can be acknowledged and affirmed by those around him/her' (3).

We begin to recognise ourselves from early on. After about eighteen months a toddler has a pretty good idea that the reflection shown in a mirror is a representation of herself (4). Before that even, babies will build a picture of themselves from the way in which they are regarded and treated, particularly by those people who are closest to them. Young babies start to form this picture from their mothers. Their mother's loving acceptance of them is the first signal that they are a person who matters. Rosemary Roberts describes this beautifully: 'The mother's face and body are like a mirror to the baby. This very early mirroring process which can reflect the mother's acceptance, forms the basis of the baby's self-concept; the mother's responses are the first "brush strokes" for the developing picture' (5).

This image of oneself as a distinct person is crucial in order to establish a sense of identity; initially it is most strongly established through ongoing contact with one person (see also Chapter 2). Dorothy Selleck argues that, only the presence of a parent (or committed regular key person in the early years setting) can provide the continuity, attention and sensuous pleasure that a baby needs to make sense of all his or her experiences and to set in motion the process of mental development (6). For children under two, particularly those who are placed in daycare, their key person offers an essential warm attachment and the assurance that, despite being one of a number, that baby or toddler is special and unique. Young babies who have been institutionalised from birth and who lack regular contact with one carer may fail to recognise the 'brush strokes' described by Roberts. In certain circumstances a person's sense of 'self' can be eroded – for example, adults imprisoned in conditions of harsh confinement. Terry Waite writes movingly of his long period in captivity and of the times when he wondered who he was: 'How I yearn with a childish, selfish longing to be understood and cared for. I am frightened. Frightened that, in growing up, my identity may slip away' (7).

As the toddler develops into the pre-school years, other people contribute to a broader view of her identity. Through their different behaviours these people will help a child to know who she is. For example, Alison knows that she is dad's little daughter and she makes him laugh; her baby brother's loving older sister when she cuddles him and gives him his bottle; her older brother's noisy little sister when she dances and sings to his records; and Alison the artist at nursery when her teacher admires her paintings. By becoming aware of the way in which others view us we build up a composite picture of ourselves. We also learn to behave in character; we get a picture of how other people regard us and then adapt our behaviour to fit this picture. Because of their immaturity, young children are very open to the opinions and views of other more experienced adults, particularly those adults who are familiar and loved, members of their immediate family, and later those others who care for and work with them. Many

FIGURE 1.1 YUICHI'S FAMILY PROVIDE HER WITH A SENSE OF PERSONAL CONTINUITY

studies highlight the importance of the secure and loving family in the child's development of self. Neil Bolton stresses the importance of having 'shared concerns' within the family. He refers to the sensitive ways in which mothers interpret and tune into their very young child's early body language and suggests that it is this interconnectedness that encourages further responses and initiates later intended communication (8).

At three and four years of age the stable family provides the child with a sense of personal continuity. Young children love to hear stories of when they were babies or to share recall of past family events. They are also keen to share and listen to predictions of 'what will happen when you are a big girl'. These shared experiences and concerns help young children to start to have a sense of self within the larger family.

The family, then, has a powerful effect on each child's sense of identity, but when the child moves to an early years setting the practitioners share this responsibility.

SELF-ESTEEM
■

When a child establishes her identity she is simply becoming aware of how others see her. Once we talk about self-esteem we start to place a value on that identity. Children do not gain a clear view of their self-worth until they are around six years of age, but their early experiences within the family and in early years settings provide the basis for them to make a judgement about themselves. Self-esteem is not fixed; it can change according to the people we are with and the situations that we find ourselves in. Alison's self-esteem is mainly secure as she recognises that she is valued in different ways by her father, by her baby brother, and in the nursery. She has a lower esteem though when she is with her older brother, who makes it clear that she is often intrusive and a nuisance to him. So the views of others not only help a young child to recognise herself as a person who is seen in different ways; they contribute to the regard she has for herself. And again it is the people who are closest to the child and who have an emotional link who will have the most profound effect on her self-esteem. These are described as the 'significant others' (9) and they include the family and primary carers, the key person and other practitioners who have early contacts with the child.

The Foundation Stage Guidance emphasises the benefits of high self-esteem which 'gives children the confidence and security to make the most of opportunities to communicate effectively and to explore the world around them' (10). One of the most important gifts we can offer young children is a positive view of themselves. Without this gift they will flounder throughout life and be constantly seeking reassurance from others as they cannot seek it from within.

When children constantly demand attention or boast about their achievements this is sometimes wrongly interpreted as an over-developed self-esteem. However, it is important to recognise that self-esteem is not conceit and this type of behaviour is more likely to reflect a lack of self-regard and a basic insecurity. In an article which stresses that self-esteem is basic to a healthy life, Murray White looks at the possible problems in later school life arising from its lack:

> If teachers examine what causes bullying and other chronic misbehaviours – the showing off, the fighting and the failure which some children have adopted – they will discover that low self-esteem is at the root of it. These children behave as they do because of strong feelings of inadequacy and internal blame, a belief that they do not possess the ability or intelligence to succeed (11).

SELF-ESTEEM IN THE EARLY YEARS SETTING

The value that we place on ourselves is also affected by how secure we feel. Both adults and children are usually secure with people they know but also when they are in familiar situations. When we start a new job or a new course of learning, most of us feel very vulnerable being placed in the position of a novice. We do not even know where to get a cup of coffee, let alone really understand aspects of new work or how others will work with us.

Studies of young children at home show them to be comfortable and in control. A young toddler will use her parent as a base to explore wider territory. She will refer to her parent when meeting new people to see if they are safe to interact with (12). Tizard and Hughes' well-known study of four-year-old girls conversing and questioning with their mothers gives a picture of children in a situation when they feel they are on sure territory (13). In nearly all families young children recognise that there are loving adults who know them and care about them. This knowledge in itself helps the child to feel secure.

When starting in an early years setting the young child faces new experiences including developing contact with people who are unknown to her and to whom she is unknown. She is placed in a similar position to an adult starting a new job but has much less experience of life to support her. Consequently, the move to a group setting can be a momentous event in the child's life, which for some can result in considerable self-doubt; even the most confident child can find this move intimidating. The setting plays a key role in maintaining each child's self-esteem when they are learning to work and play in a different environment from home.

The size and type of setting can make a difference and there is specific evidence that moving into a nursery reception class at four years is stressful. Gill Barrett's classic study of children starting school in a reception class highlighted some feelings experienced by these new young entrants. Through looking at photographs and in discussion children described feeling scared, fearful of getting things 'wrong' and not knowing what to do. Most of these feelings can be linked to not feeling in control. Barrett's work showed that, partly because of the way the pupil role is understood by young children, usually based on what they have heard from parents, other children and through television, some adopt a passive attitude, are reluctant to take risks in their learning and are anxious about their inadequacies being revealed (14).

Mary Willes' study in 1981, also in a reception class context, shows the vast array of things that young children have to learn when they make this transition:

> In taking on his new role of pupil, the newcomer to school has to be put to the test of using the language learned in interaction at home. He has to find, or to extend his resources to include, the language of a learner, one among many, in an institutionalised setting. He has to wait his turn, and recognise it when it comes, to compete, to assert his rights and sometimes to give ground. He has, in short, to discover what the rules of classroom interaction and behaviour are, what sort of priority obtains among them, and how and when and with what consequences they can be broken (15).

Both of these studies show young children facing tremendous demands, both emotional and intellectual. The fear of being wrong is a major inhibitor. Barrett suggested that too often in mainstream schools there was still emphasis placed on children needing to do things correctly and that children do need to feel that it is safe and acceptable not to know something. Since these studies took place many reception classes have made tremendous moves to recognise the needs of their youngest children in school. Despite this, too often staffing ratios remain inadequate. It is essential that, when children are newcomers to a setting, they are able to have easy access to an adult who will introduce them to the multiplicity of new experiences gently and informally and interpret new requirements for them. The close involvement of parents in this process allows children to feel emotionally supported while they learn.

The practitioner also knows that a child's self-esteem can be fragile. Self-esteem is not constant for any of us. As adults we can have a very positive view of ourselves in one circumstance only to have it knocked down in another. Given a new manager who makes unreasonable demands at work, an important project which proves to be unsuccessful or a failed relationship in our personal lives, our self-esteem can dip. A mature person with a sound self-concept should be able to cope with this over time and, indeed, to seek out self-affirming situations in which she can succeed.

A young child does not have this ability. Her self-esteem is totally dependent on the people who matter to her and the situations that they provide. A young child will only really value herself fully if she knows that she has the unconditional love of a parent or carer. This knowledge is absolutely critical, and if for some reason it has not been acquired during the early years at home then the nursery teacher has a heavy responsibility to demonstrate that love and care.

Proper caring for a child means knowing about her, including how she thinks and what interests her. In order to feel comfortable and 'at home' in a nursery, a child needs to know that she is known and that her behaviour is understood. Practitioners therefore need to have ways of tuning into what lies behind children's thoughts, comments and actions. Chapter 2 deals with the importance of closely listening to children, but we also need to recognise how young children think. Children of three and four have had limited experience of life, but on the basis of this they make incredibly sensible deductions. Their questions and comments may seem bizarre but they reflect the child's logic and constant search to make sense. 'If the sea goes in and out, why does my bath water disappear? If we have a party for baby Jesus shall we have lots of cheese (Jese)?'

Another way in is for practitioners to understand about what Piaget termed young children's 'schemes of thought'. Piaget claimed that children's patterns of thought are evident from babyhood in their early physical and sensory actions. Cathy Nutbrown describes them as 'Threads of Thought' which captures so well the fragile nature of the baby's emerging preoccupations. These schemes are strengthened as children repeat their actions; through interactions with others they begin to make connections in their thoughts and so recognise cause and effect. Children's schemes or 'schema' are dealt with extensively in other literature (16, 17, 18).

Some children have one schema while others seem to have a number. Although around thirty-six schemes have been identified, the staff at the Pen Green Centre of Excellence for Under-Fives identified the most common ones. These are those linked to straight lines (trajectory); circles (rotation); joining things (connection); covering things (enveloping); and moving things from one place to another (transporting) (19).

In order to keep in tune with children, practitioners need to listen and observe closely and then often take an imaginative leap to make sense of their meanings.

Case study

Craig at twelve months repeatedly spilt his food on to the tray of his high chair and traced up-and-down lines in the liquid. When he started at toddler club he drew mainly vertical lines when finger painting. Later at nursery school, Craig was aware of the tall trees surrounding the building. His mother had discussed this with him and had taken a photograph of Craig standing by the side of one of the trees. Craig observed that, in the photograph, 'here is my head but you can't see the head of the tree'. Craig drew a number of pictures – that is, a series of vertical lines to represent symbolically the trees. In the reception class Craig initially spent a great deal of time practising his own 'writing', which was largely composed of vertical marks of a broadly standard size. In physical education and in discussion sessions, he demonstrated a good understanding of positional language, particularly 'up and down' and 'taller and shorter' (20).

Comment

Craig's schema had been noticed by his mum from the start. She provided useful information about his interests to the nursery staff and later to his reception teacher. Craig enjoyed his early years of education. His vertical scheme of thought continued to be recognised and encouraged. He grew in confidence and strengthened his learning.

Although the child must be sure that she is loved at all times, part of the process of caring is also to help shape her behaviour (see also Chapter 6). A problem can arise where the expectations for behaviour differ from home to nursery. It may be that the basis for praise at home is 'to stand up for yourself and hit them back', or 'you make sure that you are the best in the class'. These are powerful messages for young children from people who are very important to them; all the practitioner can do is to try to modify these messages by presenting an alternative view and trying to provide the conditions in the nursery to demonstrate them. Hopefully, then, over a period of time a child learns to use language instead of fists to maintain her rights and to understand that every single person in the nursery community can be 'best' at something. Again a confident, bright, creative four-year-old whose parents have encouraged her non-contingent thinking and activity may find it difficult to conform in any group setting; she will certainly find life extremely hard in a nursery which puts very heavy emphasis on a narrow definition of correct behaviour. She risks being herself and receiving constant reprimand for her responses or complying with requirements and feeling herself to be in an alien and unreasonable environment in which she has no opportunity to show her strengths. In this situation self-belief will ebb away unless a watchful practitioner understands the behaviour that has been encouraged at home and is prepared to be flexible with the requirements in the setting.

Having a positive esteem for oneself is dependent on having a clear view of who you are; this is often difficult for children from minority groups. Tina Bruce points out that too often people from minorities are stereotyped into an identity with which they are not comfortable (21).

Case study

Kofi was black and an adopted child. His younger two brothers were white as were his parents. Kofi was only aware of being the much loved oldest child in the family – his colour was incidental, although he was proud of it. He was the only black child when he started at the nursery. When one or two children at the nursery started to call him 'black boy', Kofi was taken aback. He started to wash obsessively at home. After a week he asked his dad if he could have medicine to change colour. When the parents informed the nursery of their concerns the teachers realised that all the children needed help to see different aspects of their identities. Kofi, with others, was recognised as an important member of his family and the nursery community. Children were encouraged to describe each other in terms of their physical appearance and made a display of their differences and common features.

Comment

Kofi's teachers were initially not prepared for the reactions of the children to a child of a different colour. They felt strongly that the comment 'black boy' was simply descriptive and was not discriminatory. However, the incident made them more aware of the need to avoid stereotyping, and they were careful to avoid any possibility of discrimination when a child with cerebral palsy was admitted to the nursery shortly afterwards.

Moving a child who does not appear to be thriving during the early years at school is not to be considered lightly. Although, this was eventually seen as the right decision for James. Andrew Pollard, in his social study of five children starting school, describes James who stayed at the local state primary school for the first two years of his school career, after which his parents transferred him to an independent school. James found the move to infant school difficult and his self-esteem suffered. James was not accepted by other children although he badly wanted friends; overall he could not adapt to the robust climate of school life. His teachers supported him, but perceived him as cautious and 'nervy'. There was a clash of culture between the school and the parents who were strongly supportive of James, had high academic aspirations for him and provided home tuition for him. It was apparent that James could not meet the requirements of both school and home. When he started to be influenced by the other children at the end of the reception year, the parents became alarmed and described his new behaviour as 'rude' and 'cheeky'. Pollard suggests that this little boy's unhappiness sprang from the poor home/school communications. The parents had always aspired for James to move to an independent school where more formal teaching methods were seen to be in keeping with what they wanted for their son. Most importantly, James subsequently flourished in his new school, in his learning and social life (22).

So, optimal conditions to promote children's self-esteem, include care and respect for their ways of thinking and appreciation of difference which enables children coming from different backgrounds and cultures to experience feeling good about themselves. Self-esteem is only likely to be fostered in situations where all aspects of all children are esteemed.

SELF-KNOWLEDGE

When people are acknowledged and respected, this contributes to the regard they have for themselves. However, this must also go hand in hand with them getting to know themselves. As young children develop they start to learn about themselves and what they can do; they begin to recognise those things that they find easy and where they need help and support.

Initially, however, children have limited self-insight and they look to others to provide information. At first, young children are dependent on the adults around them to gain a view of their strengths and weaknesses. Nevertheless, although guidance should be given and boundaries for behaviour established, ultimately, as Pat Gura suggests, the main aim must be to help children develop a sense of control over their lives and build their own aspirations (23).

The way in which an early years programme is organised reflects the practitioners' beliefs about the degree of responsibility to give children and the importance of helping them to get to know themselves. Studies have shown that children can spend their time in either controlling or informational environments. In a controlling environment the emphasis is very much on the adults being in charge, and requiring children to comply. An informational environment will encourage children to take responsibility for themselves by learning to plan their work, decide what resources to use and then have a part in assessing what has been achieved (24).

In a setting where adults control, children can only respond. An informational environment will allow children to make and learn from mistakes, discover the best way of doing things and learn how to make decisions. Evidence from two longitudinal studies in the USA and Europe highlights the benefits and costs of the different learning environments. Children were studied over time having experienced one of the following three different curricular programmes:

- a skills-based programme controlled by adults

- a free choice programme

- a High Scope programme which incorporates opportunities for children to plan–do–review.

In both instances the children who were in the High Scope programmes were shown to develop more satisfying social and personal lives (25).

As always the practitioner's actions are a powerful influence on the way in which the child develops. Questions which allow children to give open-ended answers and which spring from genuine interest in all that they do will encourage individuals to think about their achievements.

The ways in which adults respond to children will also have a powerful effect on each child's developing knowledge about him or herself. For example, the skilled practitioner sensitively balances giving positive affirmation to her children, while establishing clear messages about acceptable behaviours. Drawing on studies of work with different age groups (26, 27) the following types of responses are suggested which can either hinder or help children.

■ RESPONSES WHICH HINDER CHILDREN'S SELF-KNOWLEDGE

1. *Evaluating through praise* – where adults always take the responsibility for judging what a child has done, believing that this is their job, this restricts the child from forming

her own view. Nursery settings are usually defined by constant use of praise and encouragement – comments such as 'that's wonderful', 'I'm really pleased with you' are commonly heard; however, praise can encourage conformity when it leads children to become dependent on others rather than themselves. Gura suggests that constant use of praise can be high on warmth but low in regard to information offered – this is particularly the case when the praise is general. Moreover, overdoses of lavish praise do become devalued even by nursery and infant children. Robert, age five, told me confidentially, 'It doesn't matter really what you paint because she (his teacher) always says it's really very lovely'. Young children deserve more than a comforting and benign environment. Nevertheless the use of praise is very effective when used with discretion. It is particularly helpful to encourage those children who are not well motivated, to help set the limits of behaviour and for young children who are learning to socialise and become one of a group. Use of praise is particularly helpful when children are being introduced to a nursery, but in a climate of information it should be seen as a means to an end. Praise that is focused can help children to become aware of their achievements, for example, 'using those elastic bands to fix the two boxes together is really clever Dean'.

2. *Evaluating with criticism* – negative comments are inevitably going to leave children feeling inadequate and that they have failed. Importantly, if a child is criticised this usually shuts down her thinking. Early years teachers are very aware of this and negative responses are rarely used.

RESPONSES WHICH HELP CHILDREN'S SELF-KNOWLEDGE

1. *Using silence* – often in a busy nursery, and particularly when adults feel under the pressure of time, young children are not given sufficient time to reflect and collect their thoughts. However, if when asking a question, an adult pauses to allow a child time to respond, the chances are that, as with older children, the time allowed for thinking means that the response given is of greater quality. It also demonstrates the adult's faith that the child will be able to

respond, which in turn fosters the child's confidence. Young children will learn to recognise that they are not expected to come up with quick answers and that it is more important to have time to explore what they really feel.

2. *Clarifying* – young children often find it difficult to put their thoughts into words. Sometimes, in their eagerness they rush to communicate and then tail away as they struggle to recall the sense of their message. Adults can actively accept children's contributions by paraphrasing or summarising what they have said. Although the teacher may use different words she will make sure that she maintains the child's intention and meaning. 'I know what you are saying, David. Your idea is … ' In this way a teacher shows that she has both received and understood what the child has said.

3. *Asking for information* – if practitioners show genuine interest in children's views of what they have done, this helps children to become confident in making judgements.

4. *Providing information* – if young children are helped to see how their paintings and constructions have developed over a period of time they will start to understand that achievements and progress are linked to growing up. A child will take pleasure in recalling her limitations as a baby and contrasting them with what she is doing now.

SELF-ESTEEM, SELF-KNOWLEDGE AND LINKS WITH LEARNING

It is generally accepted that a child who has sound self-esteem is well placed to learn. Positive self-esteem is not sufficient in itself; self-knowledge is important in order for people to develop not only an optimistic view of themselves but also one which is realistic. However, in order to learn, young children must believe that they are able to do so. If this belief is not secured during the early years of life it is unlikely to blossom later. In a study to accelerate learning in science with pupils of secondary age, about half made impressive progress, the others did not. One of the main reasons for this difference was that the latter group of children were afraid of failing in thinking tasks and so gave up the mental challenges required (28).

Some children on admission to an early years setting do not regard themselves as learners. Their thoughts and views may have been disregarded by adults; caring and protective parents may not have trusted children to try out things for themselves and so learn from mistakes. These children will have learned to accept that they are not important or competent to do things for themselves. By comparison, other children on admission shine as eager and capable learners. Their early experiences have included opportunities to try things out and discuss the outcomes with adults. They have been gently helped to frame their ideas in words and their increasing command of language has helped them to feel 'in control' of events.

FIGURE 3.3   FEELING IN CONTROL

The work of Carol Dweck demonstrates that children show either helpless or mastery patterns of behaviour when confronted with obstacles in learning (29). Children who follow a mastery approach are confident and have a positive view of themselves. They seek new, challenging experiences and believe that they can succeed even in the face of difficulties. Other children are unsure of themselves; because their self-esteem is not secure they constantly look for approval from others. These children show helpless behaviour in that they 'give up' easily, and when things go wrong they believe that it is their own fault because 'they are no good'. Whilst the 'mastery learners' forge ahead in learning often on their own initiative, the 'helpless children' need constant reassurance and support from parents and teachers (see also Chapter 5). Although Dweck's work was with older children, similar patterns of behaviour are evident with three- and four-year-olds as they begin to recognise who they are and what they can do.

Practitioners now have firm support from the Foundation Stage Guidance to provide well-planned play-based activities which give children scope to be creative and imaginative and have a sense of being in control. In terms of building confidence in learning, play is invaluable; Vygotsky describes this so well when he asserts that in play it is as if a child is a head taller than herself (30). However, despite the recommendations, both in schools and other early years settings there remains a degree of uncertainty about how play methodology aids learning and the practicalities of planning and provision. The DfES Foundation team are aware of the inequity in provision and plans to work with local authorities to encourage and support practitioners in providing for play.

Case study

Pascale and Jeremy were the same age, three years eleven months, and they had started nursery at the same time during the previous term. Pascale sat at a table drawing. She was clutching the pencil in a pincer grip and her movements were repetitive. Try though I might, I could not gain eye contact with her or get her to respond in any way. On mentioning this to the teacher she said that she was not surprised. When Pascale was admitted to the nursery, her name was Cheri. A month later her mother requested that the name be changed to Amanda. On returning to the nursery that term the staff were further informed that Amanda was no longer to have that name but was to be called Pascale. The little girl was not sure who she was. Her teacher reported that every day Pascale refused to move from the drawing table and join any other activities in the nursery.

On passing through to the next classroom I met Jeremy who was with a fairly large group of children listening to a story about a little boy who was walking along a very long road. Jeremy, having grasped the conventions of being a pupil in a group, raised his hand to make a comment. When invited to do so he politely asked if the road in the story went on and on into infinity! The teacher, somewhat taken aback, said that it might do but suggested that Jeremy explain what the word meant. 'Well,' said Jeremy confidently raising his voice, so that all in the group might hear 'if it goes on into infinity, it might never, ever, ever end!'

Comment

Despite being of a similar age and having had a similar amount of time in the nursery, these two children were poles apart. Pascale, alias Cheri alias Amanda, was not even able to recognise herself in her name and showed helpless behaviour in her refusal to accept new challenges. Jeremy's high regard for himself as a learner was evident in his active participation in the story. He was able to question and make links in his learning using a fascinating new word he had acquired. Jeremy showed all the elements of a master player using the teacher as a resource for further learning.

Before they arrived at the nursery, home experiences had already had a potent effect on Pascale's and Jeremy's views of themselves as learners. The staff were faced with different challenges for these two children. Pascale needed the security and consistency provided by a predictable programme and the attention and care of one adult in whom she could learn to trust. Close and sensitive links with Pascale's mother would hopefully enable her to recognise Pascale's needs and try to meet them at home. Jeremy's inner resources for learning were already firmly in place. The nursery's task here was to ensure that staff respected Jeremy's contributions, provided additional stimulus to motivate him, and extended his skills and knowledge based on what he understood already. The psychologist Carl Rogers says that children need two conditions in order to be creative learners. These are psychological safety and psychological freedom (31). Pascale's future progress depended initially on the first condition being met. Rogers suggested that psychological safety is dependent on: having total trust in a child and accepting all that the child does; encouraging the child to become self-aware; trying to see the world from the child's perspective and so getting to understand how she feels. It is only when Pascale feels safe that she will make any progress towards mastery learning. Jeremy shows that he has already benefited from positive support at home; this now needs to be sustained in the nursery; at the same time Jeremy needs the psychological freedom to try out new things and ideas.

Summary

The young child develops confidence through becoming aware of herself as a separate and worthwhile person, as well as having a realistic view of what she can achieve. Children gain their self-esteem initially from the love and recognition that they receive from their family and other significant people in their lives including their early educators. When they move into an early years setting they will gain confidence if their questions and comments are under stood and their interests recognised and strengthened as schemes of thought. They also become aware of themselves, what they are capable of doing and what is approved behaviour. Children's self-esteem and self-knowledge are closely linked to the ways in which they see themselves as learners. This leads them to show either 'mastery' or 'helpless' patterns of behaviour in the nursery. Their success as learners is dependent on them feeling secure and also having opportunities to experiment in play contexts and try things out for themselves.

Practical suggestions

Get to know your children

- Use a key person scheme to ensure that one person has the prime responsibility for establishing a relationship with each child and that parents and child are aware of this.
- Fix a clipboard and pencil in all the areas of learning. Encourage all staff to note significant comments, questions and actions from different children as they work in these areas. At the end of the day, the key person can: collect these observations in regard to his/her children; reflect on the underlying logic/scheme of thought demonstrated; and decide on any implications for action.
- Observe individual children and note those who adopt mastery and helpless patterns of behaviour.
- Plan a regular time at the end of each day/week when you meet as a staff and share any other information about children that you have gathered.

Create a climate to promote self-esteem

- Consider how your spoken and body language can affect small children, e.g. pursed lip, tensed body, toe tapping and abrupt tone of voice communicate irritability; a genuine smile, relaxed body posture, eye contact, gentle touch and warm voice communicate approachability and friendliness.
- Demonstrate that you are interested in, and have time for, each child, e.g. bend down to their level when speaking and listening to them; give them time to talk and try not to interrupt to cut across their thinking.
- Make each new child feel special, e.g. ask each new child to bring in a photograph of herself and her family. This can be displayed on a large board and used as a topic of conversation.

- If funds allow or parents will contribute, arrange for each new child to have their photograph taken and enlarged. Attach the photograph to a card and cut to form a jigsaw. Older children will enjoy working in small groups and sorting out their own photograph and those of their friends.
- Pronounce children's names correctly – if this is difficult, be honest with parents and ask for their help
- Remember and refer to important details in the child's life, e.g. How is your new kitten Isaac? Did you enjoy the fair Angelo?
- Provide mirrors in different parts of your environment to enable children to view themselves when working at different activities.
- Have artefacts and scenarios that reflect children's circumstances, e.g. books where the main characters look like them, dolls which resemble their colour and characteristics, domestic play scenarios which depict familiar contexts, posters and jigsaws which make people like them and their families appear important.

Help children to talk about themselves
- Ask children to do a painting/drawing of themselves and take time to listen to them talking about their picture.
- Ask children about their likes and dislikes about the food they eat, the clothes they wear and their favourite activities at home and in the nursery; these views can be scribed and displayed together with each child's self-portrait or made into individual books.

Provide for those children who are less secure
- Position coat pegs with the child's personal clothing so that children can see them during the day.
- Encourage children to bring a familiar toy to the nursery, in order to maintain a link with home.
- Support a child to separate from his parent/carer; suggest that he carries with him a personal memento that he can refer to during the session, e.g. a photograph of the parent or a personal item such as a scarf which carries a familiar perfume.
- Ensure that an adult is available for less secure children particularly at vulnerable times of the day, e.g. the start and the end of the session, at transition times and when children are outside.
- Make it possible for these children to be physically near to an adult during group activities.

Help children to recognise what they have learned
- Publicise children's achievements, e.g. 'Liam is really good at doing up his buttons – would you like to show everyone Liam?'

- Encourage children to teach others, e.g. showing a friend how to use the mouse on the computer; how to hang their painting to dry.
- Build into your session regular and informal recall sessions when children demonstrate and discuss with others what they have done, e.g. six children with a key worker when each child talks about and shows any outcomes of her most recent activity. It is important that each child feels free to opt out of this session or to make a minimal response. As children grow accustomed to the session they can be encouraged to offer their views on other children's work.

Professional questions

1. How do my daily routines make it possible for me to get to know and treat each child as an individual?
2. How does my environment demonstrate to children that they are welcome in the setting?
3. How are my children helped to consider critically what they achieve?
4. How do I help all my children to adopt mastery patterns of behaviour?

REFERENCES

1. Holahan, C.K. and Sears, R.R. (1999) The gifted group in later maturity, in D. Goleman (ed.), *Working with Emotional Intelligence*. London: Bloomsbury, p. 71.
2. Katz, L.G. (1995) *Talks with Teachers of Young Children*. Norwood, NJ: Ablex.
3. Sure Start (2003) *Birth to Three Matters: A Framework to Support Children in their Earliest Years*. London: DfES.
4. Smith, P.K. and Gowie, H. (1991) *Understanding Children's Development*. Oxford: Blackwell.
5. Roberts, R. (1995) *Self-esteem and Successful Early Learning*. London: Hodder & Stoughton, p. 8.
6. Selleck, D. (2001) Being under 3 years of age: Enhancing quality experiences, in Pugh, G. (ed.) *Contemporary Issues in the Early Years*. Third edition. London: Paul Chapman.
7. Waite, T. (1993) *Taken on Trust*. London: Hodder & Stoughton, p. 297.
8. Bolton, N. (1989) Developmental psychology and the early years curriculum, in C.W. Desforges (ed.), *Early Childhood Education*, Monograph Series no. 4, pp. 35–6.
9. Mead, G.H. (1934) *Mind, Self and Society*. Chicago, IL: University of Chicago Press.

10. QCA (2000) *Curriculum Guidance for the Foundation Stage.* London: QCA/DfEE, p. 29.
11. White, M. (1996) What's so silly about self-esteem? *TES*, 26 April, p. 3.
12. Sylva, K. and Lunt, I. (1982) *Child Development: A First Course.* Oxford: Blackwell.
13. Tizard, B. and Hughes, M. (1984) *Young Children Learning.* London: Fontana.
14. Barrett, G. (1986) *Starting School: An Evaluation of the Experience.* Norwich: AMMA, University of East Anglia.
15. Willes, M. (1981) Children becoming pupils, in C. Alderman (ed.), *Uttering, Muttering.* London: Grant McIntyre, p. 51.
16. Athey, G. (1990) *Extending Children's Thinking.* London: Paul Chapman.
17. Nutbrown, C. (1994) *Threads of Thinking.* London: Paul Chapman.
18. Bruce, T. (1997) *Early Childhood Education.* London: Hodder & Stoughton.
19. Pen Green Staff (1995) *A Scheme Booklet for Parents and Carers.* Pen Green Centre for Under-Fives and their Families, Corby, Northamptonshire.
20. Dowling, M. (1995) *Starting School at Four: A Joint Endeavour.* London: Paul Chapman, p. 17.
21. Bruce, T. (1998*) Early Childhood Education.* London: Hodder & Stoughton.
22. Pollard, A. and Filer, A. (1996) *The Social World of Children's Learning.* London: Cassell, pp. 225–44.
23. Gura, P. (1996) What I want for Cinderella; self-esteem and self-assessment, *Early Education*, no. 19, Summer.
24. Deci, E.L. and Ryan, R.M. (1985) Intrinsic motivation and self-determination, in *Human Behaviour.* New York: Plenum Press.
25. Sylva, K. (1998) The early years curriculum: evidence based proposals. Paper prepared for NAEIAC Conference on Early Years Education.
26. Costa, A.L. (1991) *The School as Home for the Mind.* Australia: Hawker Brownlow Education, pp. 53–66.
27. Gura, P., op. cit. (note 20).
28. Gold, K. (1999) Making order out of chaos, *Guardian Education*, 11 May, p. 2.
29. Dweck, C.S. and Leggett, E. (1988) A socio-cognitive approach to motivation and achievement, *Psychological Review*, Vol. 95, no. 2, pp. 256–73.
30. Vygotsky, L.S. (1978) *Mind and Society: The Development of Higher Psychological Processes.* Cambridge, MA: Harvard University Press.
31. Rogers, C. (1961) *On Becoming a Person.* Boston, MA: Houghton Mifflin.

CHAPTER TWO

Living and Learning with Others

'Being good with people' has always been recognised as a strength in people's work and personal lives. Perhaps this is even more crucial in today's world when the pace of life does not easily allow time for personal contacts. Professor Philip Zimbardo of Stanford University told the British Psychological Society that we are entering a new ice age of non-communication. The use of computers, faxes and mobile phones and the disappearance of shop assistants and bank tellers with whom to 'pass the time of day' are contributing to what he calls a world-wide 'epidemic of shyness'. An increase of 40–60 per cent of this condition is reported in almost every country. Zimbardo's theory is that there is now less personal contact and small talk that holds communities together (1).

This malaise is certainly not evident in early years settings. Perhaps the most noticeable aspect to any newcomer visiting a nursery is its sociability. Children are open and friendly. They chatter as they work and play. Disputes that flare up are usually settled amicably. The whole basis for young children and adults living and working together is founded on good relationships. This is clearly necessary for any successful community; the critical point is that this sociable environment is not always achieved easily. Children under five are, as with everything else, inexperienced in interpersonal skills. Considerable social learning is involved in adapting to a group, and this forms a major part of the Foundation Stage curriculum.

THE PLACE OF SOCIAL SKILLS IN EARLY PERSONAL DEVELOPMENT

To ensure their healthy growth and development, babies and very young children need to feel securely attached and become socially competent.

■ ATTACHMENT

Research indicates that where children start their lives having at least one person with whom they have a strong bond or attachment they can develop a resistance to stress in their lives (2). This bond provides a form of protection both for the early years and in their future lives and it is a basic requirement for children to establish wider social attachments as they grow up. If a baby is physically and emotionally close to one person initially (most usually his birth mother), this makes later separation from her more tolerable rather than less. From birth, every day that this significant person can be with the baby, to discover him, help him to know her, meet his needs, give him pleasure and take pleasure in him will contribute to a fund of confidence and inner peace. Even a brief few weeks of this relationship will offer the baby a good start.

Responsive and loving adults are crucial to all aspects of infant development. And you cannot overdose young infants with attention. Every time a baby receives a response to something she appears to need, the better. Penelope Leach draws attention to historical evidence of the possible consequences of the strict rationing of attention. After the Second World War, thousands of orphaned and refugee babies were kept in institutions where their physical care was excellent, but wholly impersonal. Many of these babies failed to thrive – worse, some died without, seemingly any physical reason for this. In 1990 the same dreadful situation became apparent in the packed orphanages in Romania. Quite early on, researchers concluded that these babies and small children suffered from lack of maternal care – later this was amended, recognising that it was not so much the lack of a link with their natural parent, but the deprivation of responsive and loving care. Leach stressed that this lack of attachment can of course occur within the family, for example, where a potentially loving parent becomes clinically depressed and is unable to sustain a loving bond with the child (3).

When babies and small children come to separate from their parents, the essential need is to appoint a key person with whom the small child can make a similar (but not identical) attachment. If this is made a priority it has implications for the organisation and deployment of staff. For example, in extended day provision where practitioners work on shifts, it might be necessary for two staff to share the role and for parents to be clear who is on duty at any time of the day or the week. The key person has a very complex and responsible job and should be carefully trained for the post. Above all the practitioner needs time to bond with both the baby and parents; a generous staffing ratio – where possible to exceed the minimum required for the National Standards – will ensure that the key person is not overburdened.

SOCIAL COMPETENCE

Birth to Three Matters reminds us that babies are primed to be social and to communicate. Within a very short period of time babies are 'reading' eye contacts, facial and body gestures and the tone of voice of those significant people who care for them. But we cannot help but notice that some babies and toddlers are particularly keen to interact. My experience suggests that these are the small individuals who have already had their early attempts at conversations valued; they quickly learn that what they do and the sounds they make are of interest to adults, and they want more of this affirming experience. The adult's task is to tune into the baby's intentions and efforts and maintain this social dialogue.

In order to communicate, babies, young children and indeed all of us need to have someone to communicate with. Piaget (an educational giant in his time) encouraged us to believe that the very young child was a little scientist – the role of the practitioner was simply to provide interesting and stimulating resources and then observe the child as he freely interacts with them. This belief led to marginalising the adult's work. Further study has emphasised that all of us, children and adults, grow up and learn more with others. As a result, practitioners have an important responsibility to pave the way for young children to reach out and communicate with a widening circle.

Social relationships with peers develop very early out of the family. Babies will respond to other babies. Elinor Goldschmeid and Dorothy Selleck have shown in their studies that children from a few weeks old are able to use sound, gazes and touches (later they exchange objects) to develop loyalties and attachments to other children in their group (4). From this very early start, other children continue to be important. Toddlers already show considerable interest in what people do. They tune in to how adults react to different situations and use these reactions as a point of reference for their own behaviour. All parents and caregivers will have experienced a toddler's delight when she is praised for an activity or their knowing look when the adult says 'no'. By three years friendships start to become important, although at this stage they are transitory. The development of relationships has always been a fundamental part of early childhood education. Young children are recognised not just as individuals but as part of their family. Practitioners recognise that the development of close links between the home and the nursery is above all else in the interests of the child (see

Chapter 8). Depending on their family experiences, children will also have learned a great deal already about getting on with people. They may be used to warm loving relationships within the family and have had many and varied chances to meet a wide circle of different adults and children. Other children may have been sheltered from social contacts, been reared in a culture of privacy, or may live in geographically isolated areas with no other young families nearby. Parents are usually keen for their children to spread their social wings; for most parents, an important reason for sending their child to a nursery is to help them to mix with other people, which they recognise as a key factor in living a happy and successful life.

Whatever social experiences young children have had prior to coming to an early years setting, it is likely that many relationships will have been established since babyhood and will have developed with the support of parents. The process of moving into a new environment and facing often a completely unknown group of children and adults is a challenge for any child. For those who have experienced only a small social circle of contacts at home the experience can be daunting. The vast majority of children now have some early experience in a nursery setting, but for the few who make a direct transition from home to a reception class in a mainstream school, this is probably the most challenging move for a child during her school career. In Pollard's study of five children who started school very shortly after their fourth birthday, the children's parents provided constant emotional, practical and intellectual support in the early days of school. Pollard emphasises the vital role that parents and carers play as the reference point and interpreter for their children as they move into a wider social context (5).

RELATING TO ADULTS

Young children are very concerned with themselves and they do need attention given to their particular needs. Most children will have received this at home as part of a loving upbringing. Parents and other close family members and friends will have listened, responded and demonstrated interest in all that the child does. Within this secure and interested environment children thrive. On moving to a group setting the child's first need is to develop a link with new adults whose task it is to provide a similar framework of security. When they first separate from their parents, children must be able to feel confident in the care of the people who are taking the place of their parents.

It is likely that all children will need to make this relationship with at least one adult in the setting. Where settings provide key persons this means that from the start children know that a particular adult is there for them. The importance of a key person for babies and young children is described clearly by Rosie Roberts. She suggests that a key person and significant people at home often do the same things. They help the very young child manage through the day; they think about him; they get to know him well; they sometimes worry about him; they get to know each other; they talk about the child (6).

Confident and sociable children who are already socially experienced may rapidly 'branch out' to relate to other children. The Foundation Stage Guidance points out that being with the same adults and children gives a child the time and opportunity to develop a network of relationships (7). Other children, however, continue to have a greater need for adult attention.

It may be that for various reasons, some children have been denied the time of an adult at home. Other children who initially may require a great deal of the practitioner's attention and time are those who are used to having a great deal of attention – possibly an only or first child. Some children may need the practitioner more at specific times when they are vulnerable – this may be when a new baby arrives or if there is illness or turbulence in the family. In all these cases it is important for the practitioner to be aware of and to respond to individual needs and give the message that he or she is consistently there for the child.

Good communication is at the heart of any successful relationship; Petrie suggests that 'Whether it involves children, babies or adults, interpersonal communication is a two way process. Listening to children shows our respect for them and builds their self-esteem' (8). In this context, it is a matter of the adult tuning into all that young children are trying to convey. This involves using skills and developing attitudes which are at the heart of good practice. However, a recent study initiated by the Coram Family has highlighted that this practice is far from universal. The Listening to Young Children project and training framework (9) began because of concerns, expressed particularly in national reports, that young children were not being given a voice. The project concluded that this was largely to do with a belief that children under eight years were too inexperienced to have a view or to make a useful contribution about matters that concerned them. The training framework suggests ways in which children can be encouraged to communicate both verbally and through the visual and expressive arts.

DEVELOPING UNDERSTANDINGS AND SKILLS OF FRIENDSHIP

Making friends is very important to young children; they approach other children openly often asking 'will you be my friend?'. They also show great distress if they are refused friendship. Common and heart-rending cries from some young children are 'Peter won't play with me' or 'Zareen says that she is not my friend'. One small-scale study demonstrated that when a number of children in a kindergarten left for their new school, both the group transferring and the group left behind showed signs of negative behaviour and mild distress. Although the researcher admitted that the agitation demonstrated by the leaving group may have been due to the anticipated transfer, the group of children remaining appeared to have missed their 'friends' after they had gone (10).

Studies suggest that the first six or seven years of development are critical for the development of social skills. By four years a child should easily be able to deal with several peer relationships. If a child fails during this time to learn to relate to other children, this can lead to great unhappiness. Nurseries and schools, as we have seen, are social communities. If a child is condemned to attend school daily without having the support of friends she is unlikely to learn well; studies show that lack of friends can ultimately lead children to refuse to attend school (11).

The fact that most young children in the nursery do make friends easily and quickly sometimes makes us overlook the complexities involved in establishing relationships. These include developing certain understandings which are explored below.

BECOMING AWARE OF OTHERS' VIEWPOINTS

Piaget tested young children in a formal situation and consequently found that most individuals under four were not able to appreciate any other view than their own. However, as Margaret Donaldson has shown, when they respond in everyday situations that make sense to them, children show a higher level of understanding (12). The most familiar context for children is the home. Judy Dunn's work with young families in their homes shows that even babies in their first year are sensitive to those who are close to them. Toddlers less than two years old show some understanding of how older siblings will react when teased or annoyed (13). They observe and are able to 'tune in' to quarrels between members of their family. Their own behaviour is sympathetic and supportive to the member of the family who is upset, but they are also able to recognise and join in with a shared joke. By the age of three, children in one of her studies were able to recognise, anticipate and respond to the feelings of their baby brothers or sisters (14). (See also Chapters 3 and 6.)

These studies offer powerful evidence of how, even before they can talk, very young children take a real interest in, and begin to understand, how other people behave. Although they are not able to appreciate another's perspective in an intellectual task, they already work from a sharp social intelligence. However, during these first three years of life, this understanding of people's behaviour is largely influenced by the child recognising feelings that they have themselves. In the best circumstances young children will have been able to observe family interactions and have been encouraged to take an active part in them. They are then able to take their social learning into a group setting.

Case study

Jodie brought into the nursery her new teddy bear, which she had received for her fourth birthday. She proudly showed it to the other children but became very upset when Gary, a new three-year-old, grabbed it from her and sat on it. The other children pushed Gary away and returned the bear to Jodie. Later she was observed going to Gary and offering for him to borrow the bear. Jodie explained to her teacher that Gary was only little and she knew that he really wanted a bear like hers.

Comment

Jodie's generous response showed her ability to recognise, empathise and respond positively to Gary's envy and longing for a similar toy.

FIGURE 2.1 CHILDREN COME TO UNDERSTAND WHAT IS INVOLVED IN BEING A FRIEND AND MAINTAINING THAT FRIENDSHIP

UNDERSTANDINGS ABOUT FRIENDSHIPS

Young nursery-age children regard their current playmates as their friends. When a three-year-old says 'I'm your friend now', it is likely to mean that 'I am playing with you now'. By four, a friendship is becoming more stable, based on shared experiences over a period of time. At this age children look for each other in the nursery and may spend considerable amounts of time together. It is at this stage that 'friendship' has a much more sociable meaning although a long-lasting relationship is rare until a child is around seven or eight.

These social understandings are linked to a child's level of maturation. Generally speaking, the more practice that young children have in making and playing with friends the more experiences they will have of both rejection and acceptance. In this way they come to understand what is involved in being a friend and maintaining that friendship. However, it is not always simply a matter of providing the experience, as there are powerful factors, which affect relationships. Young children are differently equipped to make friends and have friendship preferences.

Ramsey suggests that young children's social behaviour can be grouped into four different categories (15).

- *Popular* children are usually very capable and more intellectually, socially and emotionally mature than their peers. It is also a sad but evident truth that popular children are often more physically attractive and this is particularly noticeable with little girls (16).
- *Rejected* children may show aggressive or withdrawn behaviour. They may angrily retaliate against others or avoid other children.
- *Neglected* children appear to take little part in the social life of the group and are often quite content with their own company.
- *Controversial* children are described as having a major impact on the social group, being socially and intellectually talented but are often in trouble for aggressive behaviour and rule breaking. Although these children are often group leaders, they are regarded with caution by some of their peers.

Although it can be helpful to recognise these behaviours, Ramsey recognises that they are crude descriptors and many children may be socially well adjusted but not fit into these categories at all. When looking at friendship preferences research indicates that, for whatever reason, girls find it a little easier to make friends than boys. Children also tend to select friends who are like them. Thus the popularity of an individual child may be affected by the child being in a group with others of the same ethnic origin, or with those of a similar level of maturity or ability. Moreover, while little girls will play with either boys or girls, boys prefer to be with other boys.

Rubin's study of nursery-age children suggests that there are complex social skills involved in making friends. These include the ability to gain entry to group activities, to be approving and supportive of one's peers, to manage conflicts appropriately, and to exercise sensitivity and tact. The most popular children were particularly accomplished in using these skills of friendship (17).

Children seem to apply the rules for being a 'good friend' equally to children's relationships as to adults. The more experiences young children have of relationships and contacts with others in their play, the more they gain from it. Rubin's work and his reference to other studies show that the children who make friends easily show generous behaviour; they involve others in their play, praise them, show affection and care. These socially experienced children also learn that, in order to maintain a friendship, they need to recognise when others are upset and do something about it. They start to learn the skills of reconciling arguments and negotiating roles.

It is very noticeable when young children find it difficult to relate and establish friendships and it is important to distinguish between 'aloneness' as a matter of choice rather than of necessity. 'Neglected' four-year-olds may have all the social skills to communicate and play with others, but may prefer to spend time alone. Practitioners quickly learn the difference between that autonomous and self-sufficient behaviour and behaviour demonstrated by the child who is longing but unable to relate to others. The 'rejected' children are the ones who become socially isolated although this is not their choice.

Scarlett's study of nursery children suggests that socially isolated children spend a considerable amount of time 'on the sideline' observing others at play but without the strategies for joining in. When they do become involved, they are necessarily inexperienced players and they need direction from other children. This can mean that they are devalued in the group and they are very often the individuals who end up in role-play being the dog or the baby (18). When these children do try to make friends, their overtures to others are often either too timid or over-effusive and other children 'back off'. Vivien Paley vividly describes her concern about the social exclusion that operated in her class when some children announced to others 'you can't play' (19).

THE FAMILY AS A SOCIAL CONTEXT FOR LEARNING

Piaget's view of the child making sense of the world through her own investigation emphasised the importance of the environment rather than other people. Since then his views have been modified to take account of the importance of social contacts. We all need other people to help us learn and young children need adults and other children. Thus, a child's ability to form good relationships not only enhances her personal development but helps her to progress intellectually.

One of the great strengths of family relationships is that they are founded on mutual interests and shared past experiences. Tizard and Hughes vividly describe the rich and easy conversations that can take place between parents and young children as a result of daily routines (20). Children learn a whole range of social skills when they observe and imitate members of their family listening, questioning, arguing, negotiating, manipulating and agreeing. Even in volatile family circumstances there exists an intimacy between young children and the adults who have known them since birth. Any practitioner who has visited young children in their homes is aware of most children being comfortable and confident on known territory and with people who know them. One of the most challenging tasks for the educator is to develop a relationship with the child given that she knows little about her. Raven describes the difficulties of an educational home visitor when visiting a child at home. The behaviour is partly described by the adult's feeling of being accountable as a paid employee of the local authority and also being under some time pressure: 'Then there was the problem that they did not know the children sufficiently well to appreciate their interests, and were consequently unable to harness or build on these. Nor did they know how to "read" their innuendoes and body language' (21). Although it is necessary to be aware of these difficulties, nevertheless most adults involved with home visiting are extremely skilled at establishing a sensitive initial link with the child. However, once established in the nursery the child can be one among many and in some settings the adults can vary from day to day. In these circumstances each child needs help in order to learn to communicate and trust the adults around her; this will only happen if children believe that adults have time for them and are genuinely interested in what they do and think and who they are.

LEARNING WITH ADULTS IN THE NURSERY SETTING

This task of really getting inside children's minds and understanding them can only properly be achieved though observing their actions and conversing with them. This implies a certain way of working which has not always been appreciated in the past. In the Oxford Pre-School Research Study, Woods (22) reports that 'the incidence of really interesting talk is rare', and Sylva supports this by only observing very occasional coherent conversations (23). This study highlighted the many instances of managerial talk, linked with routines such as clearing up, organisation of snack time and washing hands. Certainly these studies did not suggest any absence of good relationships in the settings, but rather a lack of meaningful contact, which stems from staff not picking up messages from children.

In some studies, teachers particularly have been less successful in encouraging talk. Nine years ago, Hughes found that teachers in early years classrooms appeared to offer very limited opportunities for shared conversations. In these cases young children were mainly only required to respond to instructions and questions. This contrasted with a broader range of interactions with other adults including nursery nurses, students and parents. Hughes suggests that while the teachers took on more of a custodial role, the other adults were perceived by the children to have less authority, to be more approachable and therefore able to be questioned and sometimes interrupted (24). My own observations at the time were that different adults were not perceived so differently in private and state nursery settings. This probably reflected the fact that, over time, teachers and nursery nurses and adults in these settings had learned to work as a team, adopting a less formal deployment, and had developed a culture of all adults having an equal status. The key person system, now widely adopted, particularly in daycare, where each adult is responsible for a group of children, has also contributed to children regarding all adults as equal. Today, practice in reception classes is changing rapidly, notably with the heightened status and function of teaching assistants and with children being less aware of any distinctions in staff roles. Teachers and assistants now acknowledge the message reflected in Hughes' research and informed by the Foundation Stage Guidance (25), that children's social contact with all adults assists their learning. Although the teacher is very aware of her ultimate responsibility for all of the class, she recognises that, rather than overseeing learning from a distance, she should take a role as a talking and listening partner with children in common with the rest of her team. Where this operates well, young children benefit from being in small groups and having easy access to a known adult with whom they can share their thoughts and experiences.

Listening and responding to children's interests and concerns is vital; however, the practitioner then has to build on this information and use these social contacts to help children to gain fresh insights, reflect and move forward in learning. Findings from the REPPE project, which investigated effective pedagogy in the Foundation Stage, found that this aspect of social learning termed 'sustained shared thinking' is still relatively undeveloped and only promoted in the minority of excellent practice (26). This is perhaps understandable, in that methods of sharing and developing children's thinking have not been explored well and many practitioners are unaware of what this practice looks like. Nevertheless, some methods are in use. For example, use of open-ended questions is much more common and practitioners now more readily demonstrate their own thinking to children.

Case study

Leila in her first term in a reception class decided to make a box for her teddy to use as a hidey-hole. Margaret, a teaching assistant, observed her cutting out squares of thin cardboard to make the different faces of the box. Simon approached and commented that Leila would not be able to make a box like that because the pieces would not stick together. Leila ignored him but became upset when she was clearly not succeeding with her construction. Margaret suggested that the three of them think of an alternative approach. Simon said that he had seen boxes stacked flat in the supermarket and the sides had been folded. He suggested that folding was a good idea. Margaret collected a box and together they looked at its construction. Leila was delighted to find that she could produce a box through a combination of folding and cutting. 'We're friends aren't we,' she said. 'That's what friends do – they help each other.'

Comment

Margaret observed carefully and only intervened when Leila was upset. When she helped, it was to work alongside Leila and Simon as an equal. Her main role was to support both children. Leila's comment at the end shows how her experience of being helped confirmed in a practical way her view of what constituted friendship.

The potent role of the adults is further exemplified in the Italian pre-schools in Reggio Emilia. Warm, supportive relationships underpin all of the work with children but the scaffolding of learning is never underestimated. This scaffolding is likened to a game of ping-pong where the practitioner helps the child to clarify and articulate her ideas; she also picks up one child's idea and offers it for consideration within the group; other children throw back their responses. The practitioner also encourages conversations that help children to reflect, exchange and co-ordinate points of view; she acts as the memory of the group by making tape recordings and taking photographs of the children's discussions and activities. The continuing relationship between practitioner and child is recognised as so significant that in these schools children stay with the same teacher for three years (27).

This way of working is not limited to the Italian schools. In the best nursery settings in the UK, practitioners develop easy social relationships with children and with consummate skill use this as a means of helping children learn more.

LEARNING WITH OTHER CHILDREN

For years we have accepted the need for children to be with other children, to play together and learn how to live with others. In addition we now recognise how important children's relationships with one another are in assisting their thinking. Lev Vygotsky strongly supported social learning; he claimed that mental activity begins with social contacts and exchanges between people. Eventually these exchanges are taken on board; a child will use conversations as a basis for her own thinking. Vygotsky suggested that what the child does in co-operation with others she eventually learns to do alone (28).

Azmitia's work also highlighted the value of shared thinking. She observed five-year-olds working in pairs and produced the following conclusions. Having a partner can increase the amount of time children work on a task. The presence of a partner can prevent children from giving up in a difficult situation and it can also provide added enjoyment to the activity. Moreover, when children work together this can often increase their total work strategies as different children bring different skills to a task. Finally, when less mature or less experienced children are paired with an older or more able partner, the 'novice' learns a great deal from observing her partner and through benefiting from 'expert' guidance (29).

However, not all young children socialise naturally and for some, as we have seen, social skills are difficult to acquire. In order for children to work collaboratively they have to learn the skills of turn-taking and sharing. In the Reggio Emilia schools this is not left to chance; practical ways of fostering social knowledge are encouraged through the curriculum and the way in which the building is planned. Dressing-up areas are situated in a central area; classrooms are connected by phones, passageways and windows; both dining areas and cloakrooms are designed to encourage children to get together; the daily menu for lunch is a vivid display of close-up colour photos of the food to be served that day, encouraging children to comment on the shape of the pasta or the colour of the vegetable. Furthermore, these Italian pre-schools believe passionately in the effectiveness of learning in small groups; the staff consider that this is the most favourable type of organisation for an education which is based on relationships.

FIGURE 2.2 WHAT A CHILD LEARNS TO DO IN CO-OPERATION WITH OTHERS HE EVENTUALLY LEARNS TO DO ALONE

FIGURE 2.3 CHILDREN SHARE THEIR INTERESTS WITH OTHERS

These small groups are not set up as a convenient way of managing learning but as the best way. Staff assert that contact between children can provide opportunities for negotiation and communication that can be at least equal to that achieved when an adult is working with a child, and sometimes greater. When children are with children the contacts are equal; although children can learn a great deal with an adult there can be the relationship of authority and dependence, which can detract from a child's confidence. When children form their own groups they choose to work with others who share their interests or schemes of thinking (see also Chapter 5). Cath Arnold found that children played in this way in her family group at the Pen Green Centre; she also noted that when disputes arose, this was often because these interests or schemas conflicted (30). My own observations of four-year-olds revealed some particularly concentrated work from pairs of boys who shared the same schema.

Case study

Mark and Ben used large brushes and buckets of water to paint patterns on stone paving slabs. They painted long, straight lines and matched them for length. Mark noticed nearby pine trees and commented that their lines were like 'lying down trees'. Ben said that they could make their trees stand up and he rushed off for some drawing paper and pencils. The boys drew their trees, and compared them as horizontal lines and as vertical lines when they held the paper up. Mark drew two short vertical lines on a separate piece of paper which he described as baby trees which are still lying down.

Comment

The boys shared a strong interest in up and down (vertical schema). They rubbed ideas off against one another and Ben discovered how to transfer one means of representation to another.

MONITORING THE DEVELOPMENT OF SOCIAL SKILLS

The growth of children's social development is often dramatic during their time in the Foundation Stage. The very experience of being alongside other adults and peers means that all children 'pick up' some of the conventions of living and learning in a group. Depending on their starting point, for some individuals this is a hard and slow lesson, while others leap ahead with their interpersonal skills and show an ability to lead and influence others. Most practitioners are broadly aware on a day to day basis of their children's different levels of sociability. Others dig more deeply; they closely observe and reflect on the child's play and activity in order to acquire a properly informed and more detailed picture. The Social Play Continuum developed by Pat Broadhead (31) provides a useful tool for observing and assessing children's social play. It highlights four domains of play – associative, social, highly social and co-operative. The emphasis in the observations is on the children's activity and use of language, with a stress on continuity and progress as play moves across the four domains. Some helpful signals of progression are identified, one being when children's actions and language become reciprocal. Another sign is the impact of altercations on play; for example, in the earlier domains the adult is often called on to resolve a dispute, which inevitably halts the momentum of the play; when children play more co-operatively, they tend to resolve their own disputes rather than call on an adult to intervene.

The Social Play Continuum not only provides a good structure for observations, but also encourages practitioners to assess the level of play in a particular area of provision and to reflect on what action might help children to move into a higher social domain.

LEARNING TO BE A GOOD CITIZEN

Although the term citizenship is not included in the Foundation Stage Guidance it very applicable in the early years. If children can learn to be at ease with others and start to develop a social responsibility for them, then clearly this will affect their personal well-being, but will also better prepare them to contribute in a larger social world. Good interpersonal skills are one of the most valuable of all skills when we look to what contributes to success in life. On a broader canvas it matters as well. Every day we are confronted with examples of inhumanity: random killings, intransigent racism, callous indifference to the plight of poor people and the casual sacrifice of human lives for minor material gain. Surely, by helping our young children to develop a greater awareness and concern for others and skills to relate to them we can hope that, in some way, we are contributing to the future state of human relations.

Summary

Young children grow up in a social world which initially consists of the immediate family. They learn to relate to a wider group of adults and children when they move from the security of home into a nursery setting. Initially children need their practitioner to substitute for parents and provide them with a point of contact in their new setting.

As they grow in confidence children relate to other children. Their friendships are dependent on them acquiring and practising complex social skills.

Young children develop personally and intellectually by being with other people. They initially share social experiences of home life and learn how family members live together. They learn in a wider context in the nursery as known adults tune into their concerns and help them to make sense of new experiences. Through their friendships with other children they share their interests and thinking and learn what it means to be one of a group. The Foundation Stage is a time for practitioners to monitor and develop children's burgeoning social competence.

Practical suggestions

Support high-quality key persons to relate to very young children

- Recruit and appoint key persons who have had some life experience, who demonstrate good interpersonal skills and a genuine interest in the work.
- Link a new key person to a mentor and provide opportunities for shadowing. Provide initial and ongoing training in key aspects of work, e.g. attachment theory, listening and counselling skills.
- Establish the need for key persons to: establish an initial trusting relationship with the family through home visits and a prearranged initial meeting, understand the need for confidentiality, become informed about each child's home background in order to understand more about his/her behaviour, develop some knowledge of each child's home language in order to greet the child and parent.

Learn more about children's relationships

- Observe young children's friendships to find out who are the most popular children and those who have difficulties in making relationships.
- Observe children in role-play and note the leaders, followers and those on the sidelines. Note friendship patterns in various activities; which children are constantly together; which children share similar interests (schema) and how they share this in their construction/ drawing/painting/movement/stories.

Support children's friendships

- Give new children a 'friend' on their arrival in the nursery. Emphasise the importance of this role and encourage the 'friend' to take real responsibility for showing the new child the nursery routines.
- Provide a large stuffed animal and place it in a quiet corner of the nursery. The animal is introduced as a friend to anyone who is feeling lonely.

- Give children 'access strategies' to enable them to join a group: encourage hesitant children to join in with an activity by imitating what other children are doing. By doing this the child is often accepted as part of the group.

Help children to appreciate the effect of external events on friendships

- Support those children whose friends move away with their families. Encourage two friends to each make a gift by which they can remember one another, e.g. a special shell or stone which they found in the nursery garden or a photograph in a frame.
- Help children to accept that although they will feel lonely if they are parted from their friend (on account of holidays or illness), this is an opportunity to try out new friendships.
- Encourage a child to keep a scrapbook of nursery activities while a friend is in hospital. This can be given as a present.
- Encourage children to think of their friends whilst they are on holiday and to send them a postcard.

Provide specific support for those children who lack friendship skills

- Work with small groups of children and use puppets and miniature dolls to enact scenarios and provoke discussion. Help children to develop their understandings about relationships. Use events and comments that occur in the nursery as a starting point, e.g. taking turns, being kind and offering to play with a new child, ensuring that no one is lonely.

Provide activities and opportunities which encourage children to share and take turns

- Purchase wheeled toys which are for two children to ride. Help children to agree that each should have a set number of turns jumping down from the climbing frame. Have a large illustrated rota for cookery to allow each child to see when it is her turn.
- Provide 'treasure boxes' which contain props and dressing-up clothes to suggest different types of role-play.
- Provide for small-scale play, e.g. identify a designated and preferably secluded area. Provide a selection of attractively decorated boxes which contain small-scale people, animals and vehicles. Include ready-made floor layouts or a sheet and felt tip pens for children to create their own floor map.

Professional questions

1. How well do we communicate with babies and very young children during daily routines?
2. How does my room arrangement encourage children to talk together, to share and co-operate?
3. Have I sufficient apparatus to enable children to have reasonable opportunities to share and take turns?
4. How well does the layout of my outside area and the resources promote children's social skills?
5. How well do I tune into children's thoughts and concerns through listening to what they say, noticing their actions, reflecting on their meanings?
6. How do I extend my relationships with children to share thinking with them?
7. What model of social behaviour do I provide for my children when I interact with them, their parents and other adults?
8. How closely do I monitor children's social development and use the information gained to improve it?

REFERENCES

1. Zimbardo, P. quoted in the *Guardian*, 22 July 1997, p. 8.
2. David, T., Gooch, K., Powell, S. and Abbott, L. (2003) *Birth to Three Matters: A Review of the Literature*. London: DfES, p. 46.
3. Leach, P. (1994) *Children First*. London: Michael Joseph, p. 86.
4. Goldschmeid, E. and Selleck, D. (1996) *A Framework to Support Children in their Earliest Years*. London: DfES.
5. Pollard, A. and Filer, A. (1996) *The Social World of Children's Learning*. London: Cassell.
6. Roberts, R. (2002) *Self-Esteem and Early Learning*. Second edition. London: Paul Chapman.
7. QCA (2000) *Curriculum Guidance for the Foundation Stage*. London: QCA/DfEE, p. 29.
8. Petrie, P. (1997) *Communicating with Children and Adults: Interpersonal Skills for Early Years and Play Work*, Second edition. London: Arnold, p. 25.
9. Coram Family Sure Start (2004) *Listening to Young Children: A Training Framework*. Buckingham: Open University Press.
10. Field, T. (1984) quoted in R.K. Smith and H. Cowie (1991) *Understanding Children's Development*. Oxford: Blackwell, p. 102.
11. Parker, J. and Asher, S. (1987) Peer relations and later personal adjustment: are low accepted children at risk? *Psychological Bulletin*, Vol. 102, pp. 358–89.

12. Donaldson, M. (1978) *Children's Minds*. London: Fontana.
13. Dunn, J. and Kendrick, C. (1982) *Siblings: Love, Envy and Understanding*. Cambridge, MA: Harvard University Press.
14. Dunn, J. and Munn, P. (1985) Becoming a family member: family conflict and the development of social understanding in the second year, *Child Development*, Vol. 56, pp. 480–92.
15. Ramsey, P.C. (1991) *Making Friends in School*. New York and London: Teachers College Press.
16. Vaughan, B.E. and Langois, J.H. (1983) Physical attractiveness as a correlate of peer status and social competence in pre-school children, *Developmental Psychology*, Vol. 191, pp. 561–7.
17. Rubin, Z. (1983) The skills of friendship, in M. Donaldson (ed.), *Early Childhood Development and Education*. Oxford: Blackwell.
18. Scarlett, W.G. (1983) Social isolation from age-mates among nursery school children, in Donaldson op. cit. (note 12).
19. Paley, V.G. (1992) *You Can't Say You Can't Play*. Cambridge, MA: Harvard University Press.
20. Tizard, B. and Hughes, M. (1984) *Young Children Learning*. London: Fontana.
21. Raven, J. (1990) Parents, education and schooling, *British Journal of Educational Psychology: Early Childhood Education*, Monograph Series no. 4, p. 56.
22. Woods, D., McMahan, L. and Cranstoun, L. (1980) *Working with Under-Fives*. London: Grant McIntyre.
23. Sylva, K., Roy, C. and Painter M. (1980) *Child Watching at Playgroup and Nursery School*. London: Grant McIntyre.
24. Hughes, M. and Westgate, D. (1997) Teachers and other adults as talk partners for pupils in nursery and reception classes, *Education 3–13*, Vol. 25, no. 1, March, pp. 3–17.
25. QCA/DfEE (2000) op. cit. (note 7), pp. 25–46.
26. Siraj-Blatchford, I., Sylva, K., Muttock, S., Gilden, R. and Bell, D. (2002) *Researching Effective Pedagogy in the Early Years*. London: DfES.
27. Gandini, L. (1993) Fundamentals of the Reggio Emilia approach to early childhood education, *Young Children*, November, pp. 4–8.
28. Vygotsky, L.S. (1962) School instruction and mental development, in Donaldson op. cit. (note 12).
29. Azmitia, M. (1988) Peer interaction and problem solving: when are two heads better than one? *Child Development*, Vol. 59, pp. 87–96.
30. Arnold, C. (1990) quoted in T. Bruce (1997) *Early Childhood Education*. London: Hodder & Stoughton, p. 81.
31. Broadhead, P. (2004) *Early Years Play and Learning: Developing Social Skills and Co-operation*. London: RoutledgeFalmer.

CHAPTER THREE

Becoming Independent

Independence is an essential life skill and one that needs to be nurtured from the earliest age. There is general awareness in early years settings that young children should be encouraged to become independent; however, the term is often understood to mean different things. For example, some practitioners consider that the main aim should be to support children to be able to be apart from their families for periods of time or become self-sufficient in personal care such as toileting, washing and dressing; others believe that the priority is to develop children who can think for them-selves. In fact all aspects of independence are important in order for young children to take steps to become self-standing individuals.

THE DRIVE FOR INDEPENDENCE STARTS EARLY IN LIFE

Although very young babies are necessarily dependent on their care-givers for their physical needs, as Winnicott stresses babies are 'going concerns' whose growth and development is 'inevitable and unstoppable' (1). It quickly becomes noticeable that babies do exercise choices in what they play with, what they like to eat and when they sleep. These decisions about their physical needs and their subsequent levels of independence are significantly affected by the style of care-giving. Winnicott suggests that when adults feel responsible for shaping and forming children without being aware of these processes of developing autonomy, they make life difficult both for themselves and for the small people with whom they are living. Winnicott's views are born out when we see adults either restricting children's development or pressurising them into achieving developmental milestones too early. Two-year-old Elise was fiercely protected at home. She was never allowed to try to climb stairs or steps and only allowed to walk outside with an adult on a rein. These restrictions continued until Elise was four years. By this time her movements were poorly co-ordinated and tentative. At the other extreme some parents are very keen to accelerate their children's independence. Sitting up, walking and becoming dry at night become milestones that are immensely important to achieve early. Both of these shaping approaches stem from loving parents who genuinely want the best for their children. Elise's parents, however, failed to trust her to learn through trial and error; on the other hand, parents who push their children towards maturity before they are ready, risk them experiencing failure and losing confidence. In both cases this can lead young children to become over-dependent. Jenny Lindon states that 'We need to resist over-loading young children with stimulation and to avoid the "build better baby" type products that have emerged, especially in the United States'. Lindon suggests that babies and toddlers need time to use their physical abilities and apply their ideas. 'The clear preference of very young children for "do it again" is ideal for their learning' (2).

The early years provision in Reggio Emilia in Northern Italy has an international reputation for the excellence of its approach to the education of children from birth to six years (see also Chapter 2). Care is taken to encourage children to make decisions from the earliest age. Babies who are able to crawl are provided with individual sleep nests which resemble large dog baskets which they can crawl in and out of as they choose. This provision is a wonderful example of the respect that staff give to such young children, and also of their belief that even at this age babies are capable of deciding what is best for them.

SOCIAL AND EMOTIONAL INDEPENDENCE

The move from home or one care-giver to a group setting is a very big step for any child and will depend very much on the child's stage of readiness to be independent from his known and loved parent. In a study of four-year-old children moving into reception classes, Ghaye and Pascal identified three different activities which required children to develop degrees of independence (3). These activities – separations, transitions and incorporations – take place in any Foundation Stage setting and will be explored in turn.

Separations happen when the child leaves her parents and home for her new setting. There are considerable challenges and emotions involved for parents, children and practitioners during the early days of separations. In the study parents recounted their children's different responses. For example, one child was hesitant about lining up with others in the playground; another self-reliant child complained to his mum about her accompanying him into school. Although it is usually desirable for parents initially to spend some time in the setting with their children, this last comment highlights the need for rules to accommodate individual needs. Consideration of the child's previous experience in being separated from home and observations of her levels of confidence and adaptability in the school setting should always play a part when deciding when it is appropriate for parents to leave their child. The teachers in the reception class study made great efforts to help children into school. This was easy when admitting small groups initially on a staggered basis. One or two upsets were reported as later groups of children were admitted into a larger class group.

When a child starts in an early years setting, ideally any family should feel that the staff are doing everything possible to accommodate their needs. Initial time spent with the family may well avoid anxieties and problems arising at a later stage. In order for a new child to feel comfortable about leaving her mum or dad she must be at ease in her new setting. Such rituals as finding coat pegs, learning how to hang up a coat, moving into a room with other children and saying goodbye take time. Some small individuals will respond to these new procedures easily and rapidly; they are very ready for this new experience. Others are unsure and each new step is a burden; in this circumstance any moves to try to jolly the child into separating from her parent or carer is misguided; the child is not yet ready to make this tremendous move on her own and patience, sensitivity and more time is needed.

Transitions occur when children move from one activity or from one part of the building to another. A study of children starting school in a reception class (4) found that the following areas may cause anxiety and pose challenges for children's independence:

- The school building – in particular a vast stretch of playground, long corridors, large lavatory blocks and the complexity of building layout.
- Daily transitions – moving into the hall, being in the playground, changing for PE and lunchtimes. These times are most overwhelming when large groups of children are involved.

These potential difficulties will not be so apparent in nurseries with smaller numbers of children and buildings of a sympathetic design; moreover, provision in many reception classes now takes much greater account of young children's needs, for example by having a separate outside play space and their own toilet areas. However, in all circumstances there is a need to be aware of the changes that occur in any daily routine and the stress that this might cause to a new child.

Practitioners should expect to spend more time with the child who is still insecure in a new setting and is emotionally dependent on one adult. Although we know that young children need to be helped to make a gentle and comfortable initial transition, there are instances when children do not have enough adult support once their parent has left them. An earlier study of transition from home to pre-school found that the total adult time given to all new children was less than 10 per cent (5). Sixteen years later, my own study of pre-school settings showed that, although never neglectful, in some cases practitioners were not being sufficiently proactive; new children were more likely to be left to their own devices unless there were noticeable signs of distress. At this point a child was always comforted and often encouraged to stay with an adult for the rest of the session. However, that is often too late; experienced and good quality early years practitioners are very aware that young children can appear to be coping with situations but are in fact finding situations very stressful. During the initial days in the setting children should be closely observed. It is helpful if they know that at all times there is one adult in particular who is there for them. In this way children are reassured that they are never on their own; this reassurance prevents the bottling up of anxiety which can then lead to problems at a later stage. Over time and given initial help, children delight in learning that they can cope for themselves in many new situations.

Incorporations occur when the child learns to feel part of a group. Parents in the reception class study reported that the buying of school uniform and school bag and flask helped children to look forward to their new independent life at school. Similarly when starting in any setting, children are helped to feel independent by having some group emblem such as a badge.

Children also become more sure of their new identity as members of the setting as they become familiar with the pattern of the day. This helps them to feel in control of what they experience; they are able to predict what will happen next rather than being simply passive recipients to what is happening. Young children will demonstrate their growing familiarity with the setting by placing events into a sequenced framework. This 'script' tells a story about what happens.

Case study

I visited a reception class three days after children had started school. I wanted to find out how much of an understanding children had about school life in this short space of time. I approached Gavin and asked him 'What do you do in this school?' He paused for a moment and then told me 'Well, we paint and draw and go outside to play. Sometimes we have a story and we must try to sit and cross our legs.' After another pause, Gavin continued, 'That's not all. We have lunch and then we go to the hall. I like that. We have to take off our clothes and put them together, 'cos they will get lost. Then our mummies come to take us home.' Over the other side of the class I approached Joe with the same question. Joe avoided looking at me. He simply hung his head and muttered, 'I dunno, I dunno.'

Comment

After only three days in school Gavin has already got a wonderfully clear grasp of some main school events. His detailed script and understanding of what is required and why shows that he is rapidly feeling himself to be a member of the class community. Joe, on the other hand, is lost. He is unable to talk to me about his life at school because at this stage he has no clear understanding. Things happen during the course of the day over which he feels he has no control. For Joe school life is still a buzzing confusion; he needs considerable support from a caring adult who will help interpret events for him.

PHYSICAL AND FUNCTIONAL INDEPENDENCE

Healthy toddlers strive to develop skills that enable them to become less physically dependent upon adults. They insist on trying to dress and feed themselves, they start to control their toileting habits and they want to move to explore new territories. Three- and four-year-olds progress and refine these skills. They learn the sequence of dressing themselves and develop their fine motor skills to enable them to deal with zips and buttons on clothes. They learn to go to the lavatory unaided. Their co-ordination improves and they are able to pour a drink for themselves and carry a plate of fruit to the table. As they gain confidence they practise their physical skills using apparatus both inside and outside. The child who is physically able to climb by himself to the top of the climbing frame has achieved a considerable milestone in independence.

FIGURE 3.1 PHYSICAL INDEPENDENCE IS VERY IMPORTANT

FIGURE 3.2 SOME PARENTS PROMOTE THEIR CHILDS' AUTONOMY

Loving parents recognise that each developmental step towards physical independence is a significant achievement for their child. They proudly recount to friends and family each new example of what their child has managed to do for herself. Despite this, some parents are not always aware of their role in encouraging self-sufficiency. Although their child often surprises them they are understandably not sure of what to expect. They know that at two and three years children do not write or draw representational pictures and so it may not occur to them to give a child a pencil or crayon in order to practise making marks. Moreover, time is often the enemy. Naturally, young children's manual dexterity will not allow them to do things swiftly. Fumbling small fingers struggle with buttons when dressing and turning on the tap. In the bustle of daily life it is much easier to do things for the child than to wait for what seems endless time to allow her to try for herself. Parents and carers are also rightfully protective of their children. This sometimes leads them to be over-anxious about their physical safety. Elise, as we saw earlier, was protected from potential hazards inside and outside the home. Her parents could not bear to think of her tumbling down a step, or even falling in the garden.

In other families young children's autonomy is not only celebrated but carefully promoted. Toddlers are encouraged to feed themselves early on, even though the initial results are messy. Parents show their child how to put their vest on and do not worry if socks are first put on inside out. They provide equipment for drawing, painting and sticking and simply let their child experiment. They allow their children to take some small physical risks in learning to climb and balance on equipment in a playground, while standing by alert to prevent any real danger. Moreover, some parents help their young children to become practical and useful members of the family; they are shown how to take responsibility for small tasks such as watering the plants, laying the table and helping to wipe up pans in the kitchen. They may help to fetch and carry things for a new baby.

As a consequence of their different home experiences, when children start at a nursery their physical independence will differ vastly. Some three-year-olds will have had little opportunity to practise physical skills for themselves and may find co-ordination difficult. They have learned to be dependent; their initial drive and confidence to try for themselves has lessened and they expect others to try for them. Other children of the same age are agile and physically confident. They can cope with their personal needs and are very keen to apply their physical skills in the new experiences offered in the nursery. They are keen to extend their functional skills in the nursery and take messages or a piece of apparatus to another room or help to mix the paints. Some children are particularly adept at doing these things and become known for their reliability.

Practitioners realise that those children who are already physically independent are likely to adapt more easily to life in the setting. Children who are more dependent need time and encouragement. They also need to know that although they will be helped, it is expected that they will become physically self-reliant. Usually, once they recognise this, the vast majority of children grow in confidence and will fulfil expectations by the end of the reception year to 'dress and undress independently and manage their own personal hygiene' (6).

Case study

Andrew appeared to adapt reasonably well to the nursery except for periods of outdoor play. Whenever these times were voluntary for children, Andrew opted to stay indoors, even in very warm weather. On the one daily occasion when all children were expected to have time outside, Andrew did all he could to hide, or pretended that he had lost his shoes. His key worker Sue noticed this at an early stage and made a particular effort to stay and chat with Andrew during outside sessions. It eventually became clear that Andrew was afraid that if he played outside he would not be able to locate the lavatories (which were situated inside the building). Sue reassured him that if in need, he should simply let her know and she would return inside with him. This worked successfully; after one week when Sue accompanied Andrew to the lavatory, he told her that 'he knew the way now to have a wee' and didn't need her.

Comment

Sue's early observations of Andrew's behaviour resulted in her spending time with him to forge a relationship and gently find out the cause of his concern. Her practical support allowed Andrew to cope with outdoor play and also to practise finding his way round the new nursery building. Once Andrew became familiar with the location of the lavatories he was keen to demonstrate his independence.

A degree of physical and functional independence assists young children to feel more in control of their own lives and gives them self-respect. It is also extremely helpful to busy parents, care-givers and practitioners if children are able to cope with their own physical needs. Teachers in reception classes with less favoured staffing ratios are very aware of this. Schools have traditionally always stressed the desirability of new children having physical self-help skills and most emphasise this in school brochures for new parents. However, it does not just rest there. If we consider independence in a broader sense it should include children's development as independent learners.

INTELLECTUAL INDEPENDENCE

Most practitioners would agree that it is helpful for both children and adults if children are trained to tidy away resources after playing with them, or to take messages. There is less certainty about the extent of intellectual independence that should be encouraged. And yet, this wider issue of intellectual independence is possibly more crucial to children's futures.

Thirty years ago, Leslie Webb argued that the most important role of the nursery was to encourage children's rational personal autonomy (based on the ability of the child to think for herself). Webb also pointed out that the demands on the practitioner in helping a child think things out for herself are far greater than in encouraging physical self-help skills such as washing and dressing (7). This view was later officially supported by government, probably most famously in the Plowden Report in 1967 when Lady Plowden recommended that 'children should be agents in their own learning' (8). During the 1990s, the Plowden Report was largely discredited as being utopian. However, the belief that young children should learn to problem-solve and act for themselves is now strongly represented in the Foundation Stage Guidance (9): for children at Key Stage 1 it is included in the Non-Statutory Guidance for Citizenship (10). A recent report from the Joseph Rowntree Foundation stresses how important it is to involve young children in making decisions about all aspects of their lives. It makes the important point that often our youngest citizens are ignored. They have very different needs and interests to older children and, yet, many consultations effectively exclude anyone under the age of eight years of age (11).

Anyone who has been employed in or visited a setting where young children are working autonomously, making decisions about what they are doing with whom and where, cannot fail to be impressed with the control that these children have over the activity in their lives. It is clear that when children are supported and expected to be independent they show themselves to be very capable. It is now generally accepted that children of three and four are already powerful and persistent thinkers. Although they lack experience of the world, they compensate for this to a large extent by their inner drive to make sense of all that they experience. Given the opportunity they will self-direct themselves.

Case study

Carl had taken great care to build a construction of blocks which he proudly described as his house. He told his teacher that he wanted to show it to his mum. Rosemary, his teacher, explained gently that this would not be possible, as today his neighbour would be collecting him from the nursery at the end of the session. Carl persisted that he wanted his mum to see his work. Rosemary suggested that Carl thought carefully about how this might be possible. After a pause, Carl declared that he would draw his construction. He spent twenty minutes on his drawing ensuring that the representation was completely accurate. Rosemary provided him with ribbon and helped Carl to present his drawing as a scroll.

Comment

Instead of providing Carl with a solution to his problem, Carl's teacher made it possible for him to make his own decision. The amount of time spent on the drawing and the quality of the work reflected Carl's investment in his self-directed learning.

However, independent children do not emerge by chance. As with any learning, children have to be introduced to the skills and given the opportunity to practise and apply them. Some of the most important attributes of independent learning include children being able to use the environment for themselves, to make choices and decisions, and to reflect for themselves on what has been learned. An early years setting places high priority on helping children to develop these attributes.

USING THE ENVIRONMENT FOR LEARNING

If children are to become self-sufficient learners they must recognise that they can use space and resources for themselves without having constantly to refer to adults. Space is essential to enable children to be physically independent. A setting which is organised as a workshop can increase opportunities for children to use their initiative. The practitioner who plans her environment to promote independence will take great care with the management and layout of physical space. Children must be aware of what is available for them – this has implications for every nursery room to have designated spaces for different areas of learning. Even where the nursery is not in purpose-built accommodation, it is possible to identify learning areas using the arrangement of furniture, storage of resources, floor coverings and large pictorial notices. The Montessori philosophy emphasises self-reliance and decision-making; consequently most Montessori nurseries will encourage children to select apparatus for themselves rather than have it readily available on tables. The High Scope programme particularly stresses the importance of the physical arrangement of a room and the need for resources to be accessible to children. The programme requires that resources in each area are logically organised and clearly labelled.

Having prepared the environment, children need to be supported and trusted to use it. When young children first arrive at the setting it is likely to be their first experience of being in a group and they need to be carefully introduced to what is available for them. In order to use space and resources for themselves new children need to understand the sorts of activity that take place in each area, what they are allowed to use and how they return materials after use. The first few weeks of any induction should concentrate on helping children recognise that the environment is there for them to use.

Initially, children need to be physically helped to find and retrieve their resources and to tidy away. They need plenty of time to do this. Eventually, children who are more independent can be encouraged to help others.

MAKING CHOICES AND DECISIONS

Active learners are not dependent on just doing what others tell them but bring their own ideas and initiative to situations. Given guidance and opportunity, young children are very capable of making choices and decisions about what and how they learn, when they learn it and with whom. Alison Stallinbrass, in her classic study of the spontaneous play of young children, argues for total free choice stating that only the child is capable of knowing what activity he needs to provide the required 'nourishment' for his development (12). Thirty years later we would temper that view by acknowledging a place for some adult suggestion and indeed some activity that is teacher directed. However, young children can be involved in many decisions at the planning stage which will take account of their thoughts and interests. These may include decisions about the layout of their nursery environment, what colour paints to mix, what fruit to have at snack time or how to organise a tea party or simple outing.

Not all children find it easy initially to make decisions. For example, at first some new entrants may be overwhelmed by the amount of choice in the activities available to them in an early years setting. At this stage it is helpful to make suggestions as to what they might start to do and to watch if there are signs of children being at a loss as to what to do next. As they become comfortable and at ease in the nursery they will respond to gentle encouragement to try different options.

Within the different activities there should also be opportunities for children to select what materials or tools to use. Before children are able to describe materials, make considered choices or consider similarities and differences, they need to have had many and varied opportunities to observe and handle materials and listen to descriptive language (13). This work is best managed in small groups with a practitioner who is able to point out what is available. Initially, young children will act on impulse taking the first thing available or opting to use everything. This is a necessary stage; over time children can be encouraged to reflect on their choice and be selective.

Organisation in the setting should make it possible for children to make some decisions about with whom they wish to work (see Chapter 2) and also to determine what they do with their time. Some young children have their lives at home heavily programmed by adults; they are subjected to a relentless timetable of outings, shopping and planned activities such as swimming, dancing and music lessons; in these cases the gift of time is particularly precious. Others, of course, are provided with large chunks of time for themselves, but the only choice available to them is which television channel to view. Again, a carefully planned programme in a setting should allow scope for the child's enterprise but also provide a place for adult guidance and, when appropriate, adult involvement and intervention. As Tina Bruce suggests, 'At times the adult leads and at times the child. Each takes note of and responds to the other's actions and words' (14). Children who are given choices and real opportunities to take responsibilities for their actions are more likely to understand that adults are there as a resource to support their enterprise rather than simply allowing it to take place (15). Their confidence as decision-makers is strengthened as they begin to understand how they can have a stake in their own lives. By the end of the Foundation Stage, many children can start to make choices and decisions about aspects of their personal lives, such as healthy eating and taking exercise.

BECOMING INDEPENDENT THINKERS

The most ambitious aim in fostering young children's independence is to support and extend their thinking. Kahil Gibran in his book *The Prophet* describes this so well; he gives a profound and perceptive definition of a wise teacher who 'does not bid you enter the house of his wisdom, but rather leads you (the child) to the threshold of your (the child's) own mind' (16). Children encounter this thinking threshold when they meet something that does not fit a previous assumption; over time they have to adapt their original ideas, take account of new information and make sense of it. However, the emphasis should be on 'over time' – children have to be developmentally ready to take this intellectual leap.

Young babies and toddlers show evidence of early thinking when they remember familiar routines, games and rhymes. *Birth to Three Matters* emphasises how they need support to make and strengthen these early connections (17).

In any early years setting we see examples of children thinking, but certain conditions are needed in order for them to exercise their powerful thinking potential. Two educational thinkers, Robert Sternberg and Lev Vygotsky, help us to identify what children need in order to think well. Sternberg argues that children (and all of us) need to learn to plan, monitor, reflect and transfer in developing thinking. They also need opportunities to use these skills and strategies through problem-solving, making choices and decisions. Vygotsky stresses the role of language in thinking and making meaning from experience. Both Sternberg and Vygotsky stress that children will only be able to think well in familiar situations when they make use of previous experience and knowledge (18, 19). Clearly, the practitioner plays a key role in fostering the skills and strategies and providing the best environment for thinking.

The *Curriculum Guidance for the Foundation Stage* includes the development of language for thinking as an important aspect in the areas of communication, language and literacy (20). The Italian pre-schools in Reggio Emilia give priority to this and achieve it through the early years practitioner acting as a catalyst and fostering dialogue within the group (see Chapter 2). The High Scope programme promotes language for thinking through providing for children to review their activities and to learn over time to become reflective and self-critical.

> In the process of recalling what they've done, children attach language to their actions. This makes them more conscious of their actions and more able to refer to them and draw upon them for later use. Talking about, recalling and representing their actions helps children evaluate and learn from their experiences. When planning and doing are followed by recall, children can build on what they've done and learned and remember it for the next time they plan an activity (21).

Speaking at a recent conference, Lillian Katz reminded the audience of High Scope findings which suggest important differences between the short and long-term effects of children's experiences. 'The results of the High Scope programme suggest that although formal didactic teaching with young children can lead to good academic progress initially, a less formal, more child-centred approach is associated with longer-term success' (22).

In their search to make sense, children ask thought-provoking questions. In 1982 Dr Karin Murris developed a way of helping young children to think their way through big issues by using picture books. Murris believes that young children are able to play around and engage with ideas in a way that is more difficult for older children (23). She describes this activity as philosophical enquiry. In providing the conditions for philosophical enquiry it is important that: children set the agenda for discussion through their questions and responses to the story; each child's contribution is fully respected; and the adult remains strictly neutral and avoids steering the discussion.

Children who are encouraged to work and think for themselves come to recognise that they are free to make mistakes. Practitioners help them to reflect on their mistakes and see them as a valuable way of learning.

Case study

Richard had made a fire engine using junk materials. He proudly showed his nursery nurse and the seven other children during small group review time. 'I nearly didn't make it so good though,' Richard admitted. 'I stuck the wheels with glue but they fell off.' In response to a question from Lynda, his nursery nurse, Richard thought that he had made a good mistake. 'My good mistake helped me to fix the wheels right – and look they can turn.' (The wheels were attached with split pins.)

Comment

Richard recognised that his first solution to provide wheels for his construction was not going to work. During his activity he had seen another child use split pins to attach to pieces of card. Richard persevered with a different approach which proved to be successful. He understood that his first mistake had been useful. He had learned that one approach to attach wheels was less successful than another. Richard would use this lesson in a future activity.

Summary

Babies are born with the powerful urge to be independent although early experiences strongly affect their subsequent ability to take responsibility for themselves. A young child's independence is reflected in her readiness to separate from home and move into a group environment. It is also evident in her development of physical and practical self-help skills. Young children can be helped to have a stake in their learning through making choices and decisions, asking questions and thinking about their actions.

Practical suggestions

Support social and emotional independence

- Make it clear to each new child that she is known through referring to some aspect of her life that you shared with her during a home visit, e.g. discussing her dog, her favourite toys, or some physical detail in her house.
- Ensure that a key worker pays particular attention to each new child until it is evident that she has made a sound transition to the nursery, e.g. the key worker should be alert to occasions when a child does not understand instructions, cannot remember where to find things, cannot remember routines, is confused and tense when making a transition from one activity to another, when clearing away or going outside.
- If children are to stay full-time, invite parents or carers to join them for lunch sessions during the first week.

Support children in separating from their parents (see also Chapter 8)

- Be alert to when a parent needs to leave the nursery and be physically present when this happens.
- Agree with the parent a procedure for saying goodbye such as waving from the window or taking the child's teddy shopping with her.
- Talk through with the child the daily routines that will take place until 'mummy' returns.

Promote physical and functional independence

- Play games that need buttons, zips and buckles to be fastened.
- Encourage children to take responsibility for their own possessions, e.g. clipping wellington boots together with a named wooden peg.
- Provide individuals with areas of responsibility, e.g. keeping the book area tidy, checking that all the jigsaws are intact, checking the painting aprons for repairs.
- Encourage less confident children to take messages; as a safeguard provide a written version for the child's pocket which she can produce if she wishes.
- Help children to be tidy, e.g. sew large curtain rings onto painting aprons to make it easy to hang aprons onto pegs, provide a dustpan and brush for clearing up dry sand, provide a floor cloth or short-handled mop for coping with spillages.
- Provide pictorial notices which help children to remember self-help skills, e.g. a picture of two large hands displayed with the caption 'Please wash your hands'.

- Check how well the storage of your resources makes it possible for children to access them easily. Provide easily fitting lids on containers, low shelves with sufficient space for each piece of apparatus. Space for individual jigsaws can be marked out and symbols/colours used to match each puzzle to the space allocated.
- Check that children know where things are. Play a game in the group 'Can you find where it lives?' Prepare a drawstring bag containing various objects, e.g. pencils, blocks, counters, scissors. Ask children in turn to withdraw an item from the bag and return it to its home.

Promote intellectual independence
- Build in choice and decision-making in activities.
- *Painting*: provide a range of paper of different shapes, sizes and colours. Make the paper easily accessible by having it available on a low table in the painting area.
- *Collage*: provide a range of materials from which to select different adhesives in order for children to learn which is most effective.
- *Storytime*: provide two or three alternatives for a story and ask children to vote for their choice.
- *Snacks*: allow children to pour the amount of milk or squash they wish to drink rather than be expected to consume a standard measure.
- *Displays*: consult children about whose work is going to be displayed on walls (ensure, through gentle encouragement, that all children's work is eventually presented).
- *Outings*: provide alternative options for a walk and ask children to select.
- *Planting bulbs*: ask children to browse through bulb catalogues in order to select their favourite colour bulbs.
- *Celebrations*: consult children about what food to have for a summer picnic or Christmas party.
- Allow children choice in how they use their time:
  - make clear what resources are available by having the room clearly organised and displayed into areas of learning
  - introduce children gradually to each area in turn, making clear the activities that can take place and the resources that are available to be used
  - encourage children to record their decision of where they decide to play by sharing this with an adult who acts as a scribe for them or by asking them to attach their name card to a picture/photograph of their chosen activity.

- Encourage children to reflect on their activities:
  - help children to develop a structure to support independent thinking, e.g. provide an attractive pictorial chart with the following headings: What do I want to do? Who do I want to do it with? What do I need in order to do it? How well did we do it?
  - provide a physical area in the nursery which is specifically designed for quiet thinking; provide a number of 'thinking caps' as tangible 'props' which are helpful for those children who find it particularly difficult to concentrate
  - display models, drawing and paintings that are particularly completed and engage children in discussion about what needs to be added next
  - encourage open discussion e.g. children to ask questions or make suggestions about aspects of a story that are unresolved or that puzzle them.

Professional questions

1. How well does the storage space and labelling make clear to children where to access and return resources?
2. How many of the following things have I done today that children could have tackled just as well:
   - dressing and undressing themselves
   - sending and delivering messages
   - preparing materials, e.g. making playdough, mixing paints, combining ingredients for cookery
   - tidying away equipment?
3. What decisions and choices are my children encouraged to make about:
   - the activities they select
   - the materials/apparatus they use
   - how they use their time
   - who they work with
   - when they go to the lavatory
   - when they have a mid-morning snack
   - playing inside or outside?
4. What opportunities have my children had to:
   - make and share judgements about their work
   - respond to the work of others
   - have others respond to their work?

REFERENCES

1. Winnicott, D.W. (1964) *The Child, the Family and the Outside World.* Harmondsworth: Penguin.
2. Lindon, J. (2003) 'Good practice in working with babies, toddlers and very young children', in *Birth to Three Matters: A Framework to Support Children in their Earliest Years.* London: DfES.
3. Ghaye, A. and Pascal, C. (1988) Four-year-old children in reception classrooms: participant perceptions and practice, *Educational Studies,* Vol. 14, no. 2, pp. 187–208.
4. Cleave, S., Jowett, S. and Bate, M. (1982) *And So to School.* Slough: NFER/Nelson.
5. Batchford, P., Battle S. and Mays, J. (1974) *The First Transition: Home to Pre-School.* Slough: NFER/Nelson.
6. QCA (2000) *Curriculum Guidance for the Foundation Stage.* London: QCA/DFEE p. 40.
7. Webb, L. (1974) *Purpose and Practice in Nursery Education.* Oxford: Blackwell.
8. DES (1967) *Children and their Primary School.* Report of the Central Advisory Council for Education. London: HMSO, para. 529.
9. QCA (2000) *Curriculum Guidance for the Foundation Stage.* London: QCA/DFEE, pp. 29, 31.
10. QCA (2002) *Non-Statutory Guidance for Citizenship at KS1.* London: QCA/DFEE.
11. Willow, C., Marchant, R., Kirby, P. and Neale, B. (2004) *Young Children's Citizenship: Ideas into Practice.* York: Joseph Rowntree Foundation.
12. Stallinbrass, A. (1974) *The Self-Respecting Child.* Wokingham: Addison-Wesley.
13. Dowling M. (1995) *Starting School at Four: A Shared Endeavour.* London: Paul Chapman.
14. Bruce, T. (1987) *Early Childhood Education.* London: Hodder & Stoughton, p. 23.
15. Sylva, K. and Jowett, S. (1986) Does the kind of pre-school matter? *Educational Research,* Vol. 28, no. 1, pp. 21–31.
16. Gibran, K. (1926) *The Prophet.* London: Heinemann, p. 67.
17. SureStart (2003) *Birth to Three Matters: A Framework to Support Children in their Earliest Years.* London: DfES.
18. Sternberg, R.J. (1985) *Beyond IQ: A Triarchic Theory of Human Intelligence.* Cambridge: Cambridge University Press.
19. Vygotsky, L.S. (1978) *Mind in Society: The Development of Higher Psychological Processes.* Cambridge, MA: Harvard University Press.
20. QCA (2000) *Curriculum Guidance for the Foundation Stage.* London: QCA/DFEE.
21. Hohmann, M., Banet, B. and Weikart, D.P. (1979) *Young Children in Action.* Ypsilanti, MI: High/Scope Press, p. 88.
22. Katz, L. (2004) 'Mind the gap' talk given at a conference Celebrating Young Children's Learning, organised by the Institute of Education, University of London, 5 March.
23. Murris, K. (1992) *Teaching Philosophy with Picture Books.* London: Infonet.

CHAPTER FOUR

Emotional Well-Being

The current thrust on raising standards is in danger of ignoring children's affective development. Our education system is seen as a means of satisfying the demands of industry and commerce; this is mainly interpreted in terms of academic achievement. And yet a recent Mental Health Foundation report says that one in five young people, some as young as four, are suffering from disorders such as anxiety, depression and psychosis. The report suggests that this narrowly focused academic definition of raising standards is causing pupils distress, and 'the nation's children, the country's most important resource, are failing to thrive emotionally' (1).

Nevertheless, in other fields of corporate life and medicine there is clear acknowledgement of the significance of the emotions for people's well-being and learning. The many forms of alternative medicine take account of people's feelings and how they are linked to physical health. Holistic remedies such as yoga and aromatherapy are used increasingly as part of treatment for cancer patients. Therapists are discovering that introducing their clients to simple techniques of thought adjustment can have as much impact on the power to curb anger and aggression and cope with depression as many years of analysis. New hospital rooms are now being designed to enable patients to have the comfort and support of their families staying with them. On modern management courses we hear that 'feminine' stereotype qualities which include sensitivity and intuition are requirements for effective leaders regardless of the gender of the leader (2). Daniel Goleman summarises the view from the business world:

> The rules for work are changing. We're being judged by a new yardstick: not just by how smart we are, or by our training and expertise, but also by how well we handle ourselves and each other. This yardstick is increasingly

applied in choosing who will be hired and who will not, who will be let go and who retained, who passed over and who promoted (3).

Practitioners have always recognised the importance of young children's emotional lives in relation to their overall development. However, many staff, particularly in schools, now believe that the downward pressure on attainment has forced them into practices which they know intuitively are counter-productive for children. Some pressures come from outside; for example, when schools respond to the requirements of parents who wish to admit their children at four years into reception classes immediately on a full-time basis – this arrangement does not allow children the necessary time to adjust to new experiences. Other practices result from school requirements. The DfES Foundation team urges all practitioners to use the Guidance for the Foundation Stage, but this message is slow to filter through to all settings. Teachers in some reception classes still feel pressurised into introducing children early on in the reception year to literacy and numeracy sessions before they are ready to cope with learning in large groups. Staff in private and voluntary settings often feel intimidated by the prospect of inspection where they believe that inspectors are mainly interested in children learning to read, write and calculate; this leads them to try to accelerate younger children's attainment in early literacy and numeracy at the expense of attention being given to the other areas of learning. Sometimes these fears and practices happen as a consequence of misunderstandings of requirements. Nevertheless it is a hard and worrying fact that many practitioners continue to feel compelled to act in a way which does not recognise or value how children might feel.

Common sense and our own experiences tell us that we cannot function properly if we are unhappy, upset or angry. Our behaviour and thinking is heavily influenced by our feelings. Emotional development in young children is rapid and profound. Their feelings affect their self-esteem, the way in which they relate to others and their grasp of right and wrong. In order to equip them for living now and later, early years practitioners need to understand how children's emotional life unfolds and what is required to care for it.

EMOTIONAL INTELLIGENCE

We may be puzzled as to why a friend or family member who is academically very able fails to make a success of his career or his family life. After all, it appears that he has so much going for him. Or maybe another person who has modest intellectual qualities seems to accomplish so much in her personal and professional life. One clue may be to do with the emotional abilities these people have rather than their rational or academic competencies.

There is increasing recognition that emotional abilities have been under-rated in the role that they play in helping to ensure a successful and fulfilling life. Regardless of intellectual capacities, some people are blessed with emotional stamina which helps them to withstand the stresses and difficulties in life and have insights into and empathy with others. Others who lack this stamina and are emotionally fragile are likely to find problems in dealing with their own and others' feelings. Both rational and emotional abilities are now seen as being equally influential in determining how people enjoy and what they achieve in life.

This recognition is increasingly documented. Howard Gardner's well-known work on multiple intelligences includes reference to intrapersonal and interpersonal abilities. The first refers (albeit implicitly) to knowing about one's own feelings and the second to tuning into the feelings of others (4). Both abilities involve emotions as a means of regulating behaviour. If young children are helped to develop these abilities this will strengthen their sense of self and their relationships with a range of other people. Nowicki and Duke's study supported this. They found that children who were aware of their own feelings and sensitive to others were, not surprisingly, more emotionally stable, more popular and achieved more in school than those with similar intellectual ability but less emotional ability (5). Goleman in his work on emotional intelligence lists a number of studies that highlight both the worrying consequences when people are not emotionally competent and also the great benefits when they are. He also refers to brain studies which suggest that a person's emotional state of mind is closely linked to her ability to think more effectively (6, 7). This informed awareness tunes in well with beliefs of practitioners that, when working with young children, they are educating more than an intellect. However, the link between children's emotions and other aspects of their learning has only recently been emphasised. Past work on children's learning paid little attention to the affective aspects of development. Piaget only mentioned it as a factor which energised intellectual activity (8). Although Vygotsky stressed the importance of social relationships, he largely ignored the fact that emotions are part and parcel of those interactions (9). In 1994 Sarah Meadows described work on emotions as the 'Cinderella' of cognitive development (10). Although there is need for more work in this area, studies now increasingly recognise emotions as integral to learning.

Ferre Laevers' project 'Experiential Education' (EXE) identifies the degree of a child's emotional well-being as one of two key factors to be considered when judging the means of a child learning effectively and the quality of an educational setting. His definition of emotional well-being is broad:

> the degree to which children do feel at ease, can be spontaneous and are sat-
> isfied in their physical needs, feel the need for tenderness and affection, the
> need for safety and clarity, the need for social recognition, the need to feel
> competent and the need for meaning in life and moral value (11).

Some of these factors are explored elsewhere in this book (see Chapters 1, 2, 5 and 6); here we concentrate on the importance of regard to feelings. Laevers' work is strongly echoed in the current important action research project 'Accounting Early for Life-Long Learning'. Pascal and Bertram claim that emotional well-being is one of four factors seen in children who have potential to be effective learners (12).

Emotional well-being is now prominent in curriculum documents. It features in a number of components in *Birth to Three Matters*, where the development of very early language and involvement in imaginative play are seen to give scope for very young children to share and try out their feelings (13). The *Curriculum Guidance for the Foundation Stage* expects that, by the end of the reception year children will be able to show a range of feelings and be empathetic to how others feel (14). Sadly, there are few references in the guidance to fun and pleasure, surely fundamental emotional experiences for young children. By contrast, in the New Zealand Early Childhood Curriculum document *Te Whariki*, the section on well-being states that two of the entitlements for children are: 'an expectation that the early childhood education setting is an enjoyable place to be; a place where they have fun; and to develop a trust that their emotional needs will be responded to' (15). It also features as an ongoing thread in the collaborative work of the Early Childhood Education Forum who produced a framework for practitioners. *Quality in Diversity* is an important document in that it was produced by the representatives of the major national organisations concerned with the care and education of young children in England and Wales (16). The curriculum proposals for Northern Ireland have also drawn heavily on studies which show the impact of emotion upon learning (17).

EXPERIENCING AND EXPRESSING EMOTION

Children's experiences and expressions of feelings develop tremendously during the early years of life. Most of a child's basic emotions are in place by the time she is two years old. Young children also quickly develop their unique means of expressing their feelings and then use them deliberately to suit the occasion (18).

> **Case study**
>
> Maggie's emotions change frequently and rapidly. She can be furious one moment when her block construction collapses, but jump for joy the next moment when her childminder announces they are going out to the shops. By contrast, Kirsty's feelings are more long lasting and even. She rarely shows excitement, but plays equably by herself for most of the time. When Kirsty is upset or angry it is difficult to cheer her up. Her angry feelings (or mood) remain with her, sometimes for a whole day.
>
> **Comment**
>
> Linda, the childminder, was aware that these two three-year-old girls had different emotional styles which required a different approach. Maggie was often easier to deal with, although unpredictable. Kirsty's feelings were less easy to 'read'.

In certain situations young children may cope with their feelings in ways which are puzzling to adults. On experiencing the death of a loved relative or a close family friend, children will show their grieving through withdrawal anger or denial. Paula Alexander, a parent at the Pen Green Centre of Excellence, describes how her three-year-old son went back to bed-wetting at home after being told that his father had died:

> At nursery he kept taking things to the sandpit, burying them and digging them up to bring them back to life again. Then he'd say out of the blue 'My daddy's dead.' You have to pay close attention to what they are trying to express. The nursery did a lot of work with him through play.

Adults are usually very prepared to cope with a child's grief in the short term but may not recognise that the impact of bereavement is not always immediate. In the same article, Dr Richard Woolfson, a child psychologist, suggests that while adults feel the need to recover from their grief,

> there is no urgency in children. You tell them the news and their immediate reaction is to go and play, but it all takes time to work through. One minute a three-year-old will say granny's dead and the next minute will ask you not to forget to set a place at the table for her (19).

It is important for adults not to have any preconceptions about how children will react to grief. However, there is likely to be a time, once children have absorbed the news, when they will want to talk about their loss and, like Mrs Alexander's small son, to recreate their understanding through play. Early years practitioners can play a critical role in responding to each child's needs at a time when the child's family members are likely to be distressed and vulnerable themselves.

FIGURE 4.1 MOST THINGS ARE HAPPENING FOR THE FIRST TIME

Despite important differences in expressive style, most young children are full of raw emotion and feel acutely. The power of their emotion is heightened as their feelings are not tempered by experience. Most things are happening for the first time; as a consequence children can be desolate in their distress, pent up with fury and overbrimming with joy. They are receptive to all experiences that are offered to them. The effect of this responsiveness for those children who live turbulent lives is that they may live their lives on an emotional roller-coaster. In situations like this children can be ruled by their emotions. This is particularly noticeable with those young children who find it hard to express themselves in spoken language. It is difficult for an adult to be fluent and articulate when she is angry or distressed – how much more so for a three- or four-year-old when emotions overwhelm them.

Young children's feelings, positive and negative, will initially be best reflected through their actions. They will dance for the sheer pleasure of twirling their bodies in space; they will make marks, daub colours, stick materials, make patterns, build and construct imaginary scenarios to depict pleasures and turmoils which initially they are unable to talk about. Provision of a broad curriculum allows all children to find appropriate ways to represent what they are feeling. A narrow curriculum which only allows them to use limited materials or which places undue emphasis on representing experiences through only written symbols, is not inclusive. It is only the children who have already benefited from rich active and sensory experiences who will start to make sense of written numbers and letters; at this stage they will enjoy being helped to count and spot the letters of their name in signs and books and to practise writing them. A nursery curriculum should actively help all children to make this transition to using symbols. However, children's readiness cannot be pre-empted. Requiring all children to do things for which only some are ready will result in only some of them making any sense of what they are doing.

THE EFFECT OF TRANSITION ON CHILDREN'S FEELINGS

A young child on familiar territory at home or in a nursery is likely to feel secure and to be confident and competent. Any move means that a child is emotionally challenged. The initial effect on young children's confidence and independence of moving from a known setting has already been explored (see Chapters 1 and 2). We have seen that children experience many complex and often conflicting feelings. Excitement and anticipation of the move are tempered by anxiety, distress and confusion about the unknown. In these circumstances children's emotional well-being is not secure; this affects their ability to learn.

Negative feelings can have an effect on children's working memory. This is stressed in research from Western Australia where working memory is described as a measure of the number of things that one can cope with at one time (20). Adults all have the capacity to keep a number of ideas and skills in their minds at one time. Once these ideas and skills become familiar they become less onerous; in effect, skills which were initially learned individually and laboriously can fuse together and become automatic. Young children who are new to all learning find everything a challenge and there is so much more to remember. For example, a child who is learning to use the painting easel has to learn how to hold her paintbrush, how to apply paint and return the brush to the paint pot, what to do with the painting once it is completed, where to wash her hands and hang her apron. With practice much of this becomes routine and leaves her free to concentrate on the painting itself. However, if a child new to a nursery is worried about getting dirty or is jealous about a younger brother or sister having attention while she is away from home, these feelings can 'block' a working memory; she is literally in turmoil as a result of feeling uprooted and anxious about being abandoned. As a result, a child can become unsure, confused and forgetful about things in which she was previously competent.

Although children will initially show their feelings through what they do, their spoken language is important for them to learn to deal with emotions. In order to cope with such momentous experiences as starting school, children need to talk to express their feelings and also to make sense of what is happening to them during the school day. The following moving extract is from a teacher's informal diary of Joanne's response to starting school; it reflects the child's skills and her coping strategy with the obvious emotional difficulties that she faced.

Case study

Joanne was one of twenty-five four-and-a-half to five-year-olds who started school in a reception class.

Phase I (about a week): Joanne is very upset all the time in school. Clings to her mum and sobs when she eventually leaves. Cries for most of the day. Will try activities but joins in with tears rolling down her face. Finds out-of-class activities – music, assembly, playtime – especially difficult. She doesn't know the other children very well as yet and she's too distressed to start making friends. Typical extracts of transcripts: *'I want to go home now. Why do we have to go out? When are you coming back? I want my mum to come.'*

Phase 2 (about two weeks): Joanne seems to be starting to come to grips with school. She's begun to repeat, almost obsessively, the daily routine out loud. *'This is assembly now and then we go back to our class and we have a little play. Then it's playtime, outside isn't it? Are you going to come and play today? ... And then we come back for, we do ... have a story and another play and then it's time for my mum to come.'*

She appears to be internalising school structures and systems through verbalising her experience. She is breaking down the whole overwhelming school experience into manageable chunks, using spoken language. She is still quick to tears especially in out-of-class activities but seems to be becoming more philosophical about her daily endurance test.

Phase 3 (about a month): Joanne is starting to talk more positively about school life and by altering the pattern of her language she seems to be changing the nature of her actual experience. *'This is assembly but it doesn't last long and then we can all go back to our room don't we?'*

A constant oral delivery of her new fluctuating emotional state accompanies every new situation she is presented with. *'Oh, good ... today it's the office. I like doing the office. I'm going to go there. (Later) Mrs Knight is in the office. I'm writing, gonna do a letter for my mum. This is good. (After) I liked that Mrs Knight. I'm gonna take my letter home, give it to my mum.'*

Even more disconcerting: *'Ah ... now this is the bit I don't like but I 'spect* won't be very long will it? And then you'll come back and get us.' (Music time with the school specialist.)

By keeping her language cheery and optimistic in tone she's coping much better during the school day. Seems to be talking herself into acceptance of school attendance, sometimes talking cheerily with tears in her eyes: 'Now it's playtime again. I'm putting my coat on but I bet it's cold out there. Are you coming to play? (No) Oh ... (pause) then I'll just have to be Mrs Baker's friend and it's only for a little while and then we can come back.'

She is keeping verbal control of an almost unbearable situation and seems thereby to exercise control over her emotional responses.

Phase 4 (last five weeks of term to Christmas): becoming less verbal now and more relaxed in school. Only major changes in routine (like class assembly) are overtly distressing, although physical education is still a difficult time. Still the occasional disconcerting outburst: 'I was cross with you then Mrs Knight. I knew the answer then and I was sitting nice and you didn't ask me at all.'

I thought that the (Joanne's) problem was just about resolved so was somewhat taken aback when retrieving my talk box tapes. Joanne offered this prayer: 'Dear God, I hope it's soon time for my mummy to come and get me ... love from Joanne.'

Obviously still uncomfortable and anxious at school but less need for an active listener to provide comfort now. She's turned to the tape recorder to express her anxieties. She's now able to take a full part in all class activities and is becoming interested in all areas of the curriculum. Actively participating – not just sitting it out and surviving.

Phase 5 (the new term – Jan.): Joanne seems much happier and more settled in school. She is proud of her achievements and is making good relationships with her peers. She is especially supportive and caring when others are injured or upset and tearful. She was delighted when a younger class started after Christmas. I was encouraging my class to be extra helpful and friendly to help the new children settle in. Joanne's comment was: 'Oh, the poor things. I'm gonna be friendly, 'specially in the playtime outside. Do you remember when it was me that was the new one?' (Only too well) (21).

Comment

Joanne's fluent use of language made her difficulties instantly recognisable. Less fluent children may experience the same agonies which may not be picked up so easily. Joanne's teacher's sensitive observations made her recognise what more she could do to help children come to terms with their feelings on starting school.

THE INFLUENCE OF THE FAMILY

Young children's understandings and use of their feelings will be heavily influenced by the significant people around them, initially their parents. An important part of knowing about ourselves is to be able to recognise the different feelings that we have and that other people experience. Judy Dunn's work vividly highlights the remarkable insights that babies develop during their first year of life, as a result of noticing the emotional behaviour of family members. By the time they are two years old, children recognise that their mum, dad or brother can change from being angry to show caring behaviour, or be worried one moment and relaxed and smiling the next. At this early age children are learning rapidly what is required to alter these emotional states; for example, by comforting an unhappy younger brother (22). These studies show that even toddlers can show care and empathy in families where this is demonstrated (see also Chapter 2). By stark contrast, there is evidence of how less fortunate children learn different lessons. Daniel Goleman provides case studies of the dire emotional effects on small children who have been repeatedly physically abused (23). The most noticeable result is that these children who have suffered so much completely lack care and concern for others. At two and three years of age they typically ignore any distress shown by other children; often their responses may be violent. All they are doing is mirroring the behaviour that they have received themselves.

In families where feelings are not only expressed but are openly discussed, a young child is helped to recognise and accept his emotions and those of others. In these circumstances children are also more likely to talk freely about what they feel. These intimate contacts between parents and child involve shared experiences and loving attention over a period of time. Some parents lack this as a result of the busy lives they lead. Charles Handy points out how those adults who are in full-time and pressurised employment are starting to realise that their work is beginning to interfere with the relationships that they have with those closest to them (24). At the other extreme are parents who, because they are unemployed, have time, but the effects of overcrowded and poor housing and all the other attendant problems of poverty drain them of resources and patience to offer their small children. While the setting would never claim to be able to replace these family interactions, it can play a crucial role in working with parents and sharing the task of helping children understand what they feel (see also Chapter 10).

Case study

Karu was an attractive five-year-old, an only child, very articulate and already a competent early reader and skilled at construction. Nevertheless, he rarely talked in school and appeared to use his energies in disrupting activities for other children. He would deliberately tip over containers of apparatus while the teacher was talking, or pinch another child while she was answering the teacher. He refused to sit with other children and often tore up his drawings and early writing before his teacher could see it. By his second term in school Karu had no friends as the rest of the children disapproved of his anti-social activities.

Karu's parents admitted to having their own personal difficulties, but said that they saw very little of Karu at home as he spent most of his time watching TV in his bedroom. His father said that the one regular point of contact was at bedtime when he read Karu a story. On these occasions Karu gripped his father's hand very tightly.

Ann, his teacher, decided to try to spend more time with Karu in order to establish a closer bond. She suggested to Karu that he might meet her for a chat or a story in the library at lunchtime. (Karu had recently asked to stay in at lunchtime rather than go out into the playground where he was increasingly isolated.) Ann made these sessions chatty and welcoming. She always took a cup of tea with her and offered Karu a biscuit. Occasionally she would bring in photos of her home and her cat and tell Karu about things in her own life at weekends. At first Karu said little, but then he opened up. He expressed his terror of his father leaving home and of never being able to see him again (in fact this never happened as the parents sorted out their marital problems). Karu told Ann he felt very angry when he was made to come to school. He thought that his parents were deliberately leaving him there knowing that school made him sad. Initially Karu's behaviour was unchanged, but after two weeks of meeting daily with Ann he came to sit close beside her at group time. He gripped her skirt looking directly at her face. Ann bent down and said quietly, 'I won't leave you Karu – I am always here.' After that point Karu's progress was slow but steady. He continued to talk with Ann and sometimes talked about happy times with his parents. Eventually he made a friend (a shy newcomer to the school). By the end of term Karu was happy to go into the playground with his friend; he was becoming a sociable and equable member of the class and was able to listen and participate as one of a group.

Comment

Because of his huge anxiety about losing his father, Karu was unable to use his mind to learn from the nursery programme. His anger and resentments were not expressed verbally but were shown in his behaviour towards others. Ann's daily link with Karu helped to meet his hunger for love and security. His improved progress and behaviour was a consequence of being able to talk through his feelings and to trust his teacher.

Children's emotional understandings are dependent not only on the degree of family support but also on what sex they happen to be. Different messages about emotions are given to boys and girls. In one small study, mothers talked more often to their eighteen-month-old daughters about feelings than they did to their sons at this age. By the time they were two years old these little girls were seen as more likely to be interested in and articulate about feelings than the boys (25). Other studies offer further evidence. When parents make up stories for their small children they use more emotion words for their daughters than their sons; when mothers play with their children they show a wider range of emotions to girls than to boys. Leslie Brody and Judith Hall who summarised these studies suggest that as a result of the experiences they have, and because girls become more competent at an early age with language than do boys, this results in the girls being able to use words to explore feelings. By contrast boys are not helped so well to verbalise and so tend to be confrontational with their feelings and become less tuned in to their own and others' emotions (26). These early experiences and consequent emotional differences can very often continue into adulthood and be seen in relationships. Goleman suggests that women are well prepared to cope with the emotional aspects of a relationship; conversely, men are more inclined to minimise emotions and are less aware of the importance of discussing and expressing feelings as a way of sustaining a partnership. He argues that this emotional imbalance between the sexes is a significant factor in the break-up of marriages (27).

Given the importance that most of us attach to a stable and loving relationship in our lives, perhaps nursery education should aim to redress these differences in the emotional lessons that children learn.

YOUNG CHILDREN'S DEVELOPING UNDERSTANDINGS OF EMOTION

Young children need to have experienced a range of emotions before they begin to understand them. Using puppets with children, Denham found that those who showed both positive and negative feelings in their play were more likely to recognise and comprehend what others were feeling in different situations (28). Moreover, using puppets again, Denham suggests that children are beginning to recognise that in a given situation people may feel differently. For example, many children could understand that a puppet could be sad about going to nursery, while they would be happy (29). This ties in with other studies which indicate that young children are able to appreciate another viewpoint and are not only focused on themselves (30).

However, it is much more difficult for children to recognise that emotions can be mixed. When six-year-olds were asked to predict the feelings of a person who eventually found his lost dog but it was injured, they typically said that the owner would feel totally happy or sad, but not a mixture of both. Children at ten years acknowledged that it was possible to feel both emotions (31). Furthermore, although they may show complex feelings, they cannot predict them. However, it seems that social convention plays a part; from a young age children can be influenced to show feelings which are socially acceptable but are not genuine. In one study, four-year-old girls responded to social pressures by smiling when the researcher presented them with a disappointing toy, although when they examined their toy alone they showed their disappointment. (Interestingly, boys did not attempt to mask their feelings in the same way.) Questioned later, when they were able to swap their disappointing gift for a more exciting one, the little girls admitted to being disappointed, but thought that this would not have been recognised because of their polite words of thanks. These children made no reference to their smiling faces or the control of their real emotions and despite their behaviour were unaware of how their displayed emotion could beguile observers (32). As children grow older they begin to understand that the feelings that they show to others may not be the same as their true feelings. This lesson is a necessary one as part of becoming socialised. Nevertheless, where young children are pressurised or coerced into constantly masking their true feelings and substituting socially acceptable responses, this could lead to them misunderstanding the function of emotions in life.

Case study

Emily settled at her pre-school, seemingly without difficulty. However, she was overly polite in her responses to adults. When greeted in the morning by the nursery assistant, Emily would respond to advances with, 'I'm extremely well thank you very much.' She would thank individual staff when they supplied paper on the easel and after she had listened to a story. Emily made no advances towards other children – when they took apparatus from her and refused to allow her a turn on their wheeled toys outside she appeared to be at a loss. One day Danny took her beloved teddy from her. Emily did not protest but was later found in the cloakroom curled up in a ball. When the nursery assistant tried to talk through that matter with her, Emily repeatedly chanted 'I'm very well thank you', and refused to acknowledge her loss.

Comment

Emily had been heavily conditioned into controlling her feelings and being polite. The effect of this was that some of her behaviour was inappropriate and was regarded as bizarre by other children. When Emily experienced the loss of her teddy she was unable to give vent to her feelings, although her body language demonstrated her great distress.

The nursery worked closely with Emily's parents in order to help Emily to understand more about her feelings and to feel able to express them. She left the nursery after one year, still effusively and indiscriminately thanking adults but more able to express feelings of anger and frustration where appropriate.

SEIZING OPPORTUNITIES FOR EMOTIONAL LEARNING

We see and hear a great deal about how those adults with emotional problems can track them back to some difficulties in childhood. Goleman suggests that because early childhood is one of the very critical times for nurturing emotional growth, if this opportunity is missed or the nurturing becomes abuse it becomes progressively harder to compensate for this at a later date. If practitioners are to aim to prevent these problems in adulthood they must take advantage of the receptive nature of young children and positively help them to achieve emotional health. This means looking at a climate in the early years setting which helps children to feel, think and talk about feelings. They will think carefully about how to organise this climate. One major challenge is to help children to gradually rein in their impulses. Goleman quotes an interesting long-term study carried out in the 1960s at Stamford University. A group of four-year-olds were offered a marshmallow as a treat. If they were willing to wait for the adult to run an errand they would be allowed two marshmallows when he returned. Goleman reports that some children were unable to wait and grabbed one marshmallow almost immediately after the researcher had left the room. Other children though were able to wait for fifteen to twenty minutes for the adult to return. Some found this discipline really difficult.

to sustain themselves in their struggle they covered their eyes so they would-n't have to stare at temptation, or rested their heads in their arms, talked to themselves, sang, played games with their hands and feet, even tried to go to sleep. These plucky pre-schoolers got the two marshmallow reward.

This group of four-year-olds were tracked down at the end of their high school career and the differences between them were starkly clear. The study found that the group who had been prepared to delay their gratification early in life were as young adults more socially competent, self-assertive, personally effective and better able to cope with life's problems (33).

Young children are naturally impulsive; they can learn to wait, pause and reflect, but it is a hard lesson for some and slow progress for many. A programme of turn-taking games and activities will help to develop these skills as will a displayed time-line of routines where children can be encouraged to wait for something special to happen at the end of the session. Above all, if adults regularly share stories and model scenarios which show the benefits of resisting impulse this will influence children over time.

Circle time has become a common means of encouraging children to converse about things that matter to them. In the hands of a sensitive practitioner this can be very effective. However, circle time has tended to become accepted as a blanket method for dealing with many personal, social and emotional matters; unfortunately, there are no mechanical teaching recipes which automatically produce good outcomes. Circle times with young children can come adrift if they are organised for large groups; if they are not carefully planned and prepared; if they are not conducted by a known and trusted adult; if the adult is not already tuned into some of the children's needs and concerns; or if they become a dull and predictable routine.

Children, like adults, are more likely to talk about things that affect them with people who show that they are genuinely interested, who are prepared to give time to listen and who reciprocate with some of their experiences. Children's feelings will be stirred by sensory experiences such as listening to music, looking and touching beautiful things, tasting and smelling. If they can talk about their reactions to these positive experiences, it will alert them to recognise similar feelings on another occasion. In the same way they need to recognise negative emotions. Anger and fury which results in loss of control can be extremely frightening for a three- or four-year-old. Sensitive adults can provide safety and reassurance and encourage children to try to see patterns in their behaviour and reasons for their strong reactions. In this way children will come to accept and regulate their feelings.

Children who are emotionally vulnerable desperately need a calm and safe environment. However, occasionally the nursery that emphasises calm therapy can be in danger of repressing emotions. Children have the right both to witness and to experience different feelings. Living in a calm, bland atmosphere can produce dull people. Children's feelings should also be respected (34). It is questionable whether adults should attempt to jolly children along when they are bereft at being left in the nursery, or their friend will not play with them. This sorrow and desolation is more devastating than that experienced by an adult in a comparable situation for the simple reason that the child does not have the life experience which tells her that the cause of the distress is only temporary. A simple acknowledgement of sympathy will at least show the child that she is being taken seriously. As always, practitioners themselves play a very important role as models. A strong relationship between adults and children is founded on feeling. In such a nursery children understand that the adults care for them, laugh with them, share their tragedies and excitements and also become angry when boundaries of behaviour are broken. So long as the love and care are prevalent, children will flourish and grow given this healthy emotional repertoire.

Summary

Despite the government's current thrust on academic achievement, increasingly in other areas of work, people's emotional lives are seen to be critical factors in their success in life. Young children's emotional development is rapid and closely tied to other areas of development. Feelings are now recognised as a powerful influence on learning. In order to achieve emotional health, children need to experience and be able to express a range of emotions in their own way through a broad curriculum. They need to talk through negative emotions, particularly during times of stress, as when moving into school. Children's understandings about their feelings are heavily dependent on the support they receive from their families and also whether they happen to be a boy or a girl. Given support, they start to show empathy as toddlers and then learn to understand that people can feel differently from them. Foundation Stage settings can play an important role in aiding children's emotional well-being through their curriculum and organisation and the ways in which practitioners work with children and act as role models.

Practical suggestions

Listen and observe
- Try to catch children's responses during all parts of the school day.
- Observe how they cope with the challenges of new activities or a new member of staff.
- Ensure that you observe the body language of those children who cannot easily verbalise their feelings, particularly those with English as an additional language.

Provide an environment which enables children to acknowledge and express their feelings
- Organise a broad range of activities which enable children to express their feelings in different ways.
- Provide resources: a punch bag on which to vent angry feelings; a large soft animal or soft woolly scarves for lonely/upset children to cuddle; a large stuffed figure of a granddad sat in an armchair to whom children can confide their worries.
- Have regular displays of adults and children expressing different emotions. Use these in discussions with small groups and encourage children to identify with the feelings and to share their own experiences.
- Introduce a worry bag (a drawstring bag) and display a selection of shells (worry shells) nearby. If a child is worried he/she can be encouraged to select a shell and take it to an adult to share his/her concern. After the worry has been discussed (and hopefully resolved) the child visibly gets rid of the worry shell by placing it away in the drawstring bag.

Help children to acquire a clear and understandable picture of life in the nursery
- Make clear the daily sequence of events.
- Provide a pictorial time-line and refer to it throughout the session.
- Have a large clock and make clear the times when certain activities begin and end (with practice, many four-year-olds will learn to use the clock as a reference point).

Help children to develop coping strategies
- Use the language of feelings – suggest labels to describe children's emotions, e.g. bubbly, excited, fizzy, gloomy. Encourage them to use the vocabulary in relation to their own and others' feelings.
- Help self-contained and cautious children to recognise and open themselves to excitement, joy and wonder in the safe knowledge that these feelings are acceptable and can be controlled.

- Provide ways of talking to meet needs, e.g. instead of pushing a child off a bike in anger, suggest that the child requests to have his turn.

Demonstrate that everyone has feelings
- Talk about how you feel, what makes you angry, excited or worried.
- Use situation stories to introduce reasons for people feeling differently.

Professional questions

1. How well have new children come to terms with their feelings on admission to the nursery? How do I know?
2. What have I done today (this week) to help children be more aware of their feelings?
3. How do I help some of my older children to become less impulsive?
4. How do my feelings (impatience, frustration, pleasure, sympathy) affect how I interact with individual children?
5. What do I need to know about the children's emotional lives at home that will help me help them to become more effective learners?

REFERENCES

1. Bunting, C. (1999) Call for mental-health aid in school, *TES*, 25 June, p. 12.
2. Lightfoot, S.L. (1983) *The Good High School*. New York: Basic Books, p. 333.
3. Goleman, D. (1998) *Working with Emotional Intelligence*. London: Bloomsbury, p. 4.
4. Gardner, H. (1993) *Multiple Intelligences*. New York: Basic Books.
5. Nowicki, S. and Duke, S. (1989) *Helping the Child who Doesn't Fit In*. Atlanta, GA: Peachtree Publishers.
6. Damasio, A. (1994) *Descartes' Error: Emotion, Reason and the Human Brain*, quoted in D. Goleman (1996) *Emotional Intelligence*. London: Bloomsbury, p. 19.
7. Goleman, D. (1998) *Working with Emotional Intelligence*. London: Bloomsbury, p. 239.
8. Piaget, J. and Inhelder, B. (1968) *The Psychology of the Child*. London: Routledge and Kegan Paul.
9. Vygotsky, L. (1978) *Mind in Society*. Cambridge, MA.: Harvard University Press.
10. Meadows, S. (1994) *The Child as Thinker*. London: Routledge, p. 356.
11. Laevers, F. (1999) The Experiential Education project: well-being and involvement make the difference, *Early Education*, Vol. 27, Spring.
12. Pascal, C. and Bertram, T. (1998) Accounting Early for Life-Long Learning. Keynote talk at Early Years Conference, Dorchester, July.
13. SureStart, (2003) *Birth to Three Matters*. London: DfES p. 11.

14. QCA (2000) *Curriculum Guidance for the Foundation Stage*. London: QCA/DFEE, p. 34.
15. New Zealand Ministry of Education (1996) *Te Whariki, Early Childhood Curriculum*. Wellington: Learning Media.
16. Early Childhood Education Forum (1998) *Quality in Diversity in Early Learning*. National Children's Bureau Enterprises.
17. Northern Ireland Council for the Curriculum Examinations and Assessment (1999) *Developing the Northern Ireland Curriculum to Meet the Needs of Young People, Society and the Economy in the Twenty-First Century*. NICCEA.
18. Denham, S. (1998) *Emotional Development in Young Children*. New York: Guilford Press.
19. Williams, E. (1997) It's not bad to be sad, *TES Primary*, 12 September, p. 13.
20. Rees, D. and Shortland-Jones, B. (1996) *Reading Developmental Continuum, First Steps Project*. Department of Western Australia, Rigby Heinemann.
21. Knight, A. (1992) Starting school – a painful process, *T.A.L.K., The Journal of the National Oracy Project*, Vol. 5, Autumn, pp. 3, 4.
22. Dunn, J. (1988) *The Beginnings of Social Understanding*. Oxford: Basil Blackwell.
23. Goleman, D. (1996). *Emotional Intelligence*. London: Bloomsbury.
24. Handy, C. (1994) *The Empty Raincoat*. London: Hutchinson.
25. Dunn, J., Bretherton, I. and Munn, P. (1987) Conversations about feeling states between mothers and their young children, *Developmental Psychology*, Vol. 23, pp. 1–8.
26. Brody, L.R. and Hall, J.A. (1993) Gender and emotion, in M. Lewis and J. Haviland (eds), *Handbook of Emotions*. New York: Guilford Press.
27. Goleman, D. (1996) op. cit. (note 23).
28. Denham, S.A. (1986) Social cognition, social behaviour, and emotion in pre-schoolers: contextual validation, *Child Development*, Vol. 57, pp. 194–201.
29. Denham, S.A. and Couchard, E.A. (1990) Young pre-schoolers' understanding of emotion, *Child Study Journal*, Vol. 20, pp. 171–92.
30. Borke, H. (1983) Piaget's mountains revisited: changes in the egocentric landscape, in M. Donaldson (ed.), *Early Childhood Development and Education*. Oxford: Blackwell.
31. Harris, R.L. (1983) Children's understanding of the link between situation and emotion, *Journal of Experimental Child Psychology*, Vol. 36, pp. 490–509.
32. Cole, P.M. (1986) Children's spontaneous control of facial expression, *Child Development*, Vol. 57, pp. 1309–21
33. Goleman, D. (1996) op. cit. (note 23) pp. 60–83.
34. Scott, W. (1996) Choices in learning, in C. Nutbrown (ed.), *Children's Rights and Early Education*. London: Paul Chapman.

CHAPTER FIVE

Dispositions for Learning

We hear a great deal today about the problem of disaffection in society. Many adults become disaffected with their partners – hence the high rate of family break-up. People in all walks of life grow to be dissatisfied with their employment. Disaffected adolescents are accused of being demotivated towards study, lacking persistence and initiative. There is also a worrying trend of children being excluded from and truanting from primary schools. Yet as the term 'disaffection' implies, at one time there was a positive attitude towards what is now being rejected. All partnerships start on an optimistic note; most people feel positive when starting a new job; at one point in their lives children are strongly disposed to learn and most view starting school as an exciting venture.

This chapter does not intend to attempt to tease out why people become dissatisfied with their lot; there are many books and courses which offer advice and support for living positive and satisfying lives. However, all the literature and counselling courses emphasise that whatever the circumstances, the key to living and learning successfully lies within ourselves – it is to do with our views and attitudes and what we make of what we are given. In the previous chapter we looked at the inextricable link between the emotions and other aspects of our development. We saw how receptive young children are to emotional learning. The same messages apply to attitudes or dispositions. We know that the young brain is very receptive – the mechanisms are all present to promote powerful learning. Nevertheless, unless a young child is disposed or inclined to use what she knows, the mechanisms will not function.

WHAT ARE DISPOSITIONS?

Lillian Katz makes a useful distinction between attitudes and dispositions. She states that whereas an attitude consists of a set of beliefs, a disposition demonstrates those beliefs in behaviour. It is possible to have a positive or negative attitude towards something but not be disposed to take any action about it. Katz suggests that young children are not assumed to have attitudes because they are too young to think evaluatively. However, all we are learning about the impressionable young brain indicates that beliefs, attitudes and dispositions are being shaped in infancy. Katz further differentiates between feelings and dispositions. The former are emotional states, while the latter are habits of mind which result in patterns of behaviour (1). As we saw in the previous chapter feelings can be powerful, but with young children they can be transitory, while dispositions are likely to be more stable and long-lasting. Nevertheless, feelings will significantly affect dispositions.

Case study

Tony was constantly anxious when faced with anything new or a different routine. He looked worried and clearly felt insecure when presented with the opportunity of climbing on a new climbing frame. He was persuaded to climb onto the first rung but was not prepared to persist with the challenge of the new equipment. Tony's anxious feelings had led him to adopt a very cautious disposition.

Katz also points up the difference between predispositions – that is, the genetic gifts that are present at conception – and dispositions which are learned. Moreover, dispositions do not automatically follow on from predispositions. It is easy to believe of a friendly and outgoing baby who is bursting with curiosity that these qualities will remain with her for life. Given supportive experiences and guidance that baby will strengthen her predispositions to socialise and learn; however, if she is not given these opportunities, these early positive traits are in danger of becoming weaker.

Attention is given to attitudes and dispositions in other chapters. For example, in Chapters 2 and 6 we see how children develop sociable and moral dispositions and in Chapter 8 how attitudes of interest and tolerance towards difference are fostered. This chapter looks particularly at dispositions for learning and the messages for those who work with young children.

Babies are born with a passion to find out. Gopnik and colleagues suggest that two-year-olds have a particular drive to make sense of all around them as seen in their boundless energy to investigate and start to ask questions

(2). They lack experience of the world but their physical, intellectual, social and emotional antennae are tuned to make sense of it. This is a common endowment given to all healthy children and it happens without any formal education. However, the effects of environment influence this heritage. Children's early investigations may be nurtured or restricted and by three and four years of age the impact of children's early life experiences are already evident. It is easy to see those individuals who show signs of positive dispositions to learn such as high levels of motivation and perseverance, as well as those who are more passive or distractible.

Practitioners now have some common pointers for the dispositions that they should strengthen in young children. The *Curriculum Guidance for the Foundation Stage* identifies dispositions for learning which include independence, motivation and concentration (3). These are closely aligned with Margaret Carr's five aspects of dispositions which include: taking an interest, being involved, persisting with difficulty or uncertainty, communicating with others and taking increasing responsibility. Carr usefully suggests that these aspects can be analysed in three parts: being ready, being willing and being able (4).

DEVELOPING DISPOSITIONS AT HOME

Once again, dispositions to learn are grown in family life. Children who live in a well-organised household will observe and become accustomed to daily routines. They will learn to predict the pattern of each day, to organise their personal belongings and to value order. The effect on a small child may, of course, differ according to the impact and strength of the daily messages, the way in which parents help the child to make sense of what is happening and the child's own personality. One child may use these early lessons to develop systematic and orderly habits of learning. Another may be dominated by and become dependent upon routine which can lead to her becoming rigid and inflexible.

Case study

Chloe at eighteen months loved to draw. The crayons that she used were stored in a large biscuit tin. Chloe carefully chose her crayon, used it and then replaced it in the tin, saying 'back, back', before selecting another. She clearly enjoyed making marks but also selecting and replacing the tools.

Three-year-old Amy spent most of her time in the nursery tidying books. She smacked children's hands when they came to the book area to browse through books and use them. Directly a book was removed from the shelf

Amy replaced it. She was unable to concentrate on a group story if any books were lying around and would dart off to tidy them up. Amy disliked any change in the nursery regime. One sunny morning the nursery teacher announced that children could have their snack outside. Amy refused to go out. When gently encouraged to do so, she shouted, 'I don't like this, we don't do this.'

Comment

Chloe's mother had encouraged her to be independent and to tidy away her toys as part of a game. The toddler was already enjoying the mastery of managing her drawing tools as well as the magic effects of using them. For Amy, tidiness and routine had assumed an undue importance; so great was her need to be in control that it meant that she was unable to relate to other children or to enjoy different curriculum activities.

LEARNING IS NOT COMPULSORY

Although a very young child's learning and progress is influenced both positively and negatively by the care, stimulus, neglect or indifference from her family, in the end it is hinged to the child's own motivation. The same applies to the nursery or school age child. Her inner drive to learn remains the key factor in her subsequent achievement. This suggests that above all else practitioners need to reflect on how their provision strengthens this drive.

It is now well understood that young children learn more effectively when they are active and have regular and frequent access to adults. Many children under the age of five find it difficult to sit still even for short periods or to understand new knowledge or concepts when they are taught to a group. And yet this is still standard practice from the time that children enter many reception classes. The best literacy and numeracy sessions are creatively adapted to meet these needs through flexible timings, good staffing ratios and regular use of play methods to allow children to practise new skills and concepts. In these sessions children are supported in their learning, and are likely to want to learn more. Without this attention to young children's diverse learning needs, routine and prescriptive programmes may not reach some children and may not challenge others. Confusion and boredom will result in demotivation; in extreme cases the result could be putting children off for life from reading for leisure or delighting in numeracy patterns and problems. In short, we could end up with children who are able to read, write and calculate, but who have no desire to use these competencies. Lillian Katz points out that an appropriate pedagogy is one that takes into account the acquisition of knowledge and skills in such a way that the disposition to use them and positive feelings towards them are also strengthened (5).

Even the youngest children can show signs of disaffection towards their schooling. Gill Barratt, in her arresting study of young children starting school in reception classes, shows how they can be turned against school by a curriculum and organisation that does not take account of their interests, what they know already or the ways in which they have learned it. At this age they do not have open to them the options of older children who may try to avoid attending school. At four and five children have little choice as they accompany their parents. However, as Gill Barratt says, they do have the power to withdraw their goodwill (6). Any knowledgeable early years practitioner will recognise the body language from a three- or four-year-old who does not wish to comply with a request or take part in an activity. We may insist on attendance but we cannot require children to learn.

Case study

Kane at four years was excited about starting school. His nursery had served him well for two years, helping him to become confident and independent, but for the last term it had not offered him sufficient challenge, particularly to match his deep interest with numbers. At home Kane's dad played cards with him regularly and Kane was very able to see number patterns and to do simple number calculations. He was visibly bored with the nursery and very keen to go to 'big school'.

Kane learned school routines quickly. He was eager to show his ability in numeracy and was daunted when his responses were sometimes ignored in order for other children to contribute. He had little interest in sorting and matching activities and found the early practical recording of numbers easy and routine. After three weeks Kane's teacher, Sue, was concerned about him. He was restless and inattentive for much of the day and no longer volunteered answers in group times. In contradiction to the picture that Kane's mum had provided of his abilities, he appeared to have no interest in mathematical activities and his baseline assessment score for maths was low. Sue arranged for a Year 6 boy who was interested in maths to work with Kane for twenty minutes a day for a trial period of two weeks. Initially the boy played similar games to the ones that Kane played at home with his dad. This developed into a programme of number problems, mental arithmetic and logic. After one week Kane's behaviour had changed noticeably. He continued to look forward to sessions with his Year 6 friend (which were reduced to weekly occasions) but was now enthusiastic about other activities, particularly construction and design technology. He developed and applied his abilities in numeracy, shape and space and produced some exciting models. Kane was pleased to help other children with their work.

Comment

Before Kane was admitted to school, Sue had fortunately taken time with Kane's parents to gain a clear picture of his interests and capabilities. She rapidly noted the mismatch between Kane's reported abilities at home and what he demonstrated in the reception class. She recognised that Kane was not being challenged and her prompt and imaginative action helped to reverse Kane's early disaffection.

One of the major tasks for any early years practitioner is to identify what learning has occurred before the child starts in a group setting. Fisher (7) likens the 'composition' of each child's learning to a jigsaw puzzle, with individual pieces gradually fitting into place, so casting light on wider and deeper understandings. Following this analogy, the practitioner needs to recognise the pieces of cognition already in place and support each child in adding to their personal cognitive jigsaw. This approach to assessment and teaching respects the child's initiatives and places the practitioner in the position of a tutor. Conversely, if the practitioner ignores previous learning and attempts to 'take over' the construction of the cognitive puzzle, this damages the disposition to learn. The child is confused, the puzzle is no longer under her control and her motivation to know more is diminished.

NURTURING DISPOSITIONS TO LEARN

Lillian Katz puts forward a number of important points relating to the nurturing of dispositions in any early childhood programme (8). These will be examined in some detail.

1. *Newly acquired knowledge and skills will only be secured in learning if they are used.* Children may be able to do something but not wish to do it. On the other hand, positive attitudes by themselves are not sufficient. It is not very helpful to want to do something for which one is ill equipped.

2. *The way in which something is taught may either strengthen*

positive attitudes or damage them. For many years now, early years practitioners have become concerned that the 'paper and pencil culture' evident in primary schools had a negative influence on practice with younger children. However, recent moves have signalled that the *Curriculum Guidance for the Foundation Stage* with its emphasis on play methodology is now taken seriously. All grant-aided settings are now required to have regard to this guidance. The appointment of a team of Foundation Stage regional directors as part of the Primary National Strategy is intended to support local authorities to ensure a quality of learning and teaching with young children. Fortunately, in the best settings, particularly in nursery schools, innovative play-based learning has always been a feature.

Case Study

The staff at Tatchbrook Nursery School deliberately develop children's experience of and capacity for sustained, imaginative play; they encourage story play to develop over lengthy periods of time, often a term and sometimes longer.

In a move to deepen children's super-hero play, the headteacher, Tess, shared informally with a small group illustrations and stories of some characters from myths. The Russian story of the witch Baba Yaga Boneylegs particularly captured the children's interest and this was the start of a play theme which lasted for two terms. The play was always situated outside; children were provided with open-ended props, boxes and fabrics, and the freedom to use these as they wished. Different strands to the play included hunting Baba Yaga and other monsters such as the Minotaur and Medusa. Children also explored ideas about power and the usefulness of magic charms and potions. During the play, staff saw children coping with their fears, supporting friends, developing an understanding of cause and effect and ways to represent things through signs and symbols. They internalised the story and, using their own mark-making were able to narrate the plot onto large sheets of paper.

Comment

The children's high levels of commitment to their play is self-evident together with the tremendous benefits to their personal development. In particular it helped them delve into their deepest fears and concerns. The 'teaching' which made this possible is subtle and sensitive. Staff provide a daily time for story play and initially set the ground rules. However, importantly, adults do not dominate but 'pump-prime', encourage and help to embellish and lift children's ideas. The headteacher refers to the adult's role being to 'supply nuggets of inspiration to take the play forward' (9).

Clearly it is not possible to make learning fun all of the time but methods of teaching with young children must, above all, ensure that they strengthen positive attitudes towards what is being learned. Those positive attitudes will be needed when the learning becomes difficult.

3. *Dispositions are not easy to regenerate once they are extinguished.* Katz makes the important point that whereas knowledge and skills may be taught successfully in later life, it is more difficult to bring back to life attitudes that have been discouraged. This makes it vital to include in any early years programme a strong and explicit emphasis on nurturing the habits of mind that support learning.

Case study

Kieran, a much loved only child, attended a kindergarten from age two years. He appeared settled and his parents were very pleased with his apparent progress. From three years onwards, Kieran completed a page a day in his numeracy and English books and learned words to prepare him for entry to a reading scheme. His teacher reported to Kieran's mother that, at times, Kieran was reluctant to 'get down to work', but they had found ways of persuading him by offering lots of praise, including large Mickey Mouse stickers in his book. By age four years Kieran's record showed that he could write two sentences and tackle addition and subtraction equations. He had completed all the books in the first level of a reading scheme.

On transfer to a nursery reception class Kieran was given a choice of activities and was captivated by the construction apparatus. He spent every possible available moment building. He talked about the constructions that he had made but told the teacher that he did not like reading and that he could not write. He appeared to have no interest in numbers and actively avoided any questions to do with calculations. Kieran was keen to come to school but his parents were very dissatisfied with the teacher's comment that after one term he appeared to have made little progress in reading, writing and numeracy. The teacher made great efforts with Kieran and suggested that he needed time to work through his fascination with construction. Despite this, at the end of the year Kieran's parents removed him to a private school, which had a good 'academic' reputation. His parents explained that they felt that their son needed further challenge. At seven years Kieran was refusing to go to school and was attending a therapy clinic at the local child development centre.

Comment

Kieran's parents genuinely believed that their child was having a head start by being taught formal knowledge and skills early in life. Kieran, in turn, had learned that learning to read, write and become numerate involved dull repetition. He quickly learned that the constant praise that was offered in the nursery was not to be valued. Given the option to do more interesting things in school, Kieran was not prepared to use his time and energy doing activities that had become a chore; his reception teacher was unable to repair his damaged motivation to learn to record formally. Kieran's negative dispositions towards learning became stronger as he faced the additional stress of starting at a new school. Within one year, faced with a curriculum that emphasised the very aspects of work that he disliked, his negative attitudes had spread to an aversion to school.

Case study

As a baby and toddler Evan had been readily interested in picture books and later he had happily occupied himself making marks with large crayons on sheets of scrap paper. His mum was delighted in these early signs of interest in literacy and when he was three years old, she sent him to a nursery which stated that early development of reading and writing was a priority. Evan was required to spend some part of each day completing a workbook when he learned to copy his name and other simple words. He learned to recognise flash cards of common words and came home with lists of these words to practise. Positive reports were given of his progress.

Evan made a sound transition to his reception class at four years of age but his teacher reported that he was very reluctant to spend any time engaged in reading and writing activities. He refused to take part in any 'play writing' in role-play, claiming that he did not know the words. This attitude persisted throughout the first two terms in school despite his teacher's constant efforts and encouragement. It changed significantly when a new teaching assistant arrived. Despite many demands on her time, she spent fifteen minutes a day with Evan, playing word games, sharing writing activities in role-play and writing him a special card each day for Evan to take home to 'read'. She introduced Evan to a soft toy rabbit who 'lived' in a cardboard box. She said that the rabbit was lonely and suggested that Evan write to him. Evan's numerous written communications with the rabbit were reciprocated on 'rabbit-headed' notepaper.

By the end of the year Evan was very keen to share books; he often 'wrote' at length using many of the words he had learned previously in the nursery; he particularly enjoyed writing and illustrating cards for the teaching assistant.

Comment

Evan's initial motivation towards literacy was probably 'force-fed' at nursery.

By the end of his nursery career Evan had developed certain reading and writing skills but his enthusiasm was dampened. On starting school, because of his reluctance to enjoy books and seeming lack of confidence to practise and apply what he knew, Evan initially made slow progress in literacy. He required a one-to-one relationship with a sympathetic practitioner to help restore positive attitudes to learning. Without this prompt support Evan might well have lost his urge for learning more about literacy for a much longer period.

4. *Any early childhood curriculum must take into account how desirable dispositions can be strengthened and how negative ones can be weakened.* The receptiveness of young children to all influences means that there is just as much potential to develop unhelpful or even harmful inclinations to learning (passive, inflexible, distractible) as there is to promote the positive. A child is only likely to be well inclined to learning if the curriculum intrigues him and provides him with opportunities to learn more. At four children are very concerned with themselves, the people closest to them and the environment in which they live. They gain information through touching, tasting, smelling, listening, observing and through using their bodies. They can concentrate really well when things make sense to them. They need to try things out for themselves, practise what they have learned and be helped to clarify their thoughts through discussion. A programme which pays attention to these characteristics is likely to feed children's urge to want to learn more and to think more.

Conversely, an early years programme can be focused mainly on attainment and focused towards teaching a particular range of concepts and skills which are regarded as essential for successful attainment at a later stage in schooling. Typically this includes instructing children to learn rudimentary concepts of colour, letters and shapes often through limited pencil and paper exercises where attainment is recorded. Physical skills of cutting and sticking may be taught but with few opportunities for children to use these for their own purposes. In these circumstances children learn certain things but only on adult terms. Prescriptive activities may set a ceiling on attainment and so some children may not be challenged sufficiently. Bored children are likely to switch off any enthusiasm to learn and many will become distractible and inattentive. Even more disturbing is when children are conditioned to this type of regime; they simply comply with what is being offered. Compliant behaviour, unlike restlessness, will not provide the sharp signals of disaffection. Nevertheless, compliancy is not a mark of active learning. Young children may comply simply in order to please the adult. This becomes an easy route to 'learning'; as a consequence, other more active learning channels diminish when they are not used.

Some children may, of course, arrive at the nursery with negative inclinations towards learning. For many different reasons they may not be confident or willing to try new experiences. In these cases practitioners need time to establish a trusting relationship with the child and then gently encourage small steps towards a mastery approach. However, it is important to distinguish between a negative disposition and developmentally appropriate behaviour. For example, it is perfectly acceptable for a young three-year-old to 'flit' between activities and to be easily distracted in a small group activity; this same behaviour in a child of five may need to be considered more seriously; by the age of seven the behaviour would seriously inhibit a child's progress.

5. *Positive dispositions for learning should be strengthened as opposed to dispositions for performance.* As children become older their enthusiasm for work can differ. Those who are focused on learning are interested in it for its own sake. They are keen to gain new skills and understandings in order to improve. They are attentive and believe that their efforts in learning will pay off. Other children become

more concerned about their performance and how competent others judge them to be. This group depends on comparing their achievements with those of others – test and examination results matter more than satisfaction achieved from learning. Although these patterns are more noticeable in older children, the seeds are sown in early childhood. Katz suggests that it is reasonable to assume that if young children are regularly exposed to experiences that are intrinsically interesting and that absorb their energies, this might support a future disposition for learning. By the same token, those young children who are exhorted to compete with others and to complete tasks in order to gain adult approval, are not likely to be so disposed towards learning but rather to perform and succeed against others.

FIGURE 5.1 CHILDREN CAN CONCENTRATE REALLY WELL WHERE THINGS MAKE SENSE TO THEM

6. *There should be some means of assessing children's dispositions in an educational programme.* Although there is an increasing acknowledgement of the important role of dispositions in early education, making sure that they are in place is more difficult. It is quite easy to misconstrue young children's behaviour. Mechanical compliance when completing a task,

or a child's attraction towards a novel activity can be misinterpreted as evidence of genuine concentration and interest. Measuring these aspects of personal development is a very different matter from measuring the acquisition of skills and concepts. There is a particular danger of using simplistic methods to gather information. For example, young children may be asked to record their attitudes to aspects of daily life in a nursery through highlighting happy or sad faces. Who is to say what factors may influence the recording? The chances are that young children may guess what will please the adult and act accordingly, copy their neighbour, or record their decision impulsively, without having a clear understanding of the issues. Some of the most effective methods of finding out about children's thoughts and feelings, which underlie dispositions, are through listening, conversing with and observing the child in action. Gill Barrett's approach (see Chapter 1), using pictures depicting children's different actions, encouraged children to describe their own thoughts and feelings which they recognised and identified with some of the behaviours shown. Susan Denham used puppets effectively to gain similar information about children's emotions (see Chapter 4).

Assessment and evaluation of early years practice and children's outcomes have emerged as government initiatives largely as a consequence of public money being used to fund three- and four-year-olds in nursery settings. Major initiatives have been developed to provide a means of quality control and quality improvement. All settings in receipt of grant monies are required to make provision which will enable children to achieve certain goals by the time they leave the Foundation Stage when they become of statutory school age.

Children are assessed during their year in a reception class through the Foundation Stage Profile. The profile is well intentioned and rightly supports assessments of children's dispositions and attitudes which are based on practitioner's observations. However, the criteria for all of the six areas of learning are multiple, often confused and only focus on outcomes. This leads to very time-consuming practice and practitioners often being led into making fragmented assessments rather than gaining a complete view of the child. By contrast Mary Jane Drummond suggests that we start with the child and that, assessment is: 'the ways in which, in our everyday practice, we observe children's learning, strive to understand it, and then put our understandings to good use' (10). If we believe that children's desire to learn is paramount to their success, then surely this is a key aspect to observe and understand. Margaret Carr asks the crucial question, 'How can eager learning be described and encouraged?' (11).

Carr responds to her own question through introducing the notion of Learning Stories as a way of assessing dispositions. A Learning Story is a structured narrative which includes: the context and relationships with adults and other children, it highlights the activity and includes an interpretation from the author who knows the child well. The story concentrates on the five aspects of dispositions and gives evidence of new or sustained interest, involvement, challenge, communication and responsibility. Carr gives an example of a Learning Story for four-year-old Sean in which Sean perseveres with a difficult task even when he gets 'stuck'. Attached to the story is a photo of Sean using the carpentry drill. The teacher, Annette writes: 'the bit's too small Annette, get a bigger one.' We do, drill a hole and then use a drill to put in the screw. 'What screwdriver do we need?' 'The flat one'. Sean chooses the correct one and tries to use it. 'It's stuck.' He kept on trying even when it was difficult. Carr explains that this Learning Story will provide a focus for a discussion between Annette and Sean and, together with other Learning Stories, help both adult and child to see how well he is progressing in persisting with difficulty (12).

Other research studies have also played an important role in assessment. The Effective Early Learning (EEL) and Accounting for Life-Long Learning (AcE) projects, both from the Centre for Research in Early Childhood at Worcester College of Higher Education, have already been referred to in other parts of this book. The projects are immensely valuable because they help early years practitioners look closely at children and become aware of aspects of their behaviour. The EEL project introduced practitioners to a valuable observation instrument for identifying and measuring children's involvement. The Child Involvement Scale is based on the work of Ferre Laevers who studied how a child might be involved in deep learning as opposed to just being occupied and busy. Laevers defines the concept of Involvement as: 'a quality of human activity, characterised by concentration and persistence, a high level of motivation, intense perceptions and experiencing of meaning, a strong flow of energy – a high degree of satisfaction, and based on the exploratory drive and basic development of schemes' (13).

Laevers suggests that when children are involved in this way they show certain characteristics or signals, which can be graded to show the level at which they are working. These signals include:

- concentration
- energy
- creativity
- facial expression and posture
- persistence
- precision
- reaction time
- language
- satisfaction.

The EEL Project has very usefully adopted Laevers' work. The Child Involvement Scale enables practitioners in different settings to look closely at children and assess their level of involvement in activities through the absence or presence of the above signals (14).

The Involvement Scale which features in the EEL Project has helped practitioners to measure how well children are involved in learning – it concentrates on the process. The newly established AcE Project is concerned with the outcomes or results of effective early learning. The project recognises children's dispositions to learn as one of four important indicators of effective learning. Part of the project is to help early years practitioners to identify and nurture the characteristics which appear to be linked with dispositions to learn. Both projects have helped to make learning dispositions more visible and indicated ways of measuring them.

DISPOSITIONS ARE CAUGHT RATHER THAN TAUGHT

Katz makes it clear that while skills can be taught directly, dispositions are learned in a more subtle way. Any visitor to a nursery setting will be immediately aware how readily most young children are inclined to learn and how engrossed they can be. Indeed, for the lay person it can appear deceptively simple; young children can be seen naturally to co-operate, persevere, think carefully and be well organised in what they do. However, practitioners know only too well that these positive dispositions do not just occur; the seeds are sown at home, while in the nursery and early school days learning traits are developed through an interesting curriculum and through the behaviour and activities of practitioners.

Real learning is not something that other people can do for us. However well constructed a curriculum programme may be, it cannot ensure that young children learn. It may, of course, result in children performing. Children can be taught the alphabet song, recite rhymes and numbers. This in itself is not necessarily bad – a measure of rote learning (which is what this is) will aid working memory (see Chapter 4). The dangerous thing is that a demonstration of rote learning can seduce lay people into believing that a great deal more has been achieved than is actually the case. In a hierarchy, rote learning is lower order learning. Higher order learning requires children to have the inner drive to learn for themselves. It is more than just tacking new learning onto what we already know. In order for children to make true progress in learning they need to make sense of new information by using what they know already and modifying, updating and rethinking their ideas in the light of new knowledge. This learning is creative, active and personal. It is also very hard work. Young children must feel that it is worthwhile investing their considerable energies. It is not possible to coerce children into learning actively, only to ensure that they are disposed to do so in activities which interest and involve them.

The High Scope method of working is well known for emphasising an active approach to learning. The High Scope study tracked children from the age of five to adulthood. It found that those children who had experienced an early education from five to seven years that encouraged a mastery orientation (see Chapter 1), choice and independence, became significantly more effective learners in the long term. The study concluded that helping children to develop a sense of 'personal control' is a key factor in enabling their progress in learning and subsequent success (15).

Any curriculum which supports children's inclinations to learn will do so by having regard to their interests. This means being aware of their schemes of thought (see Chapter 1). Chris Athey describes a schema as 'a pattern of repeatable behaviour into which experiences are assimilated and that are gradually co-ordinated' (16). More simply, we might describe them as examples of children's behaviour which reflect their deep interest in something. Some children are absorbed in one scheme, others have several. Early years practitioners observe children's schemes of thought in their physical actions, particularly their drawings and constructions and through their questions. As they become older these schemes combine and strengthen and can be linked to children's interests in literacy and numeracy.

Although it is not feasible for staff to provide a curriculum which responds to each child's interests in turn, it is helpful to be aware of the aspects of a programme which will best incorporate children's interests. Following extensive in-service training, in 1997/8 a group of schools in

Northamptonshire worked with their early years advisers and explored young children's schematic play. They drew on the work of the EEL Project and used the Involvement Scale to inform their observations with regard to levels of children's initiative and involvement. The schools found that when children were allowed to choose and initiate an activity their schematic patterns of behaviour were evident. Notably, at these times children's levels of involvement were very high (17).

As we have seen, sustained imaginative play is a sure way of building on children's interests. Play methods are recognised as a central means of motivating young children to learn and should pervade the curriculum. However, a worthwhile, play-based curriculum requires considerable investment of adult time and should be carefully planned, resourced, monitored and evaluated. Children's play also requires a degree of scaffolding as does any other area of learning.

Well-planned adult stimulus will also encourage young children to dig deep into experiences and strengthen their interests. For example, a typical approach in one of the pre-primary schools in Reggio Emilia involved a group of four- and five-year-olds who undertook an extended study of a very large supermarket in their neighbourhood. They made several visits to the setting, including one when the supermarket was closed. In this way children were able to get a very close look at various features, to sketch many of the objects and features that impressed them and to have a better idea of the scale of the building when it was empty. Their remarkably detailed sketches showing the rows of baskets, the counters, the shoppers and the cashiers provided evidence of the children's scrupulous observations and what they gained by really becoming familiar with objects and events. And so children are not encouraged just to dash off a painting or complete their model quickly because the session is drawing to a close. Their work is often regarded as a first draft, an initial impression – they are encouraged to revise and adapt their initial work, to repeat activities and suggest modifications to each other's work (18).

The Reggio Emilia methods provide children with time. In his thought-provoking book, *Hare Brain, Tortoise Mind* (19), Guy Claxton suggests that there is a very important place for allowing thoughts to incubate (see Chapter 7). In work with young children, we so often emphasise the need for rapid answers, for working at a brisk pace, for keeping busy. There is undoubtedly a place for encouraging young children to keep mentally alert. However, there is also a different and more creative way of thinking which is only achieved through consideration and mulling things over. Claxton acknowledges the importance of the fast and focused thinking of the hare brain in certain circumstances; he is, though, more interested in the slower processes of the mind where reflection is central. He suggests that play is significant for the tortoise mind in that it involves 'messing about' and figuring things out. This book makes a strong case for time for day-dreaming, for toying with thoughts, for sleeping on a problem and returning to it. In Reggio Emilia and in other early years centres of excellence in this country, practitioners believe that young children should have opportunities to allow ideas to arise slowly and naturally and they make provision for it.

Thus the type of curriculum programme offered will considerably influence children's inclinations to learn. In addition, the practitioner plays a powerful role. Over the years we have experienced doubts about where the practitioner featured in nursery settings. The understandable fear of not following the hard line of prescriptive teaching has led some settings to the mistaken assumption that warm relationships are an end in themselves – that the adult's main role is to be friendly, positive and loving. Clearly, warm and positive relationships have to be the foundation for any effective work with young children, but it is now realised to be not enough. If young children are praised frequently and indiscriminately, if everything they do is always regarded as intrinsically clever, then how are they going to learn? Our young children deserve more than this benign environment because it does nothing to challenge their intellectual development. The best work by practitioners, again epitomised by the approach in Reggio Emilia, is three-pronged, based on relationships, observations and support (see Chapter 2).

The EEL Project provides an additional and similar emphasis on the role of the adult. The project includes an instrument for assessing how well practitioners nurture learning, namely the Adult Engagement Scale (20). This refers to three core elements:

- *Sensitivity*: how well the adult is 'tuned-in' and the degree of response to the feelings and well-being of the child.
- *Stimulation*: how effective the adult is when taking part in the child's learning.
- *Autonomy*: the degree of freedom which the adult provides to allow the child to experiment, make judgements, choose activities and express ideas. It also includes the boundaries established to deal with conflict and behaviour.

This useful set of descriptors is further endorsed in the National Commission on Education (21) in the introduction to *Excellence and*

Enjoyment (22) and in the EPPE project (23). The united and powerful message which emerges is that practitioners should and do impact on the way in which children approach learning. Early years staff understand that, by taking their cues from children, they are more likely to be going with the tide of their motivation – going against it is hard and often unproductive, when children show signs of withdrawing their goodwill.

Importantly, Lillian Katz reminds us that dispositions are infectious and that young children will be strongly influenced by the attitudes to learning the practitioners themselves have. She argues that adults need to think carefully about what dispositions they display. 'If teachers want their young pupils to have robust dispositions to investigate, hypothesise, experiment, conjecture and so forth, they might consider making their own such intellectual dispositions more visible to the children' (24).

Summary

Dispositions are relatively stable patterns of behaviour, which are affected by feelings. Dispositions to learn emerge from babyhood and are influenced by family life. In order to learn, young children must develop positive dispositions to do so. On entry to a nursery the inclination to learn is strongly affected when the adult acknowledges and respects the learning and achievements that have already occurred at home. Positive dispositions for learning are further strengthened through opportunities to practise them within a varied and interesting curriculum, which takes account of their interests. The practitioner plays an important role in identifying and extending these interests and through making explicit her own learning traits.

Practical suggestions

Help children to concentrate and persevere
- Where possible, provide a quiet area where children can work without distraction. Provide notices for them to use, 'Please do not disturb'.
- Provide small stand-up signs, 'Please leave', which children can place on an unfinished piece of work to which they wish to return.
- Note when a child's perseverance is flagging. Offer practical help yourself or encourage another child to support the completion of an activity.

• Make clearing up tasks manageable by delegating specific jobs to a wide range of children. Congratulate individuals when they have completed their task.

Develop memory skills
• *Kim's Game*: place four objects on a tray; remove one object in turn and invite children to identify what is missing. Gradually increase the number of objects over a period of time.
• *Pelmanism*: make a giant game with matching pictures which link to the characters and objects in a favourite story book, e.g. 'The Three Bears'. These are placed face down on a table; children in turn select a card and aim to collect a matching pair. Introduce the game with four matching pairs of pictures; increase this number over time.
• Regularly change an item of display in your room. Encourage children to spot the change. Give individual children responsibility for changing the display.

Encourage enquiry and help children to learn through their senses
• Take children on a sensory walk (wear old clothes!). Visit a quiet location; ask children to: crawl on the ground and describe what they can see; close their eyes and describe what they can feel; close their eyes and open their ears and describe what they can hear; close their eyes and open their noses and sniff and describe what they can smell (see Chapter 8).
• Provide a 'feely' bag with objects of different shapes and textiles which are changed each week. Play a guessing game when children in turn close their eyes and try to describe and identify the object.
• Play a listening game: children form a circle and a child is chosen/volunteers to be 'Peter'. 'Peter' goes into the centre of the circle and closes his eyes; the children pass a bell around and chant 'Peter, Peter, listen well. Peter, Peter who rings the bell?' When the chanting stops a child rings the bell. 'Peter' must point to the direction of the ringing.

Encourage organised approaches to learning
• Provide boundaries for using equipment/apparatus. Use circles and squares of material (small rugs can be used for larger construction) which can be laid out on a surface to provide the area on which to work.
• Help children to think sequentially when they set up, work at or clear away an activity. Ask them, what will you do first, what next?

Encourage reflection

Young children need lots of opportunities to be spontaneous and to share thoughts and experiences immediately. While adults should be available to allow this immediacy, it is also useful to help children to mull things over and to take time to think.

- Provide a thinking area in a quiet corner of the room; provide a couple of comfy chairs, interesting pictures/photographs, strange shaped stones/pieces of driftwood. Make it clear that this place is available for quietly growing thoughts; establish a culture which encourages children to share their thoughts regularly and informally.
- Help children to learn to visualise, e.g. when reading a story, stop from time to time and ask children to close their eyes and 'see the picture in their mind'.

Professional questions

1. What areas of learning do I most enjoy, what do I enjoy least? How does this affect the children's dispositions to learn?
2. When working with a group, how do I ensure that all children are actively engaged as opposed to being compliant?
3. In what activities do children most clearly demonstrate perseverance?
4. How does our daily timetable help children to concentrate and persist?
5. How does the layout of my environment encourage children to reflect?

REFERENCES

1. Katz, L. (1995) *Talks with Teachers of Young Children*. Norwood, NJ: Ablex.
2. Gopnik, A., Melzoff, A. and Kuhl, P. (1999) *How Babies Think: The Science of Childhood*. London: Weidenfeld & Nicholson.
3. QCA (2000) *Curriculum Guidance for the Foundation Stage*. London: QCA/DfES, pp. 32, 40.
4. Carr, M. (2001) *Asessment in Early Childhood Settings: Learning Stories*. London: Paul Chapman, p. 23.
5. Katz, L. (1995) op. cit. (note 1).
6. Barrett, G. (1989) Introduction, in G. Barrett (ed.), *Disaffection from School? The Early Years*. Lewes: Falmer.
7. Fisher, J. (1996) *Starting from the Child*. Buckingham: Open University Press.

8. Katz, L. (1995) op. cit. (note 1), pp. 47–56.
9. Bunting, J. (2004) *Learning through Sustained Imaginative Play at Tachbrook Nursery School*, Floor 13, Westminster City Hall, London SW1E 6QP.
10. Drummond, M.J. (1993) *Assessing Children's Learning*, London: David Fulton, p. 13.
11. Carr, M. (2001) op. cit. (note 4) p. 21.
12. Carr, M. (2001) op. cit. (note 4) p. 96.
13. Laevers, F. (1994) *The Leuven Involvement Scale for Young Children* (video and manual). Experiential Education Series No. 1, Centre for Experiential Education, Leuven, Belgium.
14. Pascal, C. and Bertram, T. (1997) *Effective Early Learning: Case Studies in Improvement.* London: Hodder & Stoughton, p. 12.
15. Schweinhart, L.J. and Weikhart, D. (1993) *A Summary of Significant Benefit: The High Scope Perry Pre-school Study through Age 27.* Ypsilanti, MI: High Scope UK.
16. Athey, C. (1990) *Extending Young Children's Thinking.* London: Paul Chapman, p. 37.
17. NIAS (1998) *Schemas.* Northampton County Council.
18. Katz, L. (1995) What can we learn from Reggio Emilia? in C. Edwards, L. Gandini and G. Forman (eds), *The Hundred Languages of Children.* Norwood, NJ: Ablex, p. 21.
19. Claxton, G. (1997) *Hare Brain, Tortoise Mind.* London: Fourth Estate.
20. Pascal, C. and Bertram, T. (1997) *Effective Early Learning.* London: Hodder & Stoughton, p. 13.
21. Ball, C. (1994) *Start Right: The Importance of Early Learning.* London: Royal Society for the Encouragement of Arts, Manufactures and Commerce (RSA).
22. DfES (2003) *Excellence and Enjoyment: A Strategy for Primary Schools.* London: DfES, p. 9, para 3.1.
23. Sylva, K., Melhuish, M., Sammons, P., Siraj-Blatchford, I., Taggart, B, and Elliot,K. (2003) *The Effective Provision of Pre-school Education (EPPE) Project: Summary of Findings.* Institute of Education, University of London.
24. Katz, L.G. (1995) op. cit. (note 1), p. 65.

CHAPTER SIX

Young Children's Behaviour

PAST AND CURRENT VIEWS ABOUT CHILDREN'S BEHAVIOUR

All parents and practitioners recognise that in the process of growing up children adopt different ways of behaving. However, views about what constitutes acceptable behaviour and how it is acquired have evolved as a result of increased knowledge and understanding about child development. Educational thinkers have held widely differing views about young children's moral development. In the fourth and fifth centuries, philosophers and theologians such as St Augustine supported the view of the child as a creature of original sin – small children were regarded as innately wicked and in need of careful moulding to lure them away from the devil. The most obvious way of suppressing the inborn tendency to sin appeared to be the use of corporal punishment. Portraits of medieval and Elizabethan schoolmasters usually show them with the birch, described as 'God's instrument to cure the evils of their condition' (1). This doctrine of original sin was widely subscribed to until the eighteenth century when Rousseau took an entirely opposite point of view. He portrayed young children as innocents – children were seen to be naturally good and in need of rescue from the bad world. He believed that children would be disciplined through natural circumstances. In some cases his suggestions are rather extreme. For example, in his most famous work *Émile* (1762) Rousseau suggests that if Émile broke his bedroom window, he would have to sleep in a draughty room and the cold which followed would alert him to his wrong action. This suggestion ignores the fact that the consequence might also be that Émile catches his death of cold (2)! However, Rousseau's denial of original sin and his statement that all is good as it comes from nature, although extreme, did have the effect of bringing about a kinder and more sympathetic way of dealing with children's misbehaviour. Modern thinking has moved forward to recognise small children as powerful learners who are beginning to make sense of situations from babyhood and to develop their own moral stances from an early age. By the end of the Foundation Stage, children are expected to recognise the difference between right and wrong and understand the consequences of their actions and words for themselves and others (3).

FACTORS WHICH AFFECT CHILDREN'S BEHAVIOUR

Newborn babies are not disposed to behave in a particular way but once exposed to the world they learn rapidly. Jenny Lindon gives a comprehensive outline of the major influences on early behaviour (4). Drawing on this work, four of these influences are examined below: family experiences, individual temperament, the way in which a child thinks and her emotional needs.

FAMILY EXPERIENCES

The first steps in learning about behaviour, are in the home. It is here that very young children begin to see how the people whom they love behave and they try to copy aspects of this behaviour. Judy Dunn's work (see Chapter 4) shows how aware a baby and young child is about how family members act. In this way, through what she terms 'affective tuning', a one-year-old baby begins to learn about other people's feelings. A two-year-old child has a good idea of what annoys, distresses or pleases others who are close to them – this is apparent when they use this knowledge as a source of power in challenging and teasing behaviour during the 'terrible two' phase. However, although a young child will learn a lot through simply observing family conduct, she will learn a great deal more if she is helped to understand it. Dunn's studies suggest that in families where arguments are followed by talk about what went wrong and resolutions, this helps a young child to grasp moral issues (5). Where young children have family members who demonstrate consistent and reasonable expectations about how to behave, it is easier for a child to respond.

As well as watching and learning from the behaviour of others, young children start to find out what they are allowed to do – what is acceptable behaviour and what is not. At this age children are dependent on older family members, and later, practitioners, to provide this information. The information provided is a crucial part of bringing up children in the home and setting, and includes establishing boundaries for behaviour. The way in which these boundaries are set will determine how children learn about rules and, eventually, how they are able to regulate their own behaviour. For example, if a child is encouraged to understand the reason for a rule there is more chance of her respecting it. Moreover, given that she has a secure and strong relationship with an adult she will be willing to please. Isabel's mum had an easy relationship with her small daughter; she responded to Isabel's questions carefully and tended to share some of her views and thinking with Isabel. At two-and-a-half, although Isabel had no real grasp of cause and effect, she trusted her mother's rule about always wearing a seatbelt in the car. The different beliefs that parents and practitioners have about how to raise children will include what they expect of their behaviour and how they intend to help their children achieve it.

Adults' views of what constitutes acceptable behaviour from young children will be influenced according to their own religious, cultural and social and moral beliefs. For some parents, the main goal is for their children to follow religious precepts such as a Christian or Muslim code of conduct. Others may want their child to work out her own way of behaving based on care and respect for others. Yet other families' beliefs might cause them to want their children to become aggressive and defend themselves, to develop prejudices and to acquire dishonest traits as a way of coping with the world.

Parents may have given a great deal of thought to the approach they will take to bringing up their children. In practice, however, emotions such as fatigue, anger and love sometimes hijack the best thought out strategies. Parents' approaches are also often influenced by memories of how they were brought up. Young mothers may admit to hearing themselves repeat what their mothers said when responding to their own children. Although the management of behaviour takes many forms, it is likely to reflect three different approaches which can be crudely categorised as the permissive, the negotiated and the directed.

Following Rousseau's philosophy, some parents and practitioners believe firmly that children should be allowed to be 'free spirits'. They feel strongly that the best way for children to achieve this 'freedom' is for them to be unfettered by adult requirements. Adults who follow this approach are fearful of crushing a child's spirit; they hold the view that it may be unnecessarily repressive to require good behaviour. Children raised in such an environment may be encouraged from a very young age to make their own decisions about matters of daily life such as what to eat and when to go to bed. Even anti-social actions may go unreprimanded as adults believe that a policy of laissez-faire will allow children to eventually come to sort out right from wrong actions for themselves.

Other families and settings may adopt negotiated approaches to managing behaviour in the belief that young children need authoritative guidance with this aspect of learning as with any other. Adults explain the reasons for rules and offer loving support to help children to achieve them. This helps the 'right' behaviour to stem from a basis of understanding. Moreover, in an easy and loving relationship, young children want to behave in a way which pleases the adults who care for them. As they practise this behaviour they grow to internalise it and, as they grow older, the behaviour stems from self-discipline.

Adults who direct young children's behaviour share the beliefs of the early thinkers who viewed children as being in need of strong moral exhortation. Strict external rules are imposed and threats of punishment used as a way of influencing how children behave. The need to control and require obedience stems from an authoritarian rather than authoritative approach. Adults may also adopt more subtle ways of directing behaviour through using emotional blackmail. In these cases young children are compelled to behave well because they are afraid of being punished or losing affection. Adults may also direct or control behaviour through heavy use of rewards. While young children need praise and encouragement to support good behaviour, too many tangible inducements will dampen children's own motivation to behave well.

Children who enter an early years setting may have experienced any one of these approaches to managing their behaviour or, more commonly, a combination of all three. It is useful for staff to gain insights into parents' views and approaches as well as making clear the approach that is adopted in the setting. Even where parents have different views about managing behaviour, they may respect a clearly argued counter-view from practitioners, which is based on the child's interests.

■ TEMPERAMENT

We may understand a child's temperament as her nature or personality. Lindon suggests that temperament influences the way in which a child reacts to her early experiences. She gives the following examples of different types of temperament and how these can impact on behaviour (6):

- *Active-passive*: some children will take initiatives for themselves, will search for new stimulus and be physically robust; others wait for things to happen to them.

Case study

On admission to the nursery it was immediately obvious that Gemma (four years) was fastidious about her clothes. She always arrived dressed in pristine outfits. Gemma refused to play with any messy materials and even after handling books she would wash her hands. On one occasion in the cloakroom, a faulty tap resulted in water being sprayed onto Gemma's dress. The little girl was inconsolable. She said that only naughty children dirtied their clothes and that the naughty children were not allowed to come to the nursery. The nursery superviser related this incident to Gemma's mum and suggested that they might work together to help Gemma to have a more relaxed attitude towards keeping clean. Gemma arrived at nursery the next day, smiling and enveloped in a pretty protective smock.

Comment

Gemma had taken very seriously her mother's strong cautions to keep her clothes clean at nursery. She clearly linked notions of right and wrong with cleanliness. Provision of a smock allowed Gemma to relax and gave her the confidence to take part in painting and water play (where she was very careful to wear additional protective clothing). However, early home influences remained. Gemma continued to disapprove of mess and was often in tears when sand or water was spilt. After two terms at the nursery, staff still needed to reassure Gemma that a mark on her clothes was acceptable and did not constitute naughty behaviour.

Case study

Four-year-old Marcus had twin baby brothers and one older sister, Rose. Rose was very caring to her young brothers; she helped to dress and feed the twins and read them all stories when she returned home from school. Her mum had told Rose on a number of occasions that she was a good older sister. When Marcus started school he insisted that he share this caring role. He carefully put on the twins' socks and shoes and cleared up their toys. Sometimes, however, Marcus found this role difficult. On these occasions he wanted sole attention from Rose and his mum. On one of these days when his mum rebuked Marcus about his demanding behaviour, Marcus said that he only wanted a sister, he did not want brothers.

Comment

Marcus had learned a great deal from Rose about caring behaviour. However, understandably because of his own need for love and attention, he sometimes found it difficult to put others first.

- *Sociability*: some children are very gregarious and need other children around them; others may be more self-contained, less outgoing, or may find it difficult to make friends (see Chapter 2)

- *Wariness*: children vary in how they deal with new situations; some may be cautious and circumspect; others unheeding

- *Negative emotions*: while all children have to deal with irritations and upsets at some time, their capacity to cope and handle feelings differs; some children have a low threshold of tolerance

- *Effort and persistence*: some children appear to have a very brief attention span and are very easily distracted while others, given interesting activities, are able to focus and become involved.

THINKING

Building on the social intelligence that they have gained from observing and experiencing the effects of family behaviour, on entry to a setting young children watch, listen and think. They note not only what adults say, but also what they do. They very quickly pick up on the expectations of adults and the overall atmosphere in a setting. Children listen not only to words, but to the way in which a request is phrased; they observe what happens if a request is not responded to – for example, what the adult does if the children do not tidy up. Generally young children are very keen to please and a warm, consistent and harmonious ethos supports adults and children to behave well towards each other. However they are very sensitive to underlying currents, for example of friction between adults or a lack of interest in the children. Thankfully these are rare occurrences, but where they exist children can feel adrift and become anxious and demanding.

EMOTIONAL NEEDS

All of us are affected by the way we feel and this is shown in our behaviour for good or ill. Many young children are emotionally robust and show the effects of positive feelings in their joyous and vigorous approach to all that they do. Others are more needy and, even given the support of a loving family, they may still show helpless and dependent behaviour. We also recognise that children's feelings will change and this is reflected in behaviour. Often the reason for the change is obvious and it is a temporary episode. For example, we expect a child to show mixed behaviour when faced with the excitement, but also the threat, of a new baby in the family. Moving to a new house, having an illness or bereavement in the family or, perhaps even worse for a child, parents separating, pose huge disruptions and may cause a child to regress and adopt babyish behaviour until she has adjusted to the change. Once the cause of the new behaviour is recognised, often, a watchful eye, patience, understanding and additional attention from the practitioner is sufficient to 'tide the child over' during this difficult and turbulent period.

TYPES OF BEHAVIOUR

Most young children are not fluent in spoken language and so the way they behave is their means of giving us messages. In a high-quality early years setting, children's joy and zest for life, their interest and involvement displayed in activities, are evidence of them feeling in harmony with their surroundings. Equally, if things go wrong for them or they feel badly within themselves, this will be reflected through their actions. We accept that most young children are still at an early stage of learning social behaviour – support for them to achieve positive social behaviour is a standard part of early years practice. Nevertheless certain worrying behaviours are increasingly evident in settings and require more understanding and attention.

1. *Distressed behaviour.* Emotional and behavioural difficulties is one of the four broad areas of special educational needs outlined in the 2001 SEN Code of Practice (7). Some children appear to be overwhelmed by emotional distress and so unable to control the way in which they behave. In extreme cases this may show itself in screaming and crying or aggressive behaviour towards other children or adults.

2. *Attention-seeking behaviour.* Some children constantly seek attention by behaviour which is difficult to ignore. Attention-seeking behaviour has negative connotations when it is probably more accurate to describe it as 'attention-needing'. For some young children (and older ones for that matter) any attention is better than no attention. And by four years a child may have learned that the one sure way of gaining attention is through negative behaviour. Demanding attention in this way may not be a conscious decision for the child, but it is what she has learned.

3. *Attention deficit behaviours and sleeplessness.* Young children are exuberant and active; this is a normal aspect of their development. However, we hear increasingly of those who are extremely fidgety, unable to concentrate and who do

not sleep well. We should be aware of changes in children's lifestyles and their responses that cause this to be highlighted. In the child's world today there is much more going on to assault the senses and so practitioners have a more difficult task to hold their attention. Moreover, there have always been those young children who have found it difficult to listen; the difference was that, in former days, these children were compliant but quietly switched off – now signs of lack of concentration are much more overt and noticeable. Whatever the reason, the effects of continual distractible behaviour and inability to sleep can be hard to deal with at home, and in a setting. Worryingly though, there seems to be a need to label this troublesome behaviour, as a first step to control it. Hence the increasing use of the terms 'Attention Deficit Disorder' (ADD), 'Attention Deficit with Hyperactivity Disorder' (ADHD) and, less used, 'Narcolepsy' to describe sleep difficulties. It is important to understand the different behaviours of children with ADD and ADHD. The former disorder may cause children to 'flit' but they may be relatively unobtrusive doing this. Those children with ADHD are much more noticeable; they are often demanding and disruptive to others. Rather than look at the underlying reasons for the problem, too often the response has been through over-ready prescription of medication, notably Ritalin, to control the symptoms. Although these drugs can help to calm behaviour, they can also produce negative side effects such as mentioned below.

4. *Depressed behaviour*. Chapter 4 drew attention to increased signs of young children showing constant anxiety, depression and withdrawal. They may persistently fret about things or appear to find life a burden – this behaviour is particularly sad when shown at such an early stage in life. One of the negative 'spin-offs' of prescribing drugs to control hyperactivity is that children often get to be lethargic and depressed – it can become a matter of exchanging one disorder for another. In extreme cases young depressed children can appear to withdraw from the world and be unable to make contact with others.

The above behaviours signal that all is not well in the child's life. We have outlined some of the contributory factors but we should not dismiss the impact of the effects of a child's experiences in an early years setting. For example, it may simply be that behaviour problems are compounded by a lack of physical activity in the programme. The most highly developed level of movement for young children is to stay still; prolonged sitting can cause undeveloped muscles to become cramped and painful; they need to use their bodies in order to focus and think (8). The lack of a strong play-based curriculum, is still too evident, despite current actions from the government. In her study entitled *Listening to Four-Year-Olds* Jacqui Cousins found that children talked of being 'too hurried to play'. When play is permitted, reception teachers admit to adopting a more controlling role. 'We cut it short … stop them … interrupt … it must be irritating for the children … ' One little girl's comments from the study poignantly sums up children's confusion about the pressure, 'Hurry up! Hurry up! It time! What it time for?' (9). An article in the *Times Educational Supplement* drew attention to the ongoing pressures on teachers and children from the continued existence of Key Stage 1 Standard Attainment Tests (SATS) and league tables. The article quotes the Liberal Democrat survey of 147 primary schools carried out in 2002 to investigate the effects of these measures. There was stark evidence of some young children's poor reactions: bed-wetting, loss of appetite, forgetfulness and signs of depression. In addition, 68 per cent of the staff involved believed that, at such a young age, formal tests are not good for children (10). At the time of writing, all these issues are receiving attention but while they continue children will show us only too clearly the effects on their well-being.

HOW CHILDREN START TO ACHIEVE INNER AND OUTER DIRECTED BEHAVIOUR

Although, as the early thinkers showed, it is possible to coerce children into 'good' behaviour, this has little to do with sound moral development. The ultimate aim must be to enable a child to understand about right and wrong and so to behave morally from her own motives. If we want children eventually to develop a strong moral code for themselves, then we must be concerned with more than them doing as they are told and parroting good manners. Their behaviour must come from the pull of their own conscience rather than from simply complying with instruction. Mia Kelmer-Pringle (11) describes this by referring to behaviour being inner or outer directed. Of course, inner-directed behaviour is a tall order for a three- or four-year-old, but it is then that the seeds are sown which are reflected in beliefs and behaviour in later life.

Before children start to regulate their behaviour they must begin to learn about cause and effect and intentions. The latter is a very difficult concept at such a young age and will only emerge over a period of time. A child starts to learn about cause and effect quite early on when she is able to project. 'If I throw that cup it will smash.' 'If I hit Carl it will hurt him.' Gradually she starts to understand about the consequences of her actions. Over time, she will come to recognise intention. Sometimes we intend to act wrongly and what we do is deliberate. At other times we do not mean to do anything wrong although the result is not good. We may not intend to drop a beautiful vase – it was an accident. Piaget's work showed that only children over eight years understood about intention (12). However, as Tina Bruce points out, more recent work with children, particularly by Margaret Donaldson, shows that these understandings can develop earlier when children are helped to learn in familiar circumstances (13).

Children also need to be able to empathise – to understand how others feel, and put themselves in their shoes. As we saw earlier, Judy Dunn shows that feelings of empathy develop very early in close family contexts. Here, babies and toddlers have had opportunities to be in close communication with people who care for them and have been with adults who share, explain and discuss feelings with them. Through growing to understand about the feelings of the people they love, children can later extend these understandings to empathise with others with whom they are less familiar.

Case study

Ibu, three years old, loved bathtime at home. He often came home from the nursery with specks of paint or clay on him and liked to wash them off in the bath. On getting out of the bath Ibu would look at himself approvingly and say, 'all clean'. Ibu made friends with a new traveller boy who had arrived at the nursery. Walter settled quickly into nursery life, but often when the two boys played, Walter would appear uncomfortable and complain of feeling itchy. On one occasion, Ibu looked at his friend and lovingly suggested 'Walt needs bath to feel nice.'

Comment

From his limited experience of being dirty, Ibu understood the reason for Walter's discomfort. He was already placing himself in Walter's position and wanted his friend to experience the same pleasures of washing that he did.

However, before children can have regard towards others they have to feel secure and loved themselves. Laevers' emphasis on the importance of personal well-being (14) is echoed by a group of primary teachers; in the context of their daily work, they recognised that the children who have positive self-esteem and a feeling of well-being will naturally recognise the work of others and praise them for it (15). This applies equally to adults. People are not likely to show this generous and caring behaviour when they lack the certainty of their own worth and so are hungry for recognition for themselves.

Case study

Three-year-old Toby was collected from playgroup by his mum who picked him up and gave him a hug. Toby looked over to where Sean was still waiting for his mum who was late arriving. 'Hug Sean as well,' Toby asked his mum.

Comment

Toby knew how much he was loved by his mum. He showed immense sensitivity in noting Sean's 'aloneness' and could afford to be generous in offering to share his mum's affection with the other little boy.

MAKING IT POSSIBLE FOR CHILDREN TO BEHAVE WELL

HAVING REALISTIC EXPECTATIONS

Young children will only be able to behave in a way which is appropriate for their stage of development. For example, if a two- or three-year-old has a temper tantrum, this is perfectly acceptable; at this age, as we have seen, emotions are powerful and difficult to control. Again, children under five find it difficult to mask feelings of frustration and boredom. Expectations both at home and in the nursery can be unrealistic. Adults may become upset or frustrated because three- and four-year-olds find it difficult to be quiet when adults converse, or to sit and listen to instructions or a story in large groups. It is important to recognise that children's social skills and powers of concentration will grow as they mature. At five and six years they may manage these things, but fidgety behaviour and interruptions before then is not necessarily a sign of poor behaviour. Although a four-year-old can be encouraged to recognise that at times other people do need to talk without her, occasionally her own need for attention will be stronger.

BEING CONSISTENT

One of the most confusing things for a young child must be to have contact with a number of adults who expect different things, or who require

FIGURE 6.1 FEELINGS OF EMPATHY DEVELOP VERY EARLY IN CLOSE FAMILY LIFE

one thing of her on one occasion and something different on another. The former can happen when home and nursery have markedly different expectations, or when adults at home or in the nursery are not of one mind. The latter is most likely to arise when adults act pragmatically rather than considering what sense the child will make of their requirement. It is all too easy, when harassed under the pressure of time, to give in to a child's insistent demand for sweets or to overlook one child hitting another; in less stressful circumstances an adult might be more able to consider the consequences of her response for the child's future behaviour.

Early years practitioners should be alert to children's understandings of how they should behave. For example, where they have been used to directive language, 'do this', 'stop that', they may find it difficult to cope with indirect requests, 'would you mind clearing up please?'

In cases where there is no single clear message about what is acceptable behaviour, children may eventually develop double standards as they learn to use the different behaviours approved in each situation. This, however, provides no basis for a child to start to internalise a moral code for himself. This internalisation is more likely to develop if a young child can learn to predict that there is one constant expectation of how she should behave.

■ PROVIDING POSITIVE ROLE MODELS

Behaviour and the development of moral values, like dispositions, are heavily influenced by what children observe from adults who are close to them. Small children learn a great deal through imitation. If they love their parents and carers they will want to be like them. This, of course, places a heavy responsibility on all of us who live and work with children. As Kelmer-Pringle points out, it is what we really are and how we behave which matters, not what we say or believe we say (16).

Case study

Carl found that the cake in his lunchbox had disappeared. He discovered that James had taken it; James was hungry because his au pair had forgotten to pack his lunchbox properly. The teacher took both upset children aside. She gently asked James to think if there might have been any other solution to the problem. Together they agreed that a better line of action would have been for James to have told an adult that he was hungry. James himself suggested that in recompense he would bring Carl a cake from home tomorrow. At the end of the day (with the permission of James and Carl) the teacher shared this episode with the other children. Everyone agreed that taking things without permission was not good and should not happen in the nursery.

Comment

Later when sharing this episode on a training course Jane, the teacher, admitted that, although she was very aware that different standards were often accepted at home, she considered that her first task was to establish a clear moral code of conduct in the nursery. At the same time she worked with parents, using examples of children's behaviour such as this one to emphasise the need for the setting's code to be reinforced at home. In order for young children to strengthen their understandings about the behaviour of other people, they need to practise roles for themselves. This is possible in play where children can explore being a powerful adult and try out different relationships in total safety. Role-play can help moral development in three ways:

- It can enable children to sort out their own feelings.
- It can help them to stand in other people's shoes (to decentre) and explore how they might feel.
- It places them in practical situations where they need to negotiate ways of behaving and treating other children.

■ PROVIDING A PROGRAMME WHICH GIVES INSIGHTS INTO BEHAVIOUR

In a setting which has developed a positive ethos or climate for children's moral development, the adults will have considered carefully the types of experiences that will both introduce and help to reinforce notions of right and wrong. Although first-hand experience of behaviour is the most powerful way of influencing young children's actions, stories are also very helpful in introducing moral dilemmas and giving moral messages.

We know now that children learn all sorts of things better in situations that they can understand. It follows then that any nursery programme should make the most of those situations that occur in daily activities and routines. It is through helping to comfort a child who has fallen and grazed her knee, or being generous to a younger child who has interrupted an activity, that moral behaviour is practised. Discussion also plays an important role. Good nurseries will skilfully turn a minor catastrophe into a moral lesson.

Case study

Patri (three-and-a-half years) had few toys at home and the nursery staff were aware that he regularly hid small items and took them home. His key worker had discussed this issue generally in her small group. She explained that although everyone was tempted, it was not right for individuals to take things for themselves as this would mean that there were not enough things to play with in the nursery. She also suggested that anyone, including herself, could store things in their pockets and forget them; it was a good idea to check each day to see if this had happened. Patri did not respond to these messages and continued to take equipment home. Soon after the discussion, however Patri was observed stuffing items under a teddy bear's blanket and whispering to teddy to hide them. Another discussion followed along the same lines. Approximately a week after this, Patri was observed again with the teddy. Using a similar tone and manner to that adopted by his key worker, Patri counselled the teddy to 'be a good boy and put things (again hidden under the blanket) back for the children to play with.' During the next month Patri was less and less inclined to take things home. He was keen to 'find' items in his pocket and share these with the staff, and was always warmly praised for his discovery.

Comment

Patri used role-play with the teddy bear to work through his behaviour. Over a period of time he was able to overcome his temptation to take things without loss of face.

DEALING WITH CRITICAL BEHAVIOUR

In 2001, 168 young children of four, five and six years were expelled from their schools (17). In 2003 a two-and-a-half-year-old child was excluded from her nursery because staff felt unable to manage her challenging behaviour (18). It is surely an indictment on society that this should occur. Moreover it is imperative that all practitioners should have the skills to deal with more severe behaviour in order to prevent a young child having this experience of failure.

The Camden Early Years Intervention Team has taken positive action in this regard. They offer training to practitioners on strategies to lesson the likelihood of a child's behaviour becoming a crisis. The team points out that, very challenging behaviour is complex and it is only too easy and not helpful to attribute blame to the child, parents or early years staff; this can be exacerbated when other parents complain about the behaviour. In fact there are always a number of factors which influence behaviour; it is both necessary to identify the underlying reasons for the child's actions and at the same time use skilled management to reduce the incidents. Basic rules require all the adults to keep calm and to reassure parents that the behaviour is being managed. Recorded observations will show the pattern and frequency of the incidents of the behaviour. It may be necessary to carry out a nursery risk assessment and, if the child is aggressive, for staff to interposition themselves between the child and other children. Sometimes a child will use her own methods of coping, for example the Camden team refer to a little girl who, at the build-up to a tantrum, would withdraw to sit on the floor in a toilet cubicle in order to calm down (19).

MANAGING BEHAVIOUR, LOVING THE CHILD

Learning to behave well is a big challenge for young children. They do need clear boundaries, and to be very clear about what behaviour is wanted; despite this they will sometimes fail to meet expectations. If these expectations have been clear and constant, a child usually knows when she has transgressed and this is accompanied by a feeling of failure. Rather than simply rebuke the misbehaviour, it is important to help the child recover to a point when she can try again. Clearly deliberate misbehaviour should be reprimanded but it should be the act that is disapproved of rather than the child. The child must be secure in the knowledge that she is loved, despite her wrong actions.

Summary

Young children should be helped to understand about right and wrong rather than simply encouraged to comply with adult requirements to behave properly. Babies and toddlers become aware of behaviour in the home and they start to tune in to the feelings of others. They learn about right and wrong behaviour through the boundaries that are set for their actions. Parents and practitioners set these boundaries in line with their own beliefs about how far children should learn to develop a conscience for themselves and how far they should be directed to behave. In order for children to develop a code of behaviour for themselves they must learn about cause and effect and motives for actions, and develop empathy. Adults can help children to behave morally by: having realistic and consistent expectations; helping children to develop moral insights from daily happenings; and showing children how to behave and that they are loved constantly even if their actions are wrong. Practitioners should be aware of factors which shape behaviour and have support, particularly in dealing with more worrying behaviour.

Practical suggestions

Monitor understandings and incidents of behaviour
- Observe children in role-play in order to gain insights into their moral understandings.

Be a step ahead
- Help children to think about their behaviour before the event; give a gentle reminder, call the child's name and make eye contact.
- Provide a special signal for a child who finds it particularly difficult to maintain social behaviour, e.g. 'Joe your teddy wants you to do this really well', or 'here is the flag Joe'.

Reinforcing rules
- Introduce the children to a naughty puppet who does 'naughty' things; explain to the children that the puppet does not know how to behave and will need to be told about the agreed rules in the nursery.
- Use puppets to play out scenarios involving different aspects of behaviour, e.g. arguments about whose turn it is to have a toy/ride a tricycle. Ask children to offer the puppets possible solutions.
- Discuss how we need to behave in the nursery. Agree two or three key rules and display them pictorially in the nursery.

Provide a supportive curriculum

- Create a programme which makes it practically possible for children to share and take turns, e.g. ensure that there is sufficient apparatus for all members of a group to have regular access; provide a 'pit-stop' and a means for children to 'sign up' (make their mark) to have a turn on a wheeled toy outside.
- Provide a substitute for very young children to release their aggression, e.g. suggest that, whenever they are angry, they hit a specific doll rather than a child.
- Help older children in the Foundation Stage to express their needs in words rather than physically. For example, Janine wants a turn on the rocking horse and is likely to push off Emma who is having a very long ride. Suggest that instead she goes to Emma and politely says that it is her turn now. Support Janine's request in order to reinforce that she has acted properly.
- Help children to settle conflicts: listen carefully to both parties and show interest and concern in what the children say and do.
- Provide children with many tangible examples of moral behaviour, e.g. discuss kind behaviour and encourage children to report their own and examples of others' kind actions.
- Start the day with a period of vigorous outside play which then helps children to use up surplus energy and be more ready to focus on quieter activities.

Professional questions

1. What aspects of my behaviour offer a positive model for young children?
2. How many rules in the nursery are totally in the interests of children's well-being?
3. How many rules in the nursery are for the convenience of adults?
4. How far do we as a staff consistently manage children's behaviour?
5. How well do we use our observations to: gain an accurate picture of young children's anti-social behaviour; plan effective action?

REFERENCES

1. Curtis, S.J. and Boultwood, M.E. (1961) *A Short History of Educational Ideas.* University Tutorial Press, p. 278.
2. Ibid.
3. QCA (2000) *Curriculum Guidance for the Foundation Stage.* London: QCA/DfEE, p. 38.
4. Lindon, J. (2003) *Childcare and Early Education.* London: Thompson.
5. Dunn, J. (1988) *The Beginnings of Social Understanding.* Oxford: Blackwell.
6. Lindon, J. (2003) op. cit, (note 4) p. 200.
7. DfES (2001) *Promoting Children's Mental Health within Early Years and School Settings.* London: Stationery Office.
8. Goddard Blythe, S. (2000) Mind and body, *Nursery World,* 15 June.
9. Cousins, J. (1999) *Listening to Four-Year-Olds.* London: National Early Years Network/National Children's Bureau.
10. TES (2003) Effects of national tests on staff and children, *Times Educational Supplement,* 2 May.
11. Kelmer-Pringle, M. (1974) *The Needs of Children.* London: Hutchinson.
12. Piaget, J. (1932) *The Moral Judgement of the Child.* Harmondsworth: Penguin.
13. Bruce, T. (1987) *Early Childhood Education.* London: Hodder & Stoughton, p. 137.
14. Laevers, F. (ed.) (1996) *An Exploration of the Concept of Involvement as an Indicator of Quality in Early Childhood Education.* Dundee: Scottish Consultative Council on the Curriculum.
15. Fountain, S. (1990) *Learning Together; Global Education 407.* Cheltenham: Stanley Thornes.
16. Kelmer-Pringle, M. (1974) op. cit. (note 11).
17. TES (2002) Your weekly guide to a whole-school issue: behaviour: part 3, *Times Educational Supplement,* 6 December, p. 15.
18. Camden Early Years Intervention Team (2004) Warning signs, *Nursery World,* 22 July, p. 13.
19 Camden Early Years Intervention Team (2004) op. cit. (note 18).

CHAPTER SEVEN

Young Children's Spirituality

There has been almost no study of young children's spiritual development, few insights as to what it comprises and little guidance on how it should be fostered. There are no explicit references to spiritual development in the *Curriculum Guidance for the Foundation Stage*. OfSTED inspections for maintained, private and voluntary provision include a required judgement on spiritual development. However inspectors are given scanty help about what constitutes evidence. They are advised that there are links to spirituality in aspects of the areas of learning that relate to children's self confidence and self esteem and understanding of cultures and beliefs (1). Although this might well be the case the generalised guidance fails to pinpoint the essence of spirituality (admittedly a difficult task and one that is only touched upon in this chapter).

Nevertheless, Wales has made a brave attempt. The new Welsh Framework for the Foundation Stage which is being piloted over four years has a section on spiritual and moral development. One of the requirements is for children to 'be still and reflect' (2). Stillness and reflection do not come naturally to young children; they are such physical beings and so full of life and vitality that the term 'spiritual' does not appear to fit. Spiritual development can seem remote from the tenets of early education which stress the importance of activity and 'being'. And yet during the early years of life children are not naturally weighed down by materialism (although some are in danger of being so, as described below) and are very receptive to thoughts and ideas. Clearly this is a good basis for beginning to recognise the things of quality and significance in life.

There is also a tendency to confuse the spiritual with the religious, although all religions share a sense of the sacred which is surely something worthwhile and precious to pass on to young children. In this chapter it is proposed that spiritual values can stand by themselves. There are different definitions about spirituality. The Office for Standards in Education suggest that

> spiritual development is the development of the non-material element of a human being which animates and sustains us and depending on our point of view, either declines or continues in some form when we die. It is about the development of a sense of identiy, self-worth, meaning and purpose. It is about the development of a pupil's 'spirit'. Some people may call it the development of a pupil's 'soul', others as the development of 'personality' or 'character' (3).

This definition includes some of the topics already covered in this book. Trying to narrow the meaning down I suggest that, for the purposes of this chapter, spirituality is about appreciating the journey through life in the deepest sense, particularly special moments, and recognising our own inner resources to help us cope with the journey. This is probably the most challenging aspect of development to promote when working with young children, but one of the most important, given that they are growing up in an increasingly soulless society. This is illustrated by three trends.

One important example is the huge emphasis on consumerism which can massively distract children from recognising and enjoying the less tangible aspects of life. Mother Teresa when visiting North America, observed that the whole society seemed to have an abundance of possessions (4) and Joanne Christolph Arnold a passionate advocate for children argues that our rich, Western society has enslaved children to consumerism.

> As advertisers tap the bottomless pockets of adults whose money is fueling the most prosperous economy in the history of the world, they are discovering the most lucrative market of all: their little (and not so little) boys and girls. At once the easiest targets and the most persuasive wheedlers, today's children and teens have been successfully harnessed to pull their parents back to the mall week after week, month after month and year after year (5).

The Archbishop of Canterbury, Rowan Williams, backs up this view. In his powerful book *Lost Icons* Williams attacks the Disney empire which, he claims is turning children into consumers by its marketing strategies (6). Despite some notable exceptions of poverty in every country, there is no doubt that most young children in Western Europe and the USA have far more things than they need. Parents seem to work longer and harder to provide children with more and more luxuries. This reaches a peak at birthday and Christmas celebrations. Amanda Craig a journalist and parent describes vividly the orgy of pre-Christmas spending.

> Going into any high street now is like walking into Toy Story: shiny boxes piled high with Barbies in fluffy tinsel-pink or Smash and Crush Hulks in flak-jacket khaki. There are multi-coloured buttons, buzzers, clashing lights and remote-controlled flights; there are bells, yells, singing fish and howling owls. Crazed by greed and ignorance, children race about in a frenzy of indiscriminate desperation or log onto web-sites such as iwantoneofthose.com. The whole enterprise is a vision of hell (7).

But as we know too well, material wealth does not necessarily feed the spirit. Having witnessed affluent lifestyles in North America, Mother Teresa offered a stark message. She commented that she also had never seen 'such a poverty of the spirit, of loneliness and of being unwanted, that is the worst disease in the world today, not tuberculosis or leprosy. It is a poverty born of a lack of love' (8). As for young children, by giving them so much and making it so easy to replace and replenish things, we are denying them the need to really cherish and value what they have.

The second trend is linked to education. Williams also points the finger at the priorities of our early educational system. He suggests that current ideas about the purpose of childhood education is to give children the skills they will need to survive and succeed in a competitive and even dangerously cut-throat world (9). By implication, the Archbishop suggests that this means an emphasis on a relentless programme designed to improve children rather than one which understands and gently steers and strengthens their natural development. Thankfully, the Primary National Strategy is supporting a relaxed, play-based curriculum in the Foundation Stage, but nevertheless many practitioners still feel under pressure to provide children with a heavy diet of literacy and numeracy too soon and some parents become too easily caught up with the need for their children to achieve as much as possible as early as possible.

This emphasis for children to acquire formal skills early is a small part of the third trend which is the move to rush them prematurely into the adult world. We hear a great deal nowadays about the 'loss of childhood' and this reflects a view that inevitably children are 'growing up' too quickly and become too knowing about the ways of the world at an early age. The media are quick to exploit this, particularly for small girls, and make-up, jewellery and sexually provocative clothes are heavily marketed. This perception of children as miniature adults becomes a vicious circle as it can affect the ways in which they are treated by parents and carers. The move has been slow and insidious. Twenty years ago Marie Winn identified this in her valuable book *Children without Childhood*:

as today's children impress adults with their sophisticated ways, adults begin to change their ideas about children and their needs; that is they form new ideas about childhood as adults act less protectively and as they expose children to the underside of their lives adult sexuality, suffering, fear of death, these former innocents grow tougher perforce, less playful and trusting, more skeptical, in short more like adults (10).

The above trends paint a grim picture and indicates some important factors that we should face and try to combat if we are to protect and strengthen children's inner lives. In doing this it is useful to consider a discussion paper published by the National Curriculum Council in 1993 (11). This attempts to highlight key aspects of spiritual development but in a way more applicable for older children. Some of the aspects they consider such as relationships and feelings and emotions have already been dealt with in other chapters. The headings below have been interpreted in a way more relevant for young children's spiritual growth.

BELIEFS

As we have seen, children will already have some firm beliefs by the time they come to school. These may include religious beliefs, including some hazy notions of deity; they will almost certainly include some values, for example, about how to treat people. It is important that children are encouraged to talk about their beliefs and values; in so doing they will start to recognise that not everyone thinks alike or attaches the same importance to particular issues. Once again this is best done in small groups where a good and trusting relationship has been established between the early educator and children.

Children know when their thoughts and beliefs are acknowledged and respected. This can sometimes be difficult when the beliefs do not accord with those of the practitioner. However, insisting that 'you don't really mean that do you?' can easily undermine the child and will not necessarily change her way of thinking. The child should at least feel that she has been given a voice and that voice is respected. As Kahil Gibran says when talking of children, 'You may house their bodies but not their souls, for their souls dwell in the house of tomorrow, which you cannot visit, not even in your dreams' (12).

A SENSE OF AWE, WONDER AND MYSTERY

The roots of spirituality are founded in early experiences of awe, wonder and mystery. This is certainly the easiest aspect of spiritual development to foster, as young children are so very impressionable. They have lived for a very short time and to them most of life is still a mystery. Young children wonder at the mundane and constantly remind us more jaundiced adults of the joy of being alive. And yet the very process of formal education can stifle the curiosity that leads to wonder and the exploration of the world. The most successful examples of encouraging awe and wonder are when the adults themselves are open to the miracles and mysteries of life.

Case study

Alice, a pre-school worker, had planned to encourage children to observe and share thoughts about growing things. She also wanted to impress the group with the power and beauty of nature. Alice passed around some sunflower seeds for each child to look at closely through a magnifying glass. They talked about the shape and feel of the seeds and what might be inside the hard shell. Alice then asked the children to close their eyes and think hard about the little seed growing. When they opened their eyes, in front of the children were two huge sunflower plants growing in pots. Jamie gazed in amazement and whispered, 'It's grown into the sun!'

EXPERIENCING FEELINGS OF TRANSCENDENCE

The word 'transcendence' derives from the Latin word *transcendere* which means 'to climb over'. Young children do 'climb over' and reach out to the limits of their world as part of growing up. A child experiences her inner strengths when she summons up courage to venture into the playground alone for the first time. When Ahmed lay on the carpet, closed his eyes and listened to a brief extract of Beethoven, he said softly afterwards, 'the music burst out of me'.

In our materialistic part of the world, children are bombarded with stimuli and invitations to expand their lives. They have sophisticated experiences at a very early age and this can lead them to look always for answers outside of themselves. We offer young children something of infinite value if we help them to look for resources within.

Although most young children are naturally noisy and exuberant, like all of us they can also thrive on peace and tranquillity. However, even if they need peace, not all find it easy to quieten themselves; some will find silence threatening and not all will be as prepared as Ahmed was to close their eyes in a group. Practitioners can help children to learn ways to relax, contemplate and concentrate but these habits will only be acquired over a period of time and in an atmosphere of trust. Many settings and schools now recognise the benefits of encouraging children to lie still and listen to music when they come into class following a noisy lunch break. Other settings teach simple yoga techniques to help relaxation. Observing these sessions it is striking to see how well young children respond, as if they crave these moments of calm. Joanna Haynes who writes about children as philosophers uses stilling techniques to help children focus. Describing how she uses the phrase 'make your bodies still and ready to listen' as a settling phrase, she says that one child commented that in order to really listen you have to be still both inside your body as well as outside. Haynes goes on to say that this led to children discussing what this comment might mean and a decision to alter the original phrase to 'make yourselves still, outside and inside' (13).

Helping children to meditate takes them a step forward to transcendence. At the Maharishi school in Lancashire, children at four are introduced to meditation and breathing exercises. Five-year-old children learn their Word of Wisdom and repeat this word as they walk to school or play with construction. At this age they do it for five minutes twice a day and after that they add one minute for every year in school (14). Caroline Sherwood in her book on meditation aptly describes it as 'making friends with ourselves' (15).

SEARCH FOR MEANING AND PURPOSE

Bruno Bettelheim writes: 'Today, as in times past, the most important and also the most difficult task in raising a child is helping him to find meaning in life. Many growth experiences are needed to achieve this' (16).

And yet young children constantly search for meaning through their questions many of which confront the big issues in life. Some of these may be related to the child's personal circumstances. 'Why doesn't my mummy live with us any more?' Others may be of a more philosophical nature – 'Why does the moon look at me?' Yet others may deal with more imponderable issues. 'Where do you go when you die?' 'Who is God?' These last questions are the most difficult to deal with and there are no set answers. However, some basic principles are helpful. The first is to keep responses simple and honest. 'God is very special to a lot of people who believe that God made the world and all the things living in it'. That should be quite sufficient to satisfy an initial question and the child will probably move on to the next burning issue such as a request to play outside. Secondly, to admit when you do not have an answer but that you are really thinking about it. A child will be satisfied if you show that it is a very important question and that you are interested in discussing possibilities and finding out what he or she thinks.

Those who work with young children are frequently pained by the traumas faced by so many during their early years of life. It is amazing how some children do appear to withstand huge disruptions, selfish and sometimes cruel behaviour shown towards them. Other children are, sadly, noticeably damaged and life is a confusion to them. Sometimes early years staff can help children deal with, and even come to terms with, aspects of suffering; a friend who is hurt or upset can be comforted and reassured; a pet dies and can be buried with suitable rituals. However, at times staff feel inadequate to deal with some hardships that children face outside the nursery. On these occasions, all that is possible is to draw on trusting relationships, to encourage children to talk, and try to point out any good and positive aspects that arise from pain. On all occasions it is helpful for children to recognise and share good memories and see them as one of life's gifts.

CREATIVITY

Bernadette Duffy reminds us of the universal human desire to be creative throughout history. She refers to how creation myths from religious and cultural groups express the profound need, satisfaction and pleasure in generating something new (17). Conversations with young children and observations of their models, drawings and paintings are a testimony to their original thinking and creativity. All but the most damaged children enter the nursery with creative talents, but it is during the early years that these talents blossom or wither. Early educators know that, like any learning, growth in creativity does not just happen, but is crucially dependent on key factors which include the curriculum and the role of the adult.

Children under five are now entitled to creative development as one of the six areas of learning. However, in the government document *All our Futures* the breadth of creative thinking is recognised. 'Creativity is not unique to the arts' (18). The Foundation Stage Guidance makes clear the potential of creativity to make links across all areas. Good nursery settings and schools have always provided this, recognising that young children need a multiplicity of ways to represent their understandings. This is expressed beautifully in the title *The Hundred Languages of Children* which describes the work of the pre-primary schools in Reggio Emilia (19). These Italian schools emphasise the ways in which young children use what the schools term 'graphic languages' to record their observations, ideas, memories and feelings. This type of curriculum is inclusive. It is worth remembering that a programme which only offers children narrow opportunities to record, perhaps simply to write or crayon, is necessarily reducing opportunities for those who may need to show their learning in different ways.

Creativity involves emotions. Calouste Gulbenkian suggests that creative and imaginative experiences help to nurture feelings and sensibilities (20). Young children can release powerful feelings and extend their emotional repertoire in dancing, stamping, twisting, in role-play and mark-making (see Chapter 4). Sternberg also suggests that negative feelings such as anxiety, can inhibit imaginative and creative thoughts and actions (21). Young children need to have a sense of emotional well-being in order to tap into their creative resources.

Creativity cannot be forced. Lesley Webb, a wise and informed educator of young children, once described the process of compost-making in the mind. Good compost, like ideas, needs time to ripen and mature. Guy Claxton echoes this when he argues that creativity is helped when people slow down and reflect; he suggests that deep and creative thinking is enhanced by serendipity (22). Probably all of us would relate to this, recognising, for example, the regenerative effect of a relaxing holiday in the midst of a busy life. The notion is particularly applicable to young children. During the early years when so much learning takes place children need to have plenty of opportunities to use and apply new ideas. In this way they become secure and confident with new information. In our current culture of targets and achievements, we are in danger of promoting a 'hurry along' curriculum. The result of this can be that children hang on by their fingertips to new knowledge without a chance to use what they know.

Given a broad and rich curriculum, the right emotional climate and time, children can become totally absorbed in creative activity. Csikszentmihalyi and colleagues observed artists, athletes, musicians and others who showed intense involvement in what they were doing. There appeared to be no extrinsic reasons for their involvement but the 'flow' of their energy or motivation. 'Whenever we are fully functioning, involved in challenging activity that requires all our skills and more, we feel a great sense of exhilaration. Because of this we want to repeat the experience. But to feel the same exhilaration again it is necessary to take on a slightly greater challenge and to develop slightly greater skills (23). When young children experience this flow they are tapping into their inner resources.

Once again, the adult is the most precious resource; she has a direct role in helping children to be creative and the role can best be described by using Bruner's term 'scaffolding'. The term implies support without constriction. Successful scaffolding requires the adult to make a sound judgement of what the child knows now, an accurate diagnosis of the next step in learning and provision of suitable support to help the child achieve it. The support could include:

- offering appropriate stimulus; this may be through provision of sensory experiences, through aiding memory skills, fostering imagination or by the provision of materials
- teaching the subskills of handling tools, mixing and managing materials
- listening, questioning and commenting, encouraging the child to bounce ideas or talk through her activity
- encouraging the child to combine materials and link different ways of representing experiences (24).

As with all talents, some children will prove to be more creative than others. Nevertheless, all have potential. Given the time and resources, access to informed adults and some good quality stimulus, this will free young children's creative abilities in, to use Robin Tanner's words, 'making the ordinary and trivial arresting, moving and memorable' (25).

THE CONTRIBUTION OF STEINER SCHOOLS

Although many Foundation Stage settings both plan and seize opportunities which support children's spirituality, some provisions make this a keystone for their work. Telling examples are seen in the Rudolph Steiner schools. Around 130 Steiner schools exist around the world. They are very child centred and the aim is for the spirit of the school to be created by the mutual co-operation of everyone. There is a heavy accent on the use of natural materials and learning about natural crafts. Imaginative play has a high profile (typically children use very simple props, such as drapes and blocks). The sense of community is tangible, through the ritual gathering around a lighted candle at the start and end of the day. Other rituals recognise and celebrate the natural cycle of life; children regularly bake their own bread and work in the garden and observe living things. The practitioner is not there to explicitly teach, but to demonstrate or model certain behaviours. According to Freya Jaffke, a renowned Steiner kindergarten teacher, these behaviours include a sense of order and rhythm, good habits and loving consistency. Jaffke suggests that when the adult exemplifies these behaviours she creates a 'mantle of warmth' which protects the child from the outside world and strengthens the child's inner resources (26).

Caroline Von Heydebrand was a distinguished teacher trainer and supporter of the Steiner philosophy in the early part of the twentieth century.

Her words capture overwhelming reverence and respect for the child and the need to trust in the power of the spirit.

> Compulsion in the life of the spirit is unendurable. If the child is given the nourishment proper to him, one which does not constrain but nurtures, then in later life, his soul will have power to investigate and discern and come to find the spiritual foundations of the world through his own reasoning and insight – the means suited to his nature and stage of development (27).

This belief remains fundamental to Steiner practice. It also has relevance for all practitioners today who are trying to balance the dictates of planning and teacher directed activities with providing space for the child.

Summary

Aspects of today's society severely constrain children's spiritual growth. Mass consumerism, the pressures on young children to achieve early in schools and the premature rush into adult life all contribute to a disenchantment with the wonder of childhood. And yet children have great potential to develop spiritually when they are young because of being open to new thoughts and ideas. If they are encouraged to talk about their early beliefs, this will in time help them to learn about others' viewpoints. Although many children are bombarded by sophisticated experiences, most are very impressionable to everyday events. Young children will grow in spirit if they are supported by warmth, order and consistency, guided to appreciate the non-materialistic aspects of life and encouraged to develop their original ideas.

Practical suggestions

- *Nurture children's inner resource.* Help young children to appreciate stillness. Establish a few moments daily when children close their eyes and are totally quiet. Help them to recognise silence as a gift of life. Encourage them to relax: lie on the floor and breathe deeply; make their bodies like flippy, floppy scarecrows; suggest that they think of beautiful things which they might share afterwards (it is always important to respect all responses, even non-contingent ones!).
- *Provide places for quiet reflection.* Make spaces available inside and outside for children to withdraw from activity and be alone. It can be a tent or curtained-off area indoors or simply a bench near some flowering shrubs or underneath a tree. It needs few resources – some comfy cushions as a minimum, but can be enhanced by a vase of flowers, scented herbs, soft lighting and music, all of which provide a

calming atmosphere. The purpose of this space needs to be made clear to children, it is there for each one of them if they want to think or just to be quiet by themselves.

- *Share precious memories.* The adult shows a small group of children her memory box. She pulls out one or two items, a photo of a dog she had when she was a little girl or a fir cone that her own child had given her some years ago as a gift. The adult talks about why these things are valuable for her although they do not cost much or any money. She introduces a memory box for the nursery. Children are invited to bring in some item that reminds them of a special time. The items are placed in the memory box and shared at a certain time each week. A sense of occasion can help to set the tone for the gathering, e.g. quiet music, lighting a candle, the box placed on a piece of carpet, the child sharing the memory sits on a particular cushion. If the item is passed around it should be handled with respect and care. It is important that each presents her 'memory' as she wishes. The adult may also continue to share her memory items with the group and share presentations with those less confident individuals.

- *Encourage a sense of values.* Encourage older children to talk about what are the most important things in life. Start a story about a girl/boy who was able to wish for the three most precious things to have for ever in her/his life. S/he could choose from (provide a tray with a selection of the following, either portrayed in photographs or the real objects): a large bar of chocolate, a bike, a loving mum/ dad/carer, a popular toy, a large ice-cream, good friends, a cat. Ask the children in turn to make their choices and so open discussion about what sorts of things are important and why. This will also give the adult useful insights into the children's developing values.

Professional questions

1. What do I do to take care of my own spiritual life?
2. How do we provide for children to reflect?
3. How strongly do beautiful things (music, art, aspects of nature) feature in our setting?
4. How do our interactions with children inspire them to be creative?
5. How well do we encourage children to value the real treasures in life – love, laughter, friendship, giving?

REFERENCES

1. OFSTED (2004) *Training for Section 10 Inspectors*, Handouts, 2, 5. London: OfSTED.
2. Hofkins, D. (2004) The play's the thing in Wales, *TES Primary Forum*, 1 October, p. 24.
3. OfSTED (2001) *Inspecting Pupils' Spiritual, Moral, Social and Cultural Development: Guidance for Inspectors*. London: OfSTED.
4. de Bertodano, T. (1993) (ed.) *Daily Readings with Mother Teresa*. London: HarperCollins, pp. 62–3.
5. Arnold, J.C. (2000) *Endangered*. Robertsbridge, E. Sussex: Plough Publishing House, p. 16.
6. Williams, R. (2000) *Lost Icons*. London: Continuum International Publishing Group.
7. Craig, A. (2003) What children really need, *Sunday Times, News Review*. 30 November p. 5.
8. de Bertondano, T. (1993) op. cit. (note 4). pp. 62–3.
9. Williams, R. (2000) op. cit. (note 6).
10. Winn, M. (1984) *Children without Childhoods*, New York: Penguin, p. 6.
11. National Curriculum Council (NCC) (1993) *Spiritual and Moral Development: A Discussion Paper*. NCC.
12. Gibran, K. (1927) *The Prophet*. London: Heinemann, p. 20.
13. Haynes, J. (2002) *Children as Philosophers*. London: RoutledgeFalmer, p. 69.
14. Anna Selby (1998) The little school of calm, *The Times Magazine*, 5 September, pp. 78–80.
15. Sherwood, C. (1997) *Making Friends with Ourselves: Introducing Children to Meditation*. Kidsmed, 10 Edward Street, Bath BA2 4DU.
16. Bettelheim, B. (1975) *The Uses of Enchantment*. New York, NY: Random House, p. 3.
17. Duffy, B. (1998) *Supporting Creativity and the Imagination in the Early Years*. Buckingham: Open University Press, p. 4.
18. National Advisory Committee on Creativity and Cultural Education (1999) *All Our Futures*. London: Department for Education and Employment and Department for Culture, Media and Sport, p. 27.
19. Edwards, C., Gandini, L. and Forman, G. (1993) *The Hundred Languages of Children*. Norwood, NJ: Ablex.
20. Gulbenkian, Calouste and Co., (1982) *The Arts in School*. London: Calouste Gulbenkian Foundation.
21. Goldberg, K. (2003) Are we all potential Einsteins? *TES Primary Campaign*. 2 May, p. 24.
22. Claxton, G. (1998) *Hare Brain, Tortoise Mind*. London: Fourth Estate, p. 52.
23. Csikszentmihalyi, M. (1988) *Optimal Experience: Psychological Studies of Flow in Consciousness*. Cambridge: Cambridge University Press, p. 367.
24. Dowling, M. (1995) *Starting School at Four: A Joint Endeavour*. London: Paul Chapman.
25. Tanner, R. (1985) The way we have come. From a talk at the opening of the Arts Centre at Bishop Grosseteste College, Lincoln.
26. Jaffke, F. (1996) *Work and Play in Early Childhood*. London: Floris Books.
27. Von Heydebrand, C. (1942) *Childhood: A Study of the Growing Soul*. London: Anthroposophical Publishing Company, p. 181.

CHAPTER EIGHT

Living in the Wider World

Babies and toddlers thrive in the love and security of their homes. The earliest environment is intimate and constant. The three- and four-year-old continues to need that secure environment, but she is very mindful of and curious about the world around her. She becomes aware of this wider world through what she hears and observes within the family, through books, the media and perhaps being taken on outings to different places; when she joins a nursery she meets other adults and children. All these experiences contribute to the child's growing understanding about herself in relation to a wider context. This chapter deals with how nursery settings can encourage young children to think and start to understand about aspects of the wider world. This includes understanding about different ways of living and matters of equality.

LEARNING ABOUT THE WORLD OUTSIDE

Early on young children recognise that there are other families apart from their own; through travel they begin to understand that people live in different places – nearby and sometimes far away. Through visits to family and friends they see at first hand people living in different ways and they learn more about this through books, stories and television. The Early Learning Goals expect that, by the end of the Foundation Stage children 'Understand that people have different needs, views, cultures and beliefs that need to be treated with respect'. Also that children 'Understand that they can expect others to treat their needs, views, cultures and beliefs with respect' (1). Some children will learn these lessons easily and naturally; others, dependent on their early lifestyles may need a lot more support. Children will have very different personal experiences of diversity; by the time they start at nursery some will have witnessed a rich cosmopolitan range of lifestyles; others may have only encountered the cultural traditions in their own community. Nevertheless, all children who will be living in the world tomorrow need to develop an understanding of how other people live. It is during the early years when children are naturally curious and receptive to new ideas that these understandings should take root. Some early years settings have a wide cultural mix of children or a deliberate policy to include children with special educational or physical needs. In these groups the issues of difference are ready to be grasped. Practitioners have a greater challenge in finding ways to raise children's awareness of diversity in settings with a more homogeneous intake, with families from only one culture or from a narrowly defined social class. However, even in these contexts children can be helped to see how others vary from them as well as what they have in common.

BEING OPEN-MINDED

Everyone builds up a set of beliefs about others. These beliefs are influenced by personal experiences but also by fear of strange or different characteristics. Beliefs may also arise from developing fixed views about others and labelling or stereotyping them.

People often fear the unknown and prejudice can flourish in a climate of ignorance. There are tales of 'closed' societies where 'outsiders' are discouraged. I encountered this in an outlying village in East Anglia in the 1960s; the staff in the school were hostile to any new families being admitted other than the locals and termed them 'foreigners'. The basis for this belief was the result of one family who had moved into the village and whose child had some difficulty in making the transition from a large town school. As a result of this experience the teachers had generalised an expectation of all new families. They were genuinely worried that standards of discipline in the school would suffer if 'foreign' children with different ways were allowed to contaminate the others. Their intolerance included a fear of dealing with strange parents and children, who they believed would have different values and lifestyles from the families they knew intimately in the village. They failed to recognise that families with young children are likely to share many things in common no matter where they come from. They also considered the idea of difference in a very negative sense in that it could only disrupt the status quo rather than add to it.

In this instance the staff had built up negative assumptions of others simply based on where they came from. Fears and suspicions also arise when people look and act differently. This may be because of the colour of their skin, a disability or their behaviour which is linked to a cultural identity.

The teachers in the village school had also developed a fixed or stereotyped view of 'outsiders'. Jenny Lindon points out some important characteristics of stereotyping, which are summarised below:

- they are usually unfavourable
- even positive stereotyping restricts, e.g. 'black boys are natural athletes'
- stereotyping depends on a belief that other groups are less varied than one's own, e.g. people are more likely to say of another social or ethnic group 'she's a typical … ' but they will say of their own group 'it all depends'
- experience of individuals who do not fit a stereotype are not thought to give any reason to adjust a view, e.g. 'you're my friend, I don't count you' (2).

The extent to which young children will learn to stereotype others and regard them with fear and suspicion depends on their own experiences and how they see people they know behaving. Children who mix with a wide variety of people from different cultures and who have encountered disability from a young age are more likely to be open-minded about differences. However, this will only happen if they see open-mindedness demonstrated by the adults they know and love. If homes do not offer this model then it is all the more important that the early years setting provides it.

EARLY INFLUENCES WHICH AFFECT UNDERSTANDINGS ABOUT BEING EQUAL

We saw in Chapter 1 how young children start to develop a picture of themselves very early through their relationships within the family. This building up of a self-image continues when a child joins a group setting; she sees then how she is regarded by a wider group of children and adults.

Young children's early life chances are deeply dependent on adults' views and behaviour towards them. This can affect all aspects of their development.

Children who are clear about who they are and are at ease with this identity will feel comfortable and positive about themselves. This is likely when children have been encouraged from the start to feel proud of themselves, their backgrounds and their early achievements. However, some children come to develop their self-esteem at the expense of others. Some families may have encouraged their children to feel naturally superior to others who are not from their social or cultural background. Other children may come from families who themselves suffer from a poor self-image. This may be for reasons of unemployment or lack of social standing. Children from these backgrounds may have been taught to boost their own position by rejecting others deemed less fortunate than themselves. They may have learned particularly to disparage other children who look different or act differently. If practitioners detect any of these signs in young children, they have a responsibility to demonstrate each child's worth and to counterbalance any feelings of superiority.

Case study

Ben, a toddler, was regarded as fragile and was physically over-protected by anxious parents. He had fewer opportunities to develop balancing and climbing skills than other children in the neighbourhood who were encouraged to play actively and take physical risks from babyhood. He also grew to be fearful of hurting himself. By the time he started at a nursery, Ben already regarded physical activity as something to avoid; when he saw other children, confident and assured in using their bodies, Ben strengthened his view of himself as physically incompetent.

After falling from a low rung of a climbing frame, for one term Ben flatly refused to use any apparatus or to use the outside play area in the nursery. By the age of four years Ben had developed a clear picture of his physical limitations which had sprung from his parents' behaviour towards him. His lack of confidence in his body led him to develop a very cautious disposition. Other children initially avoided including him in any boisterous play and then Ben started to exclude himself from any other activities apart from 'safe' pencil and paper work. Ben became increasingly isolated. He showed no interest in other children and told his mother that 'the nursery was full of nasty people who tried to make him do things'.

Comment

Three- and four-year-olds are very concerned with finding out who they are and what they can do. They need to feel that they matter. Ben's self-esteem was diminished initially by being over-protected and not being encouraged to build up his physical confidence. This led him to withdraw into himself and become negative about others.

Despite heightened awareness on the part of many people, prejudice and discrimination are still deep-rooted in British society. The grounds are widespread. They include what sex, race or ethnic group you are, your religion, age, ability/disability, social class, how you speak, what you wear and the work that you do. Some of these grounds are covered by law; all contribute to people being regarded and treated in different ways. We are concerned here with equality issues that affect young children. It is not a matter of treating children the same, but rather ensuring that, whatever their inheritance, all children have a similar entitlement in life. It is in the pre-school years that children first receive messages about how they are valued and give these messages to others. Some children are particularly vulnerable. Those children who are in a minority in a group will find it difficult if they are labelled or stereotyped by others.

It is a mistake to think that young children are immune from prejudice. Cecile Wright carried out research in 1992 when she looked at the experiences of 970 black children aged three to eight years in nursery and primary schools. She found that Asian children were subjected to racist name-calling and attacks almost daily and teachers were reluctant to deal with this formally. Afro-Caribbean children fared worse with teachers. The boys in particular were singled out more than other children for criticism; staff also stereotyped South Asian children as having poor social and cognitive skills and lacking in cognitive ability (3). The Macpherson Report on the Stephen Lawrence murder notes that inquiry members had heard 'about the racist attitudes of very young children' during the public hearings (4). These findings are immensely disturbing and practitioners need to be vigilant to all aspects of children's behaviour that indicate prejudice. Initially, however, children are simply interested in difference. Three-year-olds may comment openly that 'that man has a black face'. Four-year-olds may be socially more aware and whisper this comment to the adult they are with. In both cases this is simply an interested observation and not a value judgement. As we support young children in sharing their observations in other situations we should not encourage them to turn a blind eye to physical differences. When carefully handled, these observations can become expressions of worth. Children will learn easily about bigotry and prejudice if it is modelled for them. Parents can provide a powerful role model for children. It is only natural that they should take their values on all sorts of issues from what they observe from people who are close to them.

> **Case study**
>
> In conversation with Hugo, aged four years, he told me earnestly that he knew that he must never ever get into a car with a stranger. 'Except', he said 'if the person was driving a Volvo or Mercedes car because only rich and good people drive those cars.'
>
> **Comment**
>
> Hugo loved and admired his father very much; his one ambition was to become like his father who was a wealthy and successful businessman. I do not know the make of car that Hugo's dad drove but I could guess.

As a consequence of what very young children observe and hear and assimilate within the family setting, they will arrive at a nursery with their individual package of beliefs which influence how they view themselves and their attitudes towards others. This includes the way in which children view children with physical disabilities.

> **Case study**
>
> I was sharing with four-year-old Rosie a book about a small boy who was restricted to a wheelchair. Rosie pointed out that this was like Dom a boy in her class. 'I know that he can't walk,' she said, 'but instead of good legs he is very good at painting. I told him that.' The previous month, Andrew, a new boy to the reception class, had refused point-blank to sit next to Dom at circle time. When pressed, he protested that he was not going to sit next to someone with poorly legs – 'it's not nice.' As Andrew became used to life in the nursery he observed Dom's good relationships with the other children. He also watched Dom painting with confidence and skill. A few weeks into the term Andrew stood painting next to Dom. He looked at Dom's work and leaning over said, 'You've drawed a good man Dom – do you like my picture?'
>
> **Comment**
>
> On her first visit to the nursery Rosie had noticed Dom. She had talked about his 'bad legs' with her mum who had explained that some people have bits of their bodies that do not work very well. Rosie's rapid and genuine recognition of Dom's difficulties and talents helped Dom to see himself as a full member of the nursery group. Andrew's fear of physical disability had an equally powerful effect. Initially Dom responded to Andrew's comments by refusing to remain in the circle; he repeatedly asked to be wheeled into the book area where he sat silently watching the group. Staff rapidly realised the reason for Dom's action; Andrew's attitude had made him for the first time in the nursery feel different and deficient. As Andrew became more familiar with Dom he began to realise and admire his social skills and talents in painting. The wheelchair became irrelevant; Andrew wanted Dom for a friend.

ADULT EXPECTATIONS

The staff in an early years setting need to find out about children's beliefs about themselves and others. They will also work to strengthen each child's self-image, particularly those who may be vulnerable to bias and prejudice. One of the most effective ways of doing this is through staff demonstrating their high expectations of all children. Practitioners are invariably skilled in this aspect of work. However, occasionally where a young child is led to believe that the adult has only a low opinion of what he can do, like Ben who truly came to believe himself to be physically incompetent, the child's confidence drops and he only achieves what is expected of him. This then becomes a self-fulfilling prophecy.

Cooper distinguishes between self-fulfilling prophecies and sustaining expectations. He suggests that the self-fulfilling prophecy occurs when an inaccurate expectation of a child influences the behaviour of that child so as to make the expectation accurate. A sustaining expectation follows an initially accurate judgement, which is maintained despite other influences (5). The concern is that a self-fulfilling prophecy can lead to an expectation of a child which is sustained in later years.

Most nursery settings make shrewd and accurate judgements about their children based on skilled observations and sound information about what the child knows and understands already. However this process takes time. Staff in reception classes know that they must determine each child's starting point for learning in order to pitch experiences appropriately and provide suitable and sensitive support. Nevertheless, hasty assessments made too early often means that judgements are being made and recorded before the child has made a sound transition to school. The consequence of this is that those children are not yet sufficiently confident and settled to demonstrate their skills and competencies. This is compounded where a teacher has received insufficient information about a child's previous experiences and is unable to spend much time with individual children because of a large class size. In these situations teachers themselves know that there is a danger of making an inaccurate judgement about a child's abilities and potential for learning.

These circumstances can, of course, occur in any setting. Furthermore, without any other information, the adult's judgement may be unduly influenced by the child's social competencies rather than what he or she can do. A resulting halo effect can operate and cause over-optimistic views. For example, one Scottish study of multicultural nursery schools suggests that, in the absence of detailed observations of individual children, teachers made assessments of them based on their ethnic group membership. Thus a quiet, hardworking and well-behaved Asian child was regarded as competent and her difficulties with language were overlooked (6). The converse can also apply. A child who is awkward with people, who finds conversation difficult or who speaks colloquially, may, in the absence of other evidence, be judged to be of limited ability. Gordon Wells argues that 'Any suggestion that working-class children as a whole are "disadvantaged" in any absolute or irrevocable sense because their home experience leads them to use language differently, is certainly not appropriate' (7).

Expectations are also influenced by what people find familiar and identifiable. Val Wood suggests that teacher expectations are grounded in their own background and upbringing (8). Teachers may spot ability in middle-class children more easily than they do in children from less advantaged backgrounds, simply because they are more attuned to the former. On the other hand, children who have English as an additional language may have their behaviour misinterpreted or their abilities underestimated because of their struggle with a new language. Reflection and puzzlement may be interpreted to be sulky and uncommunicative behaviour. Children's difficulties with expressive language may lead adults to be unaware of the extent of their understanding of spoken language. Those children who are not only new to a school or nursery, but also face a new culture and have communication difficulties, need to be observed particularly carefully and given the necessary time to adapt.

Practitioners have a very real responsibility to make sensitive, informed and accurate judgements about children. Without this, some children at least will have too much or too little expected of them.

EQUALITY BETWEEN BOYS AND GIRLS

Any nursery concerned about equality should be aware of how they make it possible for boys and girls to have a similar entitlement and learn to adopt positive attitudes towards each other. Children may learn in the home how to behave differently as boys and girls and will take this behaviour into the nursery.

Families do appear to treat their sons and daughters in different ways. One study of five-year-olds shows that families encouraged girls to dance, dress-up and play quietly, while boys were given blocks and trucks and allowed boisterous play. Both girls and boys were actively discouraged from what was considered to be unsuitable responses for their sex (9). In these instances it is difficult for parents to accept that there is a very different approach in the nursery based on the belief that children should be encouraged to develop all aspects of their personality. Margy Whalley, head of the Pen Green Centre, recounts an episode one Christmas when the mother of a four-year-old child was angry and distressed as a consequence of Father Christmas presenting her son with a picnic set which was what he wanted. Whalley wisely concludes that it is necessary to move slowly when attempting to influence parents. Young children will only become confused if values at home and nursery are in direct opposition (10).

Case study

Andrea was sitting, sorting out cutlery in the kitchen area of a well-resourced role-play area. Aaron entered and settled himself in an armchair to 'read' the newspaper. He went through all the motions of a reader; turning the pages and appearing to scan the print. Glancing up from the paper he saw Andrea. 'Get off your bum and make me a cup of tea,' he ordered. Andrea promptly picked up the kettle and looked for the teapot. On observing this Ann the teaching assistant asked Andrea if she could come in to join them for a cup of tea. 'Perhaps we could ask Aaron to wash up afterwards?' she suggested. Frowning slightly, Aaron agreed.

Comment

Aaron's behaviour reflected what he had observed at home. (When the episode was recounted to his mum she wryly admitted that Aaron would have heard similar comments directed to her from his three much older brothers.) Clearly it was not consistent with the equal opportunities ethos that the nursery was trying to develop. Ann promptly invited herself into the area in order to steer the play towards giving Aaron a more equal role. Ann also hoped that she was offering a role model to encourage Andrea to be more assertive in future situations.

EQUALITY TO IMPROVE EDUCATIONAL ATTAINMENT

In the 1980s the educational performance of girls in primary and secondary schools was a high priority; as a consequence of action girls began to flourish. Now with girls out-performing boys it is the boys who are a focus of anxiety. There are many theories given as to the reasons for this – boys do not enjoy reading or girls are genetically more able. A survey of the views of secondary school pupils showed that peer pressure is one factor. Boys themselves admitted to needing not to lose face (11). However, it is too simple to look at this problem only in terms of gender. Some boys achieve well in school and still some girls do not thrive. Research by Keele

University for Ealing Council shows the influence of social class. Looking at the home life of 5,000 children from the age of four years, the study found that both girls and boys from working-class backgrounds were less likely to achieve as well as those from middle-class backgrounds. Other studies of both working-class and young black students found that the boys rejected school authority and invited confrontation although for different reasons to do with class and race. Interestingly, although black girls, distanced themselves from the school system, they were careful not to jeopardise their education (12).

Under-achievement is also a well-known problem with high attaining pupils. A study from the University of Bristol identified able boys in grammar schools as cruising. Again peer group pressure is a factor, with boys not being prepared to be seen as workers or in need of help from their teachers.

All aspects of equality in early years and later are concerned with making sure that children are enabled to do their best. This involves much more than providing the same activities for all. Any reasons for a child's lack of interest or achievement must be teased out and the curriculum and teaching styles suitably adapted.

In regard to boys' lack of attainment there is a case to be argued for some early intervention. It may be that if children in the setting are simply allowed freely to choose their activities, this in itself can set the scene for differences in later achievement. One study pointed up that it is the choices that boys and girls make from early years onwards rather than their innate ability that influences what they do later. In playgroup, given free choice, children observed selected stereotypical activities; for example, boys racing around the garden and showing an interest only in books about tractors and dumper trucks; girls engaged in role-play, and quietly drawing. On arrival in reception some boys were reluctant to draw and write having had little experience with pencils. They were also more interested in information books rather than fiction; as a result the study suggests that boys may find reading schemes which involve stories more difficult to follow. In reception classes where reading and writing are regarded highly, boys who have had little relevant experience are immediately vulnerable. As children move through school the stage is set for them to develop different styles of writing based on the books that they read (13).

However, while it is important that children are encouraged to succeed in all aspects of learning, practitioners also know that if children are able to learn in ways which suit them, they will want to learn more. Research by the Campaign for Learning on different learning styles found that small boys initially respond more to kinaesthetic or active learning (14). Annabel Dixon supports these findings and suggests that young boys find it particularly difficult to settle down to a sedentary programme. Dixon stresses the importance of using this knowledge to nurture positive attitudes from the time that children start their nursery and school careers. 'If boys gain a positive attitude to learning, in my experience they will take on a wider range of interests as they get older. So, if we are focused on difference earlier, there might be less division between boys and girls later on' (15).

These findings emphasise the need to tune in carefully and build on children's early preoccupations or schemes of thought. They also concur with Howard Gardner's conclusion that all of us have different ways of learning (16). He called these the five gateways to learning and described them as learning: through narrative or stories; through logic or mathematical thinking (these are the children who later on are so good at interpreting figures and data on graphs); through sensory and hands-on experience; through problem-solving; and through music or art. This message will resonate with many early years practitioners who have noticed how well some young children respond to identifying and making mathematical patterns, while others understand ideas conveyed in a picture or by making something.

Early years staff offer new experiences and learning in a range of forms. By using a wide repertoire of teaching styles this should ensure that every child is given the means by which they can understand best. As we know, initially young children learn mainly through their senses but then may respond particularly well to one of the learning gateways. Clearly learning approaches cannot always be matched to the needs of individual children. However, use of a broad range of methods will help to cover a range of needs and importantly also introduce children into new ways of learning.

PROMOTING A GLOBAL DIMENSION

The Foundation Stage practitioner has a huge responsibility in shaping the ideas and attitudes of our youngest children at a time when much of the world is in turmoil and peace is threatened. The future is in the hands of these children and we must prepare them in the best way to be global citizens.

RESOURCES

We know that the young brain is extremely receptive to all the experiences that we offer. This highlights the fact that all adults do, say and provide can make a difference to children's attitudes about others. For example children will respond to a setting's environment. If the environment conveys values and principles, what messages do settings offer young children and their families about different cultures and backgrounds? While young children are still struggling with written language the impact of images is strong and they will encounter many negative media images – listless, unhappy, tired and hungry families. These should be counterbalanced by affirmative posters and paintings of people from different race and culture involved in everyday events – shopping, cooking, eating and going to work.

Resources for play are important but a word of caution about dressing-up clothes. These need to reflect clothes worn for everyday life in different cultures rather than 'national costume'. As Iram Siraj Blatchford wryly observes, we might be fairly surprised if we went to an Indian nursery to find that the only English dressing-up clothes were those of Morris dancers (17). Children will play what they know. Different cooking utensils and household items need to be introduced – even better if there are children or parents who can show others how they are used in their homes.

LANGUAGE

Language powerfully influences how we think and feel about ourselves. Young children should be able to see and hear various languages and alternative scripts. Children find it easy to learn sign language and enjoy using it to respond in small groups. As they get older, they love to learn to count a few numbers, sing a song or reply to the register using different languages and identify symbols in Braille. Over time, and naturally, they come to realise that these different sounds and signs are equally useful ways of communicating.

OTHER PEOPLE

We know only too well now that young children will learn so much by themselves but they need informed adults to bring them to the next steps in understanding (see Chapter 2). Informative displays and good resources will only have good impact if they are brought to children's attention, if practitioners encourage children to explore them and to make connections between what they see and hear with their own experiences. 'Oh my daddy digs the garden like that man in Africa but he grows flowers.' Its only when children make these sorts of comments that we can see that they are beginning to recognise both similarities and differences in peoples' lifestyles.

However hard practitioners work they cannot afford to do it in isolation. Working with families is explored in Chapter 10. It is touched on here in the knowledge that some families may hold strong and fixed views on global education for their children. To quote one father, 'I want to protect my little girl from all that muck in the world – her eyes will be opened soon enough'. And yet, we cannot really succeed in influencing children's attitudes unless we work in tandem with parents and carers.

◼ WORKING IN MONO-CULTURAL AREAS

The danger of living in a closed or insular group have already been pointed out. As Elinor Lynch points out, our culture is like a second skin; most of the time we are not aware of it but it becomes visible when we encounter one that is different (18). Where children only mix with others who come from similar backgrounds their first meeting with a person who looks different or behaves differently can be a momentous experience.

In a mono-cultural setting there can be a view that it is not necessary to look outside and that 'global education is not relevant for us'. But this attitude neglects to understand that our world has shrunk: people travel easily for work and leisure across continents. Although some of our young children may not leave their locality during their lives, many more at some time in their lives will be thrown into contact with people from different walks of life. All of our children will be affected by world events and their lives will be richer as a result of thinking about the world rather than only their own little environment.

The reality is that where a setting is unable to offer children the first hand experience of living and learning within a mixed community, staff have to devise scenarios in order to raise awareness and encourage children to share their views. The obvious routes to this work are to purchase resources and focus on different celebrations. However, these approaches alone are not going to achieve real understandings. Development of global education is a process and as such it should infiltrate into all aspects of work. It can be woven into register taking, through music, songs, stories and in cooking. Different experiences of travel can be shared. A global approach to the Foundation Stage curriculum is not a bolt-on, but more another way of looking.

DEVELOPING AN INCLUSIVE NURSERY
◼

A setting which aims to help children accept and care for others must develop a climate in which everyone feels welcome and included. This is reasonably easy to achieve when the adult oversees activities and routines. In most circumstances young children respond naturally to plenty of warm encouragement for them to be generous and open to others. However, in a democratic nursery, understandably children will also choose for themselves who they play with and this may occasionally lead to exclusion. Although some children in a nursery will opt to play with others of either sex, by three and four years of age they will increasingly play in single-sex groups. Some children also have particular difficulties in joining groups because they are perceived as being different. Alice was very overweight and sometimes clumsy, Jaru had a cast in his eye and often disconcerted children by talking to them while appearing to look in another direction. Both of these children experienced being on the perimeter of the setting's activities and had at times been hurt by comments from other children.

Any hurtful or insulting remarks require sensitive but firm intervention. They should be dealt with promptly with the children concerned when the adult can make her views clear. 'I don't think that Jaru should be called "funny-eyes". It's really interesting that his eyes look different, and we have all got different coloured eyes.' Although children should be allowed to exercise their choice about who they will play with, it is a different matter if the decision stems from discrimination. It is also necessary to help those children who are vulnerable to being excluded; for example, to learn the skills of friendship and ways of entering a group (see Chapter 2).

Although the aim for any Foundation Stage setting should be for all children to be fully included in activities, when children make decisions in play they may offer only minor roles to certain individuals. Thus some children will play a full part and others may be only partially included. Typical examples in role-play are when children are regularly given token parts such as the baby or the dog. Although it seems to the outsider that these children are being marginalised, it may satisfy the children themselves. One researcher, when studying social inclusion, made the important point that inclusion is a two-way process (19). Both the person wanting to be included and the person who is the includer must agree to a situation comfortable to both parties. Even if it appears unfair that a child is always given something unimportant to do, the significant fact is that it is acceptable to the child. These issues concerning the wider world may appear remote, but young children experience many of them at a personal level. Children are regularly involved in issues of fairness and discrimination, the use and discussion of these experiences will sow seeds of understanding and codes of behaviour which can be explored in more depth at a later stage. It is unrealistic to expect early education and care to address all of society's problems. Nevertheless the foundations of equity and tolerance can be laid. Vivien Paley working with her kindergarten children in the USA suggests that 'maybe our classrooms can be nicer than the outside world' (20).

Summary

The early years setting can help young children to become aware of the world beyond their immediate environment; to learn about others from a basis of tolerance, respect and open-mindedness. In order to learn to respect others, children must see this demonstrated positively by adults. They must also respect themselves. Staff expectations have a powerful effect on what children feel they are capable of, and this in turn influences their feelings of self-worth. Staff should plan for children to have access to many different experiences; they should also follow individual children's interests and provide them with ways of learning which suit them.

Practical suggestions

Be aware of what children think
- Listen to them as they play with each other and share books; what do they notice and what observations do they make? Note any derogatory names that children use towards each other if they are angry or upset.
- Use these comments to develop teaching points, e.g. a comment overheard 'Lisa's fat' might lead to the adult bringing in posters of children and well-known media figures of different sizes in order to talk about the range of physical shapes and relative importance of body shape and size against what a person is really like.

Respect every child
- Ensure that you use children's correct names which are pronounced properly.
- Take care to record full names when a child enters the nursery. Ask parents how they and their children would like to be addressed and listen carefully to how the name is pronounced. For the benefit of other staff, a child's personal name should be underlined on the record and if necessary spelt out phonetically.
- Show a genuine interest in children's backgrounds. Ask them to bring in something that is special for them from their home. Share these precious things in circle times (most effectively organised in small groups of six to eight which will enable all children to join in and ask questions).

Help children to see themselves in relation to others
- Use images (photographs/pictures/postcards) which show children in their own homes, other children and their families in the local

environment and from other parts of the world. Use these images to interest children in other people and places and to develop balanced views.

- Display and discuss examples of similarities in the stages of growing up, in the daily aspects of life (washing, dressing, eating, celebrating) and common emotions we experience; common problems experienced in all countries (people who are homeless and poor); differences in homes, physical appearances and dress and different customs.
- Use routines to help children identify how they are alike and how they are different, e.g. when grouping children or dismissing them from a group use physical characteristics as well as items of clothing – 'all those with red socks, black, curly hair, two thumbs'.

Provide role play settings to reflect different lifestyles

- Use your home corner to depict different types of homes (tent, caravan). Help children to appreciate the special circumstances of living in these homes (cooking, washing, collecting water) in order for them to use their play to develop understandings.
- Provide examples of men and women doing different jobs. Invite adults into the nursery whose roles help to counter stereotypes, e.g. a father with a baby, a woman bus driver, a man who assists with a cookery activity.
- Use stories, jigsaw puzzles and photographic displays to show adults in different roles.

Confront exclusion

- Using photographs of the adults and children in the nursery, make stick puppets. Introduce these to the children; ask each child to select his own stick puppet and then choose other puppets whom he wants to play with that morning. This activity may identify the children who are excluded – discuss what it feels like to be left out; make brief but clear reference to any issues which involve ethnicity or disability.
- Leave the puppets in the book area for children to play with; observe any activity with the puppets or change in the children's play partners. Repeat the activity after two weeks.

Develop a global perspective

- Pick up cues and comments from parents in order to be aware of where they stand on this issue.
- Be clear and honest about the stance that you take in your setting and justify this in the children's interests.

• Use workshops, discussions and video to raise parent's interest/ awareness of the need to introduce global education at a young age – at least some parents will become interested and are then likely to support work.
• Find out what parents/family members could offer to give children insights into different ways of living; value all contributions, e.g. through thank-you cards, a thank-you picture from the children, a simple thank-you party.

Professional questions

1. How far do we as a staff understand the issues behind promoting equality of opportunity for all children?
2. How far do we as a staff work in a similar way to achieve equality?
3. Does my response to children depend on whether they are boys or girls?
4. How visible are men in the nursery; how are they used?
5. How do we identify children's preferred ways of learning and build on these preferences?
6. How aware am I of my own culture and how does it influence my behaviour with children?
7. How much do I use my knowledge of each child's cultural background in my work with the group?

REFERENCES

1. QCA (2000) *Curriculum Guidance for the Foundation Stage*. London: QCA/DfES, p. 42.
2. Lindon, J. (1998) *Equal Opportunities in Practice*. London: Hodder & Stoughton, pp. 11–12.
3. Wright, C. (1992) quoted in Reva Klein (1995) Say hello to your race relations, *TES: EXTRA Early Years*, 30 June, p. v.
4. Macpherson, W. (1999) *Inquiry into the Matters Arising from the Death of Stephen Lawrence* (The Macpherson Report): http://news.bbc.co.uk/1/hi/special_report/1999/02/99/stephen_lawrence/279746.stm
5. Cooper, H. (1985) Models of teacher expectation communication, in J.B. Dusek (ed.), *Teacher Expectancies*. London: Lawrence Erlbaum Associates.
6. Ogilvy, G.M., Boath, E.H., Cheyne, W.M., Johoda, E. and Schaffer, H.R. (1990) Staff attitudes and perceptions in multicultural nursery schools, *Early Childhood Development and Care*, Vol. 64, pp. 1–13.
7. Wells, G. (1983) Talking with children: the complementary roles of parents

and teachers, in M. Donaldson, R. Grieve and C. Pratt (eds), *Early Childhood Development and Education*. Oxford: Basil Blackwell, p. 37.

8. Wood, V. (1989) School ethos and the individual within a community, in G. Barrett (ed.), *Disaffection from School? The Early Years*. Lewes: Falmer.

9. Langois, J.H. and Downs, A.C. (1980) Mothers, fathers and peers as socialisation agents of sex typed play-behaviours in young children, *Child Development*, Vol. 51, pp. 1217–47.

10. Whalley, M. (1994) *Learning to be Strong*. London: Hodder & Stoughton, p. 53.

11. Phillips, A. (1998) 'It's just so unfair', *TES*, 13 November, pp. 14–15.

12. Hinds, D. (1998) Don't be trapped by gender stereotypes, *TES School Management UpDate*, 13 November, p. 9.

13 Macleod, D. (1997) The gender divide, *Guardian*, 17 June 1997, Schools Section, p. 3.

14. Rodd, G. (2001) Can young children learn to learn? *Early Years Educator*, Vol. 3, no. 6, pp. 16–18.

15. Dixon, A. (1998) quoted in *TES Update*, 13 November, p. 9.

16. Gardner, H. (1983) *Frames of Mind*. New York: Basic Books.

17. Siraj-Blatchford, I. (1996) Why understanding cultural difference is not enough, in G. Pugh (ed.), *Contemporary Issues in the Early Years*, London: Paul Chapman.

18. Lynch, E.W. (1998) Developing cross-cultural competence, in E.W. Lynch and M.J. Hanson (eds), *Developing Cross-cultural Competence: A Guide for Working with Children and their Families*, Baltimore, MD: Paul H. Brookes, p. 24.

19. Sherman, A. (1995) I hardly feel like I am playing: differing intentions with regards to social inclusion, *Early Years*, Vol. 16, no. 1, pp. 51–4.

20. Paley. V. (1992) *You Can't Say You Can't Play*. Cambridge, MA: Cambridge University Press, p. 22.

CHAPTER NINE

Outdoors – a Haven for Personal, Social and Emotional Development

When asked to recall their childhoods, many adults have only piecemeal memories but admit that some of their best and most vivid recollections are linked to being outside (1). They talk with pleasure about their fantasy play, making dens and using whatever was on hand as props. Messy play seemed to be understood and accepted by parents, and adults remember the joys of digging in the earth, making mud pies and, sometimes, wading in streams. Adults recall being given a lot of freedom from a young age although older children were responsible for ensuring that younger ones did not come to harm.

Dan, now 65 years, looks back on his childhood in a small midlands town as a time almost exclusively spent outside.

> We played near to the railway bank and cheered the trains as they passed by. The big boys taught us games of tag and leapfrog. They laid down the rules but we knew that they would keep us safe. We all took some food, biscuits, sandwiches and a bottle of drink – you shared what you had if someone forgot to bring their grub with them. Often I would return at the end of the day, whacked out with torn trousers and muddy shoes, but longing for tomorrow to come in order to do it all over again.

Adults such as Dan recognise only too well the value of these early experiences in helping them to enjoy a robust childhood and to grow up. In today's world it is a different story; there are many issues in young children's home lives that lead to a danger of them being deprived of the memories of outdoor play which their parents still enjoy. These issues include:

1. *Over-protection*. In today's society, many parents are worried about the safety issues of being outside. Traffic has

increased immensely in residential areas and, despite efforts to clamp down on speeding, many cars are driven too fast and pose a hazard to children playing in streets. Although there is no direct evidence that children today are in more jeopardy from encounters with strangers, the grim stories sensationalised in the media have certainly influenced parents to think that their children may be in danger, and they are understandably not prepared to allow them to play out of sight. As a consequence children are not able to enjoy 'risky freedom' – that heady feeling of tasting adventure which encourages personal growth (2).

2. *Lack of experience of being outside.* The pressure of time and the convenience of cars mean that children walk very little on a daily basis; it is common for children to be taken by car to their nursery or school even if it is located within a few minutes walking distance; walking as a weekend leisure activity for families is now rare, and particularly unusual in cold or wet weather; for those families without cars, daily journeys on foot to settings and shops can be a rushed experience in the attempt to fit in these outings with the many other demands of the day.

3. *Lack of hard physical exercise to develop young bodies.* While some families arrange physical activities for young children through attending leisure centres and clubs, many are prevented from so doing because of expense. In addition, most homes with gardens do not have facilities or space for children's energetic outside play; and not all families live near to or use the facilities of a park.

Whilst we have to face the realities of modern life and parent's concern to protect their children, the outcome is that many children do not have the opportunities to exercise their bodies or to encounter the excitement and challenges of the outdoors. As a consequence an increasing number of children have weight problems. Current figures suggest that one in ten children of four years and under are overweight, and of those one in four is obese. The Coronary Prevention Group suggests that obesity in children is becoming an epidemic and some children as young as three years are showing signs of being at risk of heart disease later in life (3).

During the early years of life when a vast amount of physical development is taking place and when habits of life are being laid down it is critical that children are able to be active. Early years settings and schools have a fundamental role to play here. This was recognised by the Chelsea Open Air Nursery opened in 1929 in order to provide challenge for over-privileged children, whom the benefactor asserted were crippled by not being allowed to take risks outside. The introduction of the Foundation Stage has emphasised the value of outside play and learning and most early years practitioners now recognise that experiences which stem from being outside are every young child's entitlement. Although it is perfectly possible for young children to make progress in all areas through learning outside, some of the main justifications for an outdoor curriculum relate to aspects of personal development.

CONFIDENCE

We know that, in the sequence of development, children first have to experience the world actively through their senses before they can think in the abstract and hold thoughts and memories of things in their heads. If we bring an interesting new object into the classroom children's responses make it clear how they need to learn about it. 'Let me touch it, let me feel, let me see, let me listen', they cry. Provision of sensory experiences is part and parcel of the early years curriculum. In a carefully planned inside environment, children are invited to receive information through tasting, smelling, touching and listening to sounds, and rich visual displays are evident in classrooms. The good practitioner will ensure that these experiences are provided inside. However, the outside area lends itself much more easily to sensory learning; such contrivance and planning is not so necessary as much of the provision is already to hand. Children can observe minibeasts in their natural environment, they can match leaves of different colours, feel their textures and listen to the sound of their feet crunching on dry leaves. They can experience the effects of different weather at first hand, smell flowers and, under supervision, they can grow and taste different herbs.

As with any other learning children need support to identify each sense and make full use of it. But the important point is that sensory learning is natural for young children; through smelling, touching, tasting, listening and looking children pick up information in a way that makes sense to them. This relevant and often intuitive learning helps them to grow in confidence and self-esteem.

Movement is initially the natural way of learning, for young children. They may be seen to be boisterous and noisy but this behaviour is entirely appropriate for their age. Sally Goddard Blythe suggests the most demanding level of movement for a child is to remain still (4). It is not that they are unwilling to do so but simply that they do not find it easy to have this degree of control over their bodies. The *Curriculum Guidance for the Foundation Stage* suggests that provision of an outside space should give scope for children to work and play on a larger scale (5). Children urgently need to become adept at using their bodies and they want to do so. Their physical skills are closely linked to other aspects of development. Those children who are clumsy, now diagnosed as developmental co-ordination disorder (DCD) are found to do less well in school than their intellectual abilities would suggest. Conversely, children who have good control of their bodies tend to have high self-esteem. Movement involves much more than just physical development. Chapter 2 referred to children's schemes of thought or preoccupations which are linked to different movements. These early patterns of behaviour help children actively to experience the world. Children use their bodies in all areas of learning. Children will use and extend gross and fine motor skills when working practically and creatively; over time their gross motor movements become refined and support mark-making; they also learn to solve problems through practice, trial and error. All these efforts result in children experiencing achievement and developing a positive view of themselves (6).

INDEPENDENCE

A well-planned outdoor area, like an indoor area, can offer tremendous scope for children to become self-reliant and make choices and decisions. The outside area can, however, offer the child more scope for challenge: opportunities to take risks in climbing and balancing, in having more spaces to hide, in experiencing the weather, in building and constructing on a larger scale than possible inside. Moreover, the nature of outside play means that children are more likely to instigate activities for themselves rather than being reliant on the adult. At a basic level, if outside play is available throughout the session children are able to select where they want to play. As they get used to setting their own challenges and making decisions when playing outside, children will strengthen their powers of independence and grow in responsibility.

SOCIAL SKILLS

Although some younger children are not yet ready to play with others and some are naturally inclined to play alone, much outside play is social and co-operative. Almost thirty years ago Tizard's study of the play of four-year-olds in pre-school centres found that children from 'working-class' backgrounds opted to spend 75 per cent of their time outside, and that here their co-operative play was more evident than indoors (7). Most young children will play together naturally but the practitioner can encourage more reluctant children to join in with large-scale building projects or to partner games of throwing and catching.

EMOTIONAL DEVELOPMENT

The indoor environment, particularly where there is a confined space, often means that there is concern to button up children's emotional expression in the interests of the rest of the group. When children work in over-crowded conditions they can become irritable and aggressive (8). Outdoor space is more accommodating and allows children to express their feelings more openly; they can squeal with pleasure and excitement or explode with a temper tantrum without undue disruption. Superhero play is a contentious issue but one that needs to be faced. Practitioners, whilst sympathetic to the need for young boys in particular to take part in vigorous, superhero play, admit to finding it difficult to cater for in classrooms. Outside it is easier, not only to allow this play but to enter into it – noise and vigorous activity is able to be accommodated. Outside play is also very inclusive. There are certain groups of children who feel more at ease out of doors. Helen Bilton refers to traveller and refugee children: 'for them, they need to be outside as this is where they feel empowered' (9).

One of the most profound lessons that children can start to learn outside is about the pattern of life, of birth, death and renewal. It is important for them to understand that their environment is forever changing, even in the depths of winter. As they sweep away dead growth in the winter they start to find new shoots underneath. In one nursery children found a dead sparrow and planned its funeral in some detail. One child suggested that other birds were looking at the burial from the single tree in the garden and they felt sad.

MOTIVATION

Perhaps the greatest justification for outdoor learning is that children are strongly inclined to learn outside – studies show that it is a preferred activity and invites curiosity, investigation and the pleasure of growing things. Learning through Landscapes suggests that the freedom involved is a great incentive. 'Because of the freedom the outdoors offers to move on a large scale, to be active, noisy and messy and to use all their senses with their whole body, young children engage in the way they most need to explore, make sense of life and express their feelings and ideas (10).' One small-scale study provided young children with Polaroid cameras and asked them to record what they liked best about their nursery. The children voted firmly for being outside. 'One little boy took a picture of a crawl-through tunnel and another photographed a football. They really valued the open space, especially if there were things like climbing frames and bikes … ' (11).

Case study

The practitioners read the story of *The Tale of Mr Jeremy Fisher* by Beatrix Potter to a group of seven four-year-old children, who were immensely interested and discussed the illustrations. Two children mentioned that their dads went fishing. One girl said that he had fished in a lake when he went camping. The teacher suggested that they set up a camping site with fishing facilities outside.

A large bath of water was placed under the climbing frame. Children brought in pebbles and water weed from home and created a pond. They were invited to fish from the top of the frame using home-made fishing rods with magnets attached. An array of plastic fish with paper clips to attract the magnets were placed in the bath. A rowing boat was already fixed in the grounds and this was used for further fishing activities.

The camping site consisted of two small pop-up tents and two old wooden clothes horses covered with blankets. The children set up camp themselves (with a little help from an adult). Night time was simulated when window flaps and blankets were pulled down and children used torches inside their dens. All children contributed ideas about the camping equipment necessary and together made lists of what they required (some children wrote their own lists – others had their ideas scribed for them). The lists were posted on the parents' noticeboard and parents responded by sending in items requested. A large cardboard box served as a kiosk to sell tickets for the campsite and fishing permits (both made by the children). Nathan insisted that visitors must sign their permits and he showed the others how to make permit badges (with the aid of safety pins).

After two days the play appeared to flag. The practitioner invited the initial group together and three others who wanted to join in to think further about what people did when they went camping. How did they travel to the site and what did they eat?

Dale suggested that a camp shop be set up where campers could buy food. The group organised by themselves using a large cardboard box as the

---

shop and small boxes and containers from a collection kept for junk. Dale initially refused to allow anyone else to become the shopkeeper until Nathan persuaded him to 'come fishing and let others have a turn in the shop because that's fair'.

The group also set up a parking area for wheeled vehicles. Two children made signs directing people to the different areas on the site.

Comment

All in the group developed social skills of working together, negotiating, sharing equipment and taking turns. They were curious and persistent in their approach to the project. Effie and Huda brought in further information from home, e.g. different sorts of bait that can be used to catch fish. The group made decisions and were largely responsible in physically establishing the play environment. Sean and Nathan were encouraged to talk about their fear of the dark. They played through 'going to be at night time' in the dark tent and Bruno reassured them that 'it's cosy and nothing to be frightened about'.

Given these undoubted benefits, Foundation Stage settings have a very real responsibility to offer children experience of outside activity but as with any provision the quality of learning and development will be dependent on amount of thought and preparation that is invested. Any planning for outdoor play will need to consider provision of a safe environment which is accessible to children. This should ensure many gains in personal development, one of the main ones being early experiences in caring for the world that they live in.

GETTING SAFETY IN PERSPECTIVE

Recognising that practitioners have the serious responsibility of being *in loco parentis*, it is reasonable to accept that, during the time they are in educational settings priority must go to keeping young children safe. The outside early years environment needs to be a particular focus for safety as children are likely to be more active. However, whilst this means protecting a child from obvious hazards there is also a dual and longer-term responsibility, which is to help children to learn about keeping safe and dealing with possible danger. As Jenny Lindon suggests, if we want to protect children in the longer-term it is not sensible to keep them away from every risk. Children, from an early age, need to gently learn from trusted adults about some of the dangers in their environment and how to deal with them (12). In one sense if we wrap children up in cotton wool we are not so much protecting them, but ourselves from taking the responsibility of helping them to understand what it means to grow up and to be safety conscious.

Even at a young age children can understand the need to be safe, to check for themselves if a structure is secure or a plank is properly balanced. Most will take this responsibility very seriously and grow in self-confidence as they make the decisions.

Not only is it undesirable, it is impossible to create an environment that is risk-free. However, staff have to be aware of liability and now it is standard and recognised practice to undertake a risk assessment. This should apply to the layout of the grounds, different surfaces and the type and positioning of equipment. A risk is usually assessed through careful observation and shared information about incidents or perceived potential to harm children. While it is not acceptable to tolerate high risk, any environment that provides opportunities for challenge and excitement will, for some children, be slightly risky.

MAKING THE MOST OF WHAT YOU HAVE GOT

There have always been lots of good reasons for not providing an early years curriculum outdoors. Some common ones are a lack of space, limited staffing and insufficient time. However, with increasing recognition of the value of the outdoor environment these limitations are being faced and dealt with.

SPACE

Many nurseries have very limited outdoor provision but with imagination they can provide for a range of experiences in a very small area. The aim should be as far as possible for the outside area to complement what is available for children inside and to make it as accessible as possible. One benefit of a small outside area is that it is likely to be easier to supervise.

STAFFING

Staffing ratios can vary from 1–4 to 1–15 and this is clearly going to influence the amount of oversight and degree of involvement of adults with outside activities. Staff who restrict outside provision to set times in the day might be persuaded to allow more access if they recognise that:

- a well-planned outside environment should involve no higher risk and thus no greater level of care for children than if they work inside
- free access to outside will mean an end to the rush to go out

en masse, which can create difficulties for children sharing provision and for adults in allocating their time fairly.

■ TIME

Practitioners never complain of excess of time – there is always a scarcity and often a feeling that we rush young children through activities each day. However, if we focus on what children are learning rather than what they are doing, this helps us to look at the curriculum in a holistic way, hopefully to plan a little less content but to concentrate on providing the most fruitful experiences that will help children to grow personally. As with indoor activities, children will be more inclined to concentrate and persevere if they have time to pursue interests. The brief playtime is not conducive to this and McAuley and Jackson suggest that interrupting 'children's absorbed activity' can subvert learning almost as much as allowing disruptive behaviour (13).

Time is a finite commodity. There is of course time for anything but not time for everything. If we recognise the rich benefits of outside experiences for children, this leads to the conclusion that we cannot afford to reduce time for this provision even if it means less time spent on other daily routines.

Case study

A nursery class in an inner city area had limited space inside and access to only a tiny yard outside, which until then had been used as a space for three wheeled toys. The arrangement was not satisfactory as each child only had access to a vehicle twice a week and then could only ride it in a small circle round and round the yard, which caused both staff and children frustration. The nursery staff recognised the need for change. Having the children's play closely observed they decided that they had very little scope to play imaginatively in the classroom. The 'home corner' occupied a corner of the classroom, and the small space meant that it was very poorly resourced. When asked what they would like to do outside if they did not ride the vehicles, some children said that they would love to make dens.

Staff started to share stories with children about dens, hidey-holes and caves. One of the favourites was *Can't You Sleep Little Bear* by Martin Waddell. The children thought that the bear's cave looked very cosy. They were invited to draw pictures and plans for building a cave and to decide what they might need to have inside it. Together, staff and children made a 'cave' which took up the entire outside space. They built a willow construction which they covered with waterproof cloth. Inside it was equipped with bedding, torches, cushions and a large stuffed bear sitting on a chair. Children had free access to the cave and the play that developed was complex and focused. The home corner inside was dismantled and this freed up some much needed inside space to be used for construction and small-scale play.

One child reflected the views of many others when he commented that 'our bear cave is the very best thing in school and it's our very own'.

Comment

The nursery staff had sensibly researched through observations and through discussions with children what they needed outside. They also made the most of two small spaces by regarding them as a total environment. The children's close involvement in setting up the cave is reflected in their high-quality play and their expressed sense of personal satisfaction.

HELPING CHILDREN TO LOOK AFTER THE WORLD OUTSIDE

The need to respect and conserve our environment is now acute and is a recognised aspect of the National Curriculum. Most young children have a strong affinity with the natural world. A two-year-old will amble along a road and stop for a maddeningly long period to examine a weed growing out of a wall. The attractions of water, mud and minibeasts never fails. This early interest provides a very sound basis for extending their understanding and developing a respect for the environment in which they live. Even given a small patch of earth children can still learn how important it is to care for it, to keep it looking beautiful by being careful, tidy, gentle in handling things and leaving nature to grow.

However, some nurseries will be interested in catering in more depth for this aspect of personal development. Three successful approaches working with young children outside are described briefly below.

EARTH EDUCATION

The institute for Earth Education was set up in America in the 1980s as a non-profit volunteer organisation. It aims to provide programmes to help individuals 'live more harmoniously with the earth'. The basic programme is one of acclimatization, which in summary is to feel at home with the natural world, to be aware of ones place in life's processes, and to become more aware and understand more of the natural world.

Although the programmes are designed for all age groups, many aspects are particularly suitable for young children, as there is a heavy focus on feelings and learning through the senses. Some of the main principles of an acclimatization programme reflect the tenets of early childhood practice. These are that: people learn best when they feel what they are learning; the best learning starts where the learner is; the wide worlds of perception and emotion cannot be measured or described in words; in a good learning experience the medium should be the magic of discovery and wonder and joy (14). The programme of activities is designed to take place out of doors and to be organised for small groups. With under-fives, one adult for every four children is desirable. This enables easy conversation and for the adult to respond to each child's discoveries and observations. An essential requirement is that the adults themselves enjoy the wonders of the natural world. (See below for practical suggestions for an earthwalk.)

■ FOREST SCHOOLS

In Denmark, Forest Schools have been an important aspect of early years education for the past fifteen years. They were introduced initially for children of five and six years in Copenhagen to provide them with some nursery experience in the year before they attended school; a bus would collect children daily and take them into the local forests simply because there was no space to build conventional nursery units. The benefits of this type of provision were quickly recognised. The Forest School developed based on the belief that young children could be educated to appreciate the natural world and to begin to understand the need to care for nature. There is also a heavy emphasis on helping children to become autonomous – to become physically independent, explore for themselves and not be afraid of getting dirty.

In 1995 Bridgwater College Early Years Centre of Excellence followed the Danish model and started its own Forest School for three- and four-year-olds and the centre now leases a secure woodland site and a minibus. The children visit the forest for one day nearly every week they are in the nursery and in all sorts of weather. The aim is to encourage them to grow in confidence and independence, to learn to take risks and to gain skills in, and knowledge of aspects of, the outside environment. They develop observational skills, learn how to whittle sticks, light a fire and extinguish it safely. After one year of these experiences the children camp in the woodland, with some of the parents, staff and students. Over the last nine years the project has expanded vastly and Forest School centres are established in many parts of the country (15).

■ THE RISING SUN WOODLAND PROJECT

This project drew both on the philosophies of the Forest Schools and the Reggio Emilia pre-schools. With the aid of a grant, children from a nursery

FIGURE 9.1 LOOKING AFTER OUR WORLD

FIGURE 9.2 YOUNG CHILDREN DEVELOP SKILLS IN THE FOREST SCHOOL

class in Northern England were transported to a countryside park with a team of specialist workers (including artists, environmental officer and early years staff). The richness of their experiences depicted in beautiful video materials shows opportunities for children to gather and collect natural objects, encounter water, ice, mud and fire, challenge their physical skills in climbing banks and trees, build dens and live with an imaginary dragon in the woodland. The project records the children's huge range of personal development. Caring attitudes were encouraged in protecting plants and trees. This ethos influenced children's attitudes to each other, for example when one child stung his arm on a nettle, his friend said 'don't worry, I'll look after you, we'll find Mrs B or Mrs N' (16).

Summary

There are rich opportunities for children to grow and develop personally when playing outside. However the realities of modern life mean that many have too little chance in their home lives to encounter and enjoy the outside environment. Early years practitioners have a responsibility to offer an outside curriculum to children in the knowledge that it will offer them skills and attitudes that will hold them in good stead for their future personal development. Each setting should make its outside accommodation and resources fully accessible to children. Where young children are involved in planning and developing their outside environment they are likely to be more motivated to use it.

Practical suggestions

Start from the child's perspective
- List the things that you enjoyed doing outside as a child – climbing, jumping, digging, make-believe, making dens, hiding, collecting.
- Discuss with your children what they would like to include in an outdoor play area; ask them to tell you or draw a picture of this.
- Take a small group of children to visit a neighbouring early years setting which has a good outside area; walk around and discuss the different features; provide them with cameras and ask them to take a photograph of a favourite feature outside that they would like to include in their setting.

Develop a quiet sanctuary
- Provide a sheltered/screened area for children to rest from activity and reflect; provide low seating/rugs and cushions; make sure that children recognise that the purpose of this place is to be able to

withdraw from noise and activity to enjoy peace.

Provide transportable resources which encourage children to work together and give vent to their feelings
• Have a trolley on wheels with transparent or wire baskets; label and resource each basket with different equipment, e.g. for gardening – small forks, rakes, trowels, watering cans, gardening gloves, plastic kneelers; for windy days – streamers, windmills, bubble mixture and wands, paper for making paper planes, small kites; for imagining – small play scenarios and mats.

Plan your outside area to teach about environmental issues
• Even a very limited space can provide for a raised bed or tubs of plants and bird feeders or a bird table; trees and vegetation to attract butterflies and insects; rocks or logs as homes for minibeasts; an area sectioned off to contain cobbles and stones for children to arrange in different patterns; regular activities which include looking at shadows at different times of the day, noting the different position of the sun and clouds at different times of the day.
• Think carefully about what environmental experiences you want to provide for children, rather than simply what you want to grow.

Plan specific activities to nurture acclimatisation with the earth
• Prepare a series of simple activities to allow children to experience and enjoy the environment through their senses. The following three activities have been adapted from the Earth Education Acclimatization Institute. The walk should be for no longer than twenty-five minutes on the first occasion and ideally there should be one adult available for a group of three children. The venue would ideally be a patch of woodland but it is possible to use a 'wild' area in a local park. It does not have to be an extensive area; you do not have to walk very far but do ensure that the environment is suitable for the activities. You should aim to link the activities to provide the children with an enjoyable and unified experience of the natural world.

Explain to the children that you are going on a very special walk when they will be using their eyes, ears, fingers and noses to explore things.

Activity 1: Using your nose. Start the walk if possible near a fragrant spot (damp moss, bluebells, wild garlic). Explain to the children that some things are easy to smell but others have secret scents; show them how to scratch a root or patch of damp soil in order to allow it to share its perfume. Encourage them to share their favourite 'smells' with their helper and others in their small groups.

Activity 2: The little people's garden. Resources required: cardboard tubes which are cut down to provide a viewfinder for each child. Prepare for this activity in advance by identifying the little garden, a mossy and secluded patch with interesting features such as boulders, ferns, pieces of bark and fungus. Cover this with a black cloth. Tell the children a story about a group of little people who have a garden nearby and lead them towards the cloth. When you arrive explain to the children that in order to see the garden they must first collect a gift for the little people – it should be the smallest thing they can find nearby – a twig, leaf, tiny stone. When the children have gathered their gifts they return to the cloth. Before you reveal the little people's garden you give a viewfinder to each child. Show them how they can have their own special view of the garden. Encourage each child to decide where to place their gift in the garden.

Activity 3: Wind dancers. Demonstrate to the children how a leaf twirls through the air. Talk about all the little things that dance in the wind. Suggest that children find their own. They have to look carefully for twigs, blades of grass, seedpods and feathers, and test them to see which are the best dancers. They return to the group and each child demonstrates his or her dancer.

Professional questions

1. How well informed are you about your children's previous experiences of being outside?
2. What messages does your outside area give to children as users; how do you know?
3. How much do you know of parent's attitudes to their children being outside; how have you managed to reassure and convince more reluctant parents of the benefits of outside play?
4. How well does your outside area challenge your oldest and most experienced children?

REFERENCES

1. Edgington, M. (2002) *The Great Outdoors*. Early Education, 136 Cavell Street, London, E1 2JA.
2. Ouvry, M. (2000) *Exercising Muscles and Minds*. National Early Years Network.

3. James, P. (2003) Planning policies that work for the prevention of obesity. Meeting convened by the International Obesity Task Force and the Coronary Prevention Group, 11 November.
4. Goddard-Blythe, S. (2000) Mind and body, *Nursery World*, 15 June.
5. QCA (2000) *Curriculum Guidance for the Foundation Stage*. London: QCA/DfEE, p. 15.
6. Gallahue, D.L. (1989) *Understanding Motor Development, Infants, Children, Adolescents*. 2nd edn. Indianapolis, IN: Benchmark Press.
7. Tizard, B., Philps, J. and Plewis, I. (1976b) Play in pre-school centres – 11. Effects on play of the child's social class and of the educational orientation of the centre, *Journal of Child Psychology and Psychiatry*, Vol. 18, pp. 21–38.
8. Bates, B. (1996) Like rats in a rage, *The Times Educational Supplement*, Vol. 2, 20 September, p. 11.
9. Bilton, H. (2004) *Playing Outside: activities, ideas and inspiration for the Early Years*. London: David Fulton, p. 5.
10. Learning through Landscapes (2004) *Early Years Outdoors' Vision and Values for Outdoor Play*. Winchester: Learning through Landscapes.
11. Finch, S. (1999) quoted by J. Moorhead in Out of the mouths of babes, *Guardian*, 2 June, p. 9.
12. Lindon, J. (1999) *Too Safe for their Own Good*. London: National Early Years Network.
13. McAuley, H. and Jackson, P. (1992) *Educating Young Children: A Structural Approach*. London: David Fulton, pp. 46–7.
14. Van Matre, S. (1979) *Sunship Earth*. Earth Education Acclimatization Institute, PO Box 288, Warrenville, IL 60555, p. 11.
15. Bridgwater College Children's Centre Brochure, Bath Road, Bridgwater, Somerset TA6 4PZ.
16. Rising Sun Pre-school Project (2000) *Time Out in the Woodland*. Newcastle: Sightlines Initiatives, p. 24.

CHAPTER TEN

Working with Families to Support Young Children's Personal Growth

Every child and family is unique. We now accept that only a minority of children live in a family with parents who have remained married. Christine Pascal refers to the plurality of families which now include one parent families (both men and women), same sex families, unmarried partners, divorced and married partners with families. Families are also smaller and the role of the extended family has dwindled (1). For children their family consists of the people who are closest to them and who care for them on a daily basis. These may include neighbours, family friends and partners or birth parents. Any one of these may be the 'significant' person for the child; these are the people that we as adults remember so vividly when recalling major influences in our childhood.

Early years staff are also significant for young children but they can never take the place of the family. However, if families and staff work closely together the child will benefit. This chapter explores the particular role of families in the young child's personal and social development. It also considers how early years staff can learn from families, support them and work closely with them.

FAMILIES MATTER

However it is made up and however imperfect, for a young child her family is critically important. The relationship between a young child and her immediate family is by its very nature personal and intense. Parents invest so much in their children because they matter to them. Lillian Katz emphasises the passionate relationship between parents and children, which inevitably involves a range of emotions including love and care, anger and frustration (2). Parents are, and should be biased in favour of their child. The Newsons, writing over twenty years ago, stressed how important this is.

> The best that community care can offer is impartiality – to be fair to every child in its care. But a developing personality needs more than that; it needs to know that to someone it matters more than other children; that someone will go to unreasonable lengths, not just reasonable ones, for its sake (3).

Throughout this book we see how adult models of behaviour impact on the way children think and behave. Long before a child starts at a nursery, her early personal experiences in her family will be a powerful influence on her attitudes to living and learning as one of a group.

Case study

Rick was used to making decisions about how to use his time in play and sharing with others while he stayed with a neighbour who was his childminder; his dad, a single parent, encouraged Rick to help with the daily chores of clearing up after meals and sorting clothes out for washing. Rick and his dad also talked about what they had done each day and sang songs and looked at books before bedtime. Dad took Rick and the neighbour's child swimming every Saturday morning. Rick was used to taking some responsibility and being treated with respect. At four Rick was confident and secure within himself.

Jez was seemingly also confident but at four years of age he was learning different lessons. His older brother shoplifted regularly and he taught Jez how to easily transfer a bar of chocolate from the shop counter into his pocket. When these episodes were recounted at home Jez's dad was tolerant and amused, saying that he 'had done the same as a kid'. Jez initially settled into a nursery well but was confused and angry when he was gently taken to task for taking toys and sweets from other children's pockets and lunchboxes.

We can be sure that the family provides the young child with an influential example of what things are important and interesting in life, how to conduct oneself and how to live with others. Most significantly, the ways in which the family members regard and treat the child provide her with a view of herself. The value of the home and family life in helping young children to develop emotional insights and to learn about right and wrong behaviour has already been discussed (see Chapters 4 and 6). In addition, studies have shown the significance of daily life at home where children listen, converse, interrupt, question and learn from members of their family (4, 5). The EPPE study found that the quality of the home environment was the key factor – in short, what parents do with their children is more important than who they are. For example, one of the numerous factors that seemed to lead to children developing higher intellectual, behaviour and social skills is the opportunity to have friends to play with at home (6). Charles Desforges' study for the DfES suggests that parental engagement can account for up to 12 per cent difference between the outcomes for individual children (7). Finally, even though family members work, or are at school, in the long-term most of them have a lot of contact with young children. Apart from those in full-time daycare, children spend the bulk of their time at home.

APPROACHES TO PARENTING

We have all had parents, and if and when we become parents, our experience of being 'parented' is probably the strongest influence on our attitudes and behaviour. This can work in two ways. Some people may, consciously or not, dismiss their parents' approach, believing that their own style of parenting is preferable to what they had. Others, deliberately or unconsciously, will base their style of child management on what they have known.

The Commission for Racial Equality reminds us that ethnic differences can also play a part in determining how children are brought up. It suggests, for example, that when different family members collect children at the end of the day, these arrangements may be condemned as failing to give a child sufficient continuity or security. This judgement may not take into account that these children come from families where several members, all of whom are trusted, care for them and share the responsibility for meeting them. 'There is no single "best" way to bring up a child, and there are as many differences in child-rearing practices among white and among black families as there are between them' (8).

Parents may also have different views between them about how to raise their children. Blamires reminds us of this with particular reference to those parents who have children with special educational needs. She suggests that when parents are faced with highly emotional issues and significant issues regarding provision for their child who has difficulties, they may think and react very differently (9).

Whatever parents believe about and do with their children, it cannot be assumed that this will coincide with what happens in early years settings. Unless staff and parents are aware of each other's beliefs and practices, they could be working at cross-purposes. Tina Bruce rightly points out that it is not for early childhood staff to tell families how to bring up their children or indeed to insist that the setting's way is the right way (10). However, both parties need to know about each other's views. Schools in particular, and now all nursery settings, take great pains to inform parents about their priorities and practices. It is less common, though, for settings to find out about what families consider to be important for their children. Surely this is important in order to meet the requirement in the QCA Curriculum Guidance for 'practitioners to show respect and understanding for the role of the parent in their child's education'. (11)

Case study

Four-year-old Wang-Hoi was waited on heavily by his three older sisters at home. They tidied away his toys and clothes and responded to all his needs. At the nursery Wang was required to learn to be self-sufficient; he found this very difficult and resisted all attempts to encourage him to fend for himself. When changing clothes to go outside, Wang would dangle his wellington boots in front of a member of staff; he became confused and cross when asked to tidy equipment away and started to hide at tidy-up time. It was not until his mother and teacher discussed Wang's behaviour that they became aware of each other's different expectations. After that they agreed that Wang should be helped to conform with nursery practices and his family would encourage him to 'do as his friends did'. However, his mother insisted that at home Wang would remain the 'little prince' and his sisters would continue to do things for him.

Comment

The nursery and the family respected each others viewpoint, although initially Wang-Hoi found it difficult to adjust to these dual expectations. However, he carefully observed what other children did. Three weeks later Wang joyfully pulled at one of the helper's hands and showed her how he had stacked bricks away. After that he appeared to have accepted the nursery routines and took great pleasure in learning how to cope for himself. Wang's mother laughed when she heard this development and reported that his dependent behaviour was unchanged at home.

PRESSURES ON PARENTS

Being a parent of a young child is an unmatched wonder; all parents experience the joy, excitement and fun of sharing life with a newly emerging personality. These are the precious rewards for the difficulties and challenges of parenting. It is tempting for professionals working for limited and planned periods of time with children who do not belong to them, to criticise what parents do and do not do. The reality is that bringing up children today is not easy even when one has the support of a loving partner or family, no financial worries and your children are loved and wanted. Being a parent can be a frightening, exhausting and lonely job if the parent concerned is young, inexperienced or alone. Most parents, whatever their circumstances, find the job a heady combination of delight and frustration and despair; some of the time it is simply tedious. Being a parent has always meant responsibilities; in a complex and fast-changing world the job has become even more demanding. Lillian Katz wrote that

> Many of the stresses of parenting stem from the wide range of choices, alternatives and options available to modern Americans in virtually every aspect of life. It is not difficult to imagine how many fewer arguments, heated discussions and reductions in demanding behaviour on the part of children would follow from having to live with minimal or even no choices in such things as food, television shows, toys, clothes, and so forth (12).

These stresses are evident in the UK and have certainly not lessened in the last twenty-five years. Parents are not helped by society where often we see dual standards. For example, there are pressures for all parents to contribute to the workforce, and yet the public finger is still pointed at parents who place their children in daycare in order to remain in employment. People like to see young children behaving properly in public; they complain that today's children are 'spoilt' by being given too much. And yet the media bombard children with messages about the latest toy that they should have; children are constantly beset by temptations in supermarkets where sweets and toys are set out on low-level shelves accessible to small hands. Busy parents, sometimes only too aware of the lack of time they can spend with their children, try to compensate by providing their children with material possessions whether it be sweets or other goodies advertised by the media as essential to make every little boy or girl happy. Asha Phillips, an experienced child psychiatrist, while sympathising with the parents' need to indulge their children, suggests that this may actually deprive a child of learning the important lesson in life of doing without. 'Without this ability, he (the child) will always be at the mercy of wants that can never all be satisfied. Having and discarding possessions easily also robs him of the feeling that anything is special' (13).

Parents invariably want the best for their children but sometimes their own circumstances prevent them from acting in their child's interests. Financial burdens can take their toll on young families; unemployment and poor housing can lead to adults having low self-esteem and seeing little point in striving for improved conditions for them and their children. Often these families live in areas with weak community links and general acceptance of anti-social behaviour. Many women are now more assertive about achieving what they want in life while men are less certain of their role in the home, particularly where they are no longer the breadwinner. In turn these circumstances can cause stress and family rows which are so damaging emotionally for young children. Family members may also suffer from poor mental health shown in symptoms of anxiety, depression and erratic behaviour. Masud Hoghughi, professor of parenting and child development, suggests that approximately 15 per cent of children, despite the efforts of schools, are drifting towards social exclusion. These children come from families who are beset with the problems described above.

> Such families are unable to provide 'good enough parenting'. Their children do not receive adequate physical, emotional and social nurture or protection from harm. They are brought up without any sensitive help to develop internal standards of behaviour; they acquire little idea of their own potential and how to fulfil it. These families do not have the motivation, resources or opportunity to help their children benefit from schooling (14).

There are then a minority of families who are most vulnerable. A wider group of parents cope with the turbulence and demands of separated partnerships, single parenthood and full-time jobs and careers. While none of these factors in themselves are necessarily harmful for children, they can mean that it becomes difficult at times for parents to provide their young child with the undivided attention and unqualified love that is needed. Constant disharmony between parents can be particularly disturbing. When parents stay together, but in an acrimonious relationship, children can be hurt emotionally. Goleman's work shows that the way a couple handle feelings between them will have a clear effect on their children, who from a young age are very sensitive to the feelings of people close to them (see Chapter 4). The alternative – parental separation – can also damage, particularly if children are faced with this as a fait accompli. If parents do decide to go their separate ways, even young children need to have matters explained to them and to feel involved in decisions if at all possible. This is proposed in a government consultation paper on parental separation (15). The challenges of being a parent go across all sectors of society; with grossly unequal distribution of work, children may be living with parents who, as Charles Handy describes, may have plenty of resources and no time, or plenty of time and no resources (16). Young children need access to both.

In wanting the best, some parents are very ambitious for their children to achieve academically. Tizard's study of young children in the inner city showed that virtually all mothers of children in reception classes interviewed wanted their children to have a better education than themselves (17). These positive aspirations are surely helpful for children who are likely to be better motivated by the encouragement and support from parents. However, in a culture of competition, aspirations can cause pressure. Eleven years ago, Tricia David pointed out how parents of young children had been made more anxious about their child's educational failure since the introduction of the National Curriculum (18). Since then there has been plenty of anecdotal evidence from parents and practitioners and from the results of national surveys to show that young children do feel pressurised by targets and having to undertake tests at as young as seven years (19). Some children are required to jump the first hurdle even earlier. Joan Clanchy, former head of North London Collegiate School, describes her observations of young parents in the park with their three-year-olds as they discuss selection procedure.

> They exchange data on the success rates of different primary schools and pre-preps, on which teachers they have decided are 'simply hopeless', on where to send Little Treasure for beginners' French, tennis, ballet, swimming, violin and, often, speech therapy … The time on the swing seems to be a rare moment of peace for some three-year-olds.

Clanchy's sympathy is for these parents who, she suggests, are driven by the message that early achievement is all that matters. However, she ends her article on a warning note: 'Most of the current small victims … will brush it (the pressure) all off and cope. But some will long resent the hurdles that are constantly erected in front of them and the hurt will go deep. Teenagers can exact a terrible revenge' (20).

Penelope Leach shares the concern for those young children whose parents are only interested in their offspring achieving things. She paints a picture of the child who comes to recognise that she is only loved for what she does rather than for who she is. Leach suggests that this has extremely damaging consequences for any child's self-esteem (21).

OFFERING SUPPORT FOR PARENTS

In the Open University publication, *Confident Parents, Confident Children*, the introduction states: 'Helping people become confident parents may be the best way to ensure that the next generation grows up to be capable and confident. There is more to parenting than just looking after a growing child. As adults we too "grow" as we become more experienced and skilful parents' (22). There is increasing acknowledgement that raising a child in today's world is not easy. Despite this it is only very recently that there has been anything done by the government to intervene in the family. Until 1997 there was very little support for childcare. Tricia David suggests that British family policy has been dominated by the belief that 'an Englishman's home is his castle' and that any state intervention has been thought to intrude on and erode family life (23). However, in recent years there have been moves to make more explicit the responsibilities that parents have for their children. The government's encouragement for home/school agreements, the published guidelines for children to spend time on homework and the recommended curfews for children out at night signal an official view that parents should assert their authority in the long-term interests of their children (24). This hard-headed approach is counter-balanced by a range of initiatives designed to offer practical help for families.

SOME MAJOR ACHIEVEMENTS

■ MORE AFFORDABLE CHILDCARE AND EDUCATION

Despite increasing government expenditure on childcare, the most important contributions come from parents, who in 2003–4 paid around £3 billion a year for their children to be cared for (25). Childcare is understandably particularly expensive for the youngest children. The Daycare Trust's 2004 childcare costs survey found that the typical cost for a full time nursery place for a child under two is £134 a week, or almost £7,000 a year (26). The cost of childcare continues to be a main concern for parents who wish or need to return to work or to train. Lone parents find it particularly difficult. Seventy-eight per cent of non-working lone mothers (and 63 per cent of non-working mothers) say they would prefer to go out to work or study if they had access to good quality, convenient, reliable and affordable childcare (27). Since 1998/9 public funding for childcare costs has steadily increased.

- The childcare element of the Working Tax Credit introduced in 2003 is available for parents on lower incomes. In April 2004 approximately 263,000 parents were benefiting from the tax credit.

- New Deal – childcare support is an approach to get parents with children under 16 years to return to work. There is advice from a personal adviser and funding available towards the costs of training, travel and childcare.

- Care to learn – childcare support for young parents. This scheme offers financial support for childcare to teenage parents who want to return to or continue their education or training. From August 2004 the scheme includes all young parents under 19 years.

- Childcare support for students gives priority to lone parents and those on low incomes.

- Employers' support towards childcare costs. As from 2005, changes in the existing tax and National Insurance exemptions will create more incentives for employers to support the provision of childcare for their employers (28).

MORE LINKED-UP CHILDCARE AND EDUCATION

Historically, social care, health, childcare and education have operated separately; too often parents have had to negotiate their way through different services, replicate information for different professionals, and often receive conflicting advice and support. The notion of bringing together agencies to support families in a unified way gained impetus in the late 1990s with the introduction of early excellence centres. By 2003 there were 107 centres. The Office for Standards in Education inspected a sample of excellence centres between 2001 and 2003, and the report highlighted the benefits for parents and families of effective integrated practice. Strengths included: very well managed services for family support, adult education and children with special educational needs. Several excellence centres were reported to provide excellent outreach services where workers take active steps to link with vulnerable and isolated families (29). Early excellence centres have paved the way for children's centres with their central agenda to pull services together to work for families.

IMPROVED OPTIONS FOR PARENTS DURING THEIR CHILDREN'S START IN LIFE

In 2003, new legislation on maternity and paternity leave and flexible working made it more possible financially for parents to stay at home with their children from birth to two years. Alternatively, if parents do return to work early, rather than look to group childcare, some prefer to have their babies and toddlers cared for in their own homes or to be with a childminder. From April 2005 this will be easier when parents will be able to claim tax credits for home-based childcare.

■ GUIDANCE FOR PARENTS TO SUPPORT THEIR CHILDREN

At times, being a parent can be difficult, distressing and confusing, particularly for young and inexperienced adults. General and specialist help may now be sought from five funded parent helplines (30). In addition, all new Sure Start ventures include a wide range of courses for parents to help them to understand and support their child's positive learning and behaviour. In centres where this type of support is well established, parents grow to lead discussion groups and meetings for themselves to share some of the problems and pleasures of bringing up young children. Government grants coupled with the skills and dedication of skilled trainers have had considerable impact on families. Early evaluations of work with parents in early excellence centres suggested that the lives of parents and children were genuinely transformed (31).

In summary, some parents are already receiving considerable financial help for childcare, others are gaining from easier access to different services, some parents of very young children are beginning to have choice of home care and the task of parenting is now recognised as worthy of support.

NURSERIES AND FAMILIES WORKING TOGETHER
■

Against this picture of government backing, the nursery and school have the responsibility and challenge of working with families practically on a daily basis. All parents should certainly benefit in some way from the scope of the government schemes, but it is the direct contact that they have with the practitioners that can influence the way in which parents feel supported to bring up their children. Similarly, the effect of the setting on what happens to children is largely dependent on what parents are prepared to condone or actively support.

Staff in nursery settings have traditionally understood the inextricable links that exist between the young child and her family. When Margaret McMillan opened her nursery school in Deptford in 1911, she was a firm believer that parents should take a strong role in all aspects of the work (32). Margaret McMillan was ahead of her time. Although over the years nursery settings have developed some exciting and innovative ways of working with families, it has taken most of the century to ensure that this work is beginning to become common practice. Even now, terms such as 'parental involvement', 'partnership' and 'open door policy' are used in a variety of contexts and to cover different purposes in discussing and documenting aspects of nursery life. Some nurseries and schools cautiously acknowledge that parents have a right of access but little more. Others are proud of the daily presence of a number of parents tackling different tasks with children during the nursery day. When one looks more closely, though, it is often difficult to see any planning or purpose to this involvement, other than the view that 'an extra pair of hands is always useful'. Yet other nurseries may have a detailed written policy for parents – a stack of paperwork may be produced to keep parents informed but this does little to generate the spirit of working together. Work with parents can take many forms and will be undertaken for different and legitimate reasons. These can include meeting the requirements of government in order to be eligible to receive nursery grants, or capitalising on parents' fundraising initiatives. However, if staff really wish to work closely with parents and share in the upbringing of their child during the critical early years, this requires an approach with three important ingredients:

- exchanging information with families
- tuning in together to understand children's personal and social development
- respecting and supporting families.

■ EXCHANGING INFORMATION WITH FAMILIES

All settings and schools are required by law to provide information for parents. The schedules used in inspections require that parents are informed about what is on offer to their children and that they also get to know what progress their child is making (33, 34). However, no legislation is likely to meet the real concerns any new parent will have when their child moves from home for the first time. These may include the worry of how their child will adapt to a new regime and environment; what will be expected of the child; how he or she will get on with other children and adults; how much the child will miss the familiarity of home life. When parents hand over their child they are demonstrating a great act of faith in the people who will be acting *in loco parentis*; in turn, they should be informed about what they regard as important. It is not surprising that their child's welfare, personal development and behaviour feature highly. When questioned about their views of a good school, a large group of parents regarded good relationships among parents, teachers and children, the aptitude and attitudes of staff, a positive ethos and good discipline as all important. By comparison the physical resources of the school and academic results were not so highly regarded (35). Essentially, although parents need to be given information about curriculum principles and practices, what they want is reassurance about the staff who will be working with their child. This has always been the case. In a transition study of children moving from home to pre-school, two-thirds of new parents interviewed said that they wanted to meet the nursery staff (36). It seems, then, that in order to respond to parents' real questions and concerns, the nursery must try to communicate the ways in which staff work with children, manage their behaviour and help them to develop good relationships. The member of staff who will be mainly responsible for the child should be available to talk informally; in this way parents will to get to know the staff member as a person and see how their child might relate to her or him.

Settings are also aware that the exchange of information is two way. Staff need to tap into the fund of knowledge that families have about their children; for example, how children have spent their time during the earliest years of life. Have they been used to being parted from parents – perhaps staying at granny's for occasional nights, spending weekdays with a childminder, or staying with a whole range of neighbours or friends on account of parents' busy social or work lives? The establishment of children's hotels means that some young children will have had the experience of being 'boarded out' while their parents are away. Contrast this with children who have never been separated from their parents until they join a nursery.

Parents potentially play the ace card when it comes to having information about their children's personal development. Because of the close relationship that they have, they know about their child as a person in a way that no outsider could. Parents and other close family members are aware when children feel pleased with themselves, when they are confident or fearful and when they are truly interested. Unless parents are estranged from their children they know how they tick and can predict how they might feel and act. They may not be aware of how their child is prepared for early literacy and numeracy but they have invaluable and intuitive knowledge about their child's personal attributes. It is unlikely that an adult working with children in a group setting will easily have access to such intimate information. Early years staff sorely need this information from parents in order to help them to form a rapid and meaningful bond with each child. The information can highlight children's behaviour in different situations and throw light on a completely different world of learning at home. It can complement the information that staff glean in the nursery or school and can contribute towards a three-dimensional view of each individual. Staff and parents need time together in order to encourage parents to respond to the question, 'tell me about your child'? Parents will respond if they are convinced that their knowledge is not only valuable for staff, but important to help their child to settle happily, to feel that she is known, and to make progress. 'The key ingredient to a successful meeting will be the teacher's evident and genuine interest in getting to know their child' (37).

TUNING IN TOGETHER TO YOUNG CHILDREN'S PERSONAL AND SOCIAL ■ DEVELOPMENT

Although parents and carers are likely to have unparalleled information about their children, there are times when they find it difficult to interpret why they behave as they do. As children struggle to find out and understand their world they become absorbed in certain activities and ask what appear to be bizarre questions. Parents love their children; they find many of their responses endearing and amusing as they repeat them to friends. However, they do not always recognise the significance or the underlying messages behind what they are describing. Early years staff who have been trained in child development may understand better the reasons for a child's actions; nevertheless, they only see a very limited slice of behaviour while the child is in the nursery. If staff and parents share their observations of children in the nursery and at home they will be in a stronger position to understand what is happening.

Chris Athey's work with parents in 1990 introduced them to their children's schemes of thought (see Chapter 5). The study aimed at gaining further information about how young children developed their understandings at home and in the nursery. Information was shared freely with parents who were asked to attend discussions and outings with their children. Parents were also asked to note what their children did and said at home. Chris Athey admits that initially parents treated the professionals as the experts. However, as they became better informed and gained confidence, parents were able to take an equal part with staff in tracing their children's patterns of understanding. Although parents' levels of understanding and participation in the project varied, Athey stresses that all became more and more interested in observing their child. 'Nothing gets under a parent's skin more quickly or permanently than the illumination of his or her own child's behaviour' (38).

Since then many nurseries have introduced parents to children's schemes of thought. The Pen Green Early Excellence Centre has worked particularly hard in this area and has produced a straightforward and illuminating introduction to schema which is designed to help parents become more aware of some of the reasons for what their children do and say (39).

■ RESPECTING AND SUPPORTING FAMILIES

Tricia David suggests that different and complex views of society have made the job of parenting particularly difficult (40). Perhaps it was always naive to assume that the biological fact of producing a child made for good parenting. However, now parents are urged to consider their responsibilities and to capitalise on their child's responses from birth to such a degree that the joy and spontaneity of the role is in danger of disappearing. Some parents are confused as they become steeped in literature which may offer conflicting advice; others are isolated and in danger of feeling desperate and powerless as a small child appears to take over their lives. By sharing the child with parents the early years setting is in a key position to help.

Adults can indulge children as a consequence of their own guilt. They may naturally be worried about the effects on a young child of family break-up or the lack of time that they spend with their child as a result of their long working hours. As a result they may condone behaviour which they would normally regard as unacceptable. This can lead a child to feeling in an uncomfortable position of holding power. Parents sometimes need reassurance that the best way of showing their love for their children is to establish clear rules. This helps young children to feel secure and cared for, while a lack of guidance can lead a young child to a freedom which is heady but frightening. Lillian Katz reminds us that it is not so much the different family pattern that the child grows up with that will affect her psychological and social development, as the way in which she regards that arrangement (41).

Despite the unique role that they have, parents are at least very modest about their influence, and in some cases still remain unaware of how essential they are to their children's personal growth. Perhaps the one most important thing that staff, particularly key persons, can offer all parents is to help them recognise this.

Work with families is complex and sometimes frustrating. Despite this, as Edwards points out, many nursery staff see this aspect of their work as a long-term investment (42). If parents are respected, supported and informed during the earliest years of their child's education, they are likely to be stronger parents as their child grows older, and their parenting skills will also be used with younger children in the family.

Summary

Whatever form a family may take, it is immensely important for each child; the intensity of family relationships provides a powerful influence on the child's view of herself and how she should behave. Parents will have their own views about bringing up their children and these may not always coincide with the aims of the nursery. However, if each party knows where the other stands, this is more likely to lead to shared tolerance and respect.

If early years settings are to support parents, they need to fully acknowledge the pressures of parenthood; these can arise as a result of the changes in and expectations of society including family turbulence, the demands of work and lack of money. Although recent government initiatives are providing an infrastructure and increased funding to help families, the successful nurturing of young children is largely dependent on practitioners and parents working closely together on a day-to-day basis.

Practical suggestions

Share respective standpoints about young children's personal and social development
- Through informal chats/discussions/seminars (whatever term is likely to appeal to your family group), invite parents and carers to share their views about how they would like their children to develop, e.g. how important is it for their children to become self-confident, assertive, sensitive, competitive, obedient, self-critical?
- Ensure that families are clearly informed about the nursery's aims for fostering personal and social development.
- You may never reach a full consensus but open discussion can help all parties to reflect on their views.

Help families to support their children in personal and social development
When you have established a trusting relationship with parents it may be helpful if you encourage them to consider some of the following questions (it is extremely important that these are offered in a spirit of mutual discussion and that any suggestion of 'testing' parents is avoided):
- *Helping confidence.* How carefully do you listen to what your child is telling you? How do you show that you respect (i) your child's views (ii) your child's drawings/paintings/models? How do you show your child that she is very special?
- *Supporting behaviour.* How consistent are you in how you expect your child to behave? When are you likely to be too hard on your child?

When are you likely to be over-indulgent? What rules are non-negotiable? How often do you praise/give attention to your child when she is behaving well?

- *Aiding independence.* How well do you encourage your child to be personally independent, e.g. dressing/washing/going to the lavatory? How much choice does your child have in daily routines, e.g. choosing a cereal for breakfast, clothes to wear, which walk to take? What decisions does your child have in how she uses her time at home?

- *Developing social skills.* How many other adults and children does your child meet during the week? How often do you invite other children to play with your child at home? How often does your child visit other people's homes?

- *Encouraging tolerance and interest in others.* How well does your own social circle reflect a mix of people from different backgrounds and cultures? How do you help your child to learn about how other people are different and similar, e.g. from within your neighbourhood, through your family accommodating foreign students, from books, pictures and television?

- *Encouraging care for the environment.* How do you help your child care for growing things, e.g. through having her own patch of garden/window box, providing food for the birds, helping to care for a pet? How do you help them to become responsible for keeping the environment tidy, e.g. through picking up litter in the park, on camping holidays?

- *Priority.* How much of your time do you show that you really enjoy being with your child?

Set up communication links to suit parents

- Parents' very different circumstances will influence the way in which they will wish to exchange information about their child with the nursery. For example, some will prefer a daily and informal personal contact with their child's early years practitioner; others will relish completing a home diary or having a visit at home. It is helpful if the nursery makes clear that there are a number of options. The most effective link will have good regard to family preferences.

> **Professional questions**
> 1. How much do you know about parents' aspirations for their children?
> 2. How well do you manage to convince all your parents of their importance to their children?
> 3. How do you show parents that you use the information they share with you about their children?
> 4. How do know that parents are fully satisfied with what you offer their children?

REFERENCES

1. Pascal, C. (1998) Accounting Early for Life-Long Learning. Lecture at Early Years Dorset Conference, Dorchester, July.
2. Katz, L. (1995) *Talks with Teachers of Young Children*. Norwood, NJ: Ablex.
3. Newson, J. and Newson, E. (1976) *Seven Years Old in the Home Environment*. London: Allen and Unwin.
4. Tizard, B. and Hughes, M. (1984) *Young Children Learning*. London: Fontana.
5. Wells, G. (1984) *Language Development in the Pre-School Years*. Cambridge: Cambridge University Press.
6. Sylva, K., Melhuish, M., Sammons, P., Siraj-Blatchford, I., Taggart, B, and Elliot, K. (2003) *The Effective Provision of Pre-school Education (EPPE) Project: Summary of Findings*. Institute of Education, University of London.
7. Desforges, C. and Abouchaar, A. (2003) *The Impact of Parental Involvement on Pupil Achievement*. DfES Report 433.
8. Commission for Racial Equality (1989) *From Cradle to School: A Practical Guide to Race Equality and Childcare*. London: CRE, pp. 22–3.
9. Blamires, M., Robertson, C. and Blamires, J. (1997) *Parent-Teacher Partnership: Practical Approaches to Meeting Special Educational Needs*. London: David Fulton.
10. Bruce, T. (1997) *Early Childhood Education*. London: Hodder & Stoughton.
11. QCA (2000) *Curriculum Guidance for the Foundation Stage*. London: QCA/DfES, p. 9.
12. Katz, L. (1995) op. cit. (note 2), p. 162.
13. Phillips, A. (1999) How to raise a confident child, *The Times*, 18 February, p. 21.
14. Hoghughi, M. (1999) Families hold the key, *TES*, 12 February, p. 2.
15. DfES (2004) *Parental Separation: Children's Needs and Parents' Responsibilities*. www.dfes/gov.uk/childrensneeds.
16. Handy, C. (1994) *The Empty Raincoat: Making Sense of the Future*. London: Hutchinson.
17. Tizard, B., Blatchford, P., Burke, J., Clare, E. and Plewis, J. (1988) *Young Children in the Inner City*. Hove and London: Lawrence Erlbaum Associates.
18. David, T. (ed.) (1993) *Educating our Youngest Children: European Perspectives*.

London: Paul Chapman.

19. Northern, S. (2003). Play, *Times Educational Supplement*, 2 April, p. 7.

20. Clanchy, I. (1998) I'm late! I'm late! I'm only three, but I must achieve, *Independent*, 8 October.

21. Leach, P. (1994) *Children First*. London: Michael Joseph.

22. Open University Community Education Pack (1997) *Confident Parents, Confident Children*. Milton Keynes: Open University Press.

23. David, T. (ed.) (1999) *Young Children Learning*. London: Paul Chapman, p. 209.

24. DfEE (1997) *Excellence in Schools*. London: Stationery Office, pp. 58–9.

25. National Audit Office (2004) *Early Years Progress in Developing High Quality Childcare and Education Accessible to All*. London: Stationery Office.

26. Moss, P. (2004) *A New Era for Universal Childcare. Childcare and Early Years Services in 2004*. London: Daycare Trust, p. 4.

27. Woodland, S., Miller, M. and Tipping, S. (2002) *Repeat Study of Parents' Demand for Childcare*. DfES Research Report 348.

28. Moss, P. (2004) op. cit. (note 26), p. 9.

29. OfSTED (2004) *Children at the Centre: an Evaluation of Early Excellence Centres*, London: OfSTED.

30. DfES (2004) *Funds for Parents Helplines*.
    www.dfes.gov.uk/pns/DisplayPN.cg?pn id= 20040121

31. Bertram, T and Pascal, C. (1999) *Early Excellence Centres: First Findings*. London: DfEE.

32. Dowling, M. (1992) *Education 3–5*. London: Paul Chapman, p. 6.

33. OfSTED (2003) *The OfSTED Handbook and Guidance on the Inspection of Nursery and Primary Schools*. London: Stationery Office.

34. OfSTED (1998) *The OfSTED Handbook and Guidance on the Inspection of Nursery Education in the Private, Voluntary and Independent Sectors*. London: Stationery Office.

35. Hughes, M., Wilkeley, E. and Nash, T. (1994) Parents' choice of school, in A. Pollard and E. Bourne (eds), *Teaching and Learning in the Primary School*. London: Routledge/Open University.

36. Blatchford, P., Battle, S. and Mays, J. (1982) *The First Transition: Home to Pre-School*. Slough: NFER/Nelson.

37. Dowling, M. (1995) *Starting School at Four: A Joint Endeavour*. London: Paul Chapman, p. 148.

38. Athey, C. (1990) *Young Children Thinking*. London: Paul Chapman, p. 66.

39. Mairs, K. (1990) *A Schema Booklet for Parents*. (Obtainable from the Pen Green Centre, Corby, Northants.)

40. David, T. (1995) Being a parent of a four-year-old: pleasure and pain, in T. David and C. Nutbrown (eds), *Four-Year-Olds in School? Learning Properly*. OMEP UK.

41. Katz, L. (1995) op. cit. (note 2).

42. Edwards, E. and Knight, P. (1994) *Effective Early Years Education*. Buckingham: Open University Press, p. 111.

CHAPTER ELEVEN

Some Important Ingredients

In reviewing most curriculum aspects there are usually resource requirements, and often implications for buying more things. When promoting
personal, social and emotional development it is rather different.
Nurturing young children's personal growth is primarily dependent on
practitioners who are both disposed to do this work and skilled in doing it.
These staff find ways to strengthen children's resilience and start them on
the road to becoming good citizens. Of course this does not happen in a
vacuum and some effective methods and activities to achieve this have
been highlighted in the book. In this concluding chapter the focus is on
more powerful ways of supporting children's personal development
through books, storytelling and fantasy play. Although there are a few suggestions for making purchases, the emphasis is more on how they are used.
And this is in the hands of the practitioner.

THE INFLUENCE OF BOOKS AND STORIES

Literature plays a very important role in personal development for most
people. We read books for relaxation, comfort and enlightenment. Reading
a good book can reduce stress; we can often identify with a character and
so recognise motives for our actions, or begin to understand how others
operate. Stories also stick in the mind. We may listen to a lecture and strain
to remember the facts but we will have no difficulty in remembering illustrations or anecdotes. We often tell ourselves a story as a way of making
sense of a situation, or reliving an experience.

For young children books and stories play an even more crucial role. As we
have seen, children have powerful feelings but may not be able fully to
understand or articulate them – an appropriate story may help put their
feelings into words and pictures. Cathy Nutbrown confirms this: 'Many
books can help to support children's emotional development, reflecting
and affirming their feelings by challenging their thinking and presenting

characters with different emotions including fear, sadness, excitement, love and care' (1).

Literature also plays a very important role in teaching. Books can help to introduce or reinforce for children important issues such as fairness, other ways of living and care for the environment. Of course, children need to experience these issues for themselves. However, if they have had only four or five years' experience of life, this first-hand knowledge will be limited; through stories and pictures they will extend and clarify what they are just beginning to know for themselves.

THE CONTEXT FOR SHARING BOOKS AND STORIES

At the beginning of the twenty-first century there is a wealth of information available for young children through television, film and computerised programmes. Some would consider that the attraction of sophisticated media approaches can mean that books pall in comparison. However, the power of story is age-old; it is simple, immediate and the method can be used flexibly. Young children will respond best if they share books and listen to stories with people they care for and in a comfortable environment. A sleepy young child knows that she is loved and secure when she shares a familiar storybook at bedtime while cuddling up to her parent or carer. At other times children can enter different worlds and experience excitement and danger in the safety of a group story. In a nursery setting the book area needs to tempt young children into selecting and tasting books for themselves and sharing them with friends. Many nursery settings transform their book areas into beautiful and imaginative spaces using furniture and soft furnishings and pictures. The illusion of privacy can be created through a den or cave. The continual presence of an adult in the book area can provide a lap for those children who most need this physical contact. Stories can also be offered 'on demand' and shared informally with small groups; in these cases children will select their choice of book rather than receiving one selected by the adult, which is more likely to happen in a set storytelling session. If children are offered this type of provision and interaction then books come to offer much more than development in literacy. Stories will be associated with feelings of pleasure, intimacy and sharing thoughts, ideas and memories with others.

ENCOURAGING A PERSONAL RESPONSE FROM CHILDREN

Children invariably listen with rapt attention to a well-read story. Despite this, it takes careful planning to find out how much they have understood and what ideas they have about the characters and issues, and also to help them make links with their own experiences.

The Development Education Centre in Birmingham (2) introduced a range of ways to help children respond to stories. The suggestions below draw on some of this work.

- *Asking questions about the story*: sensitive questions from the adult can encourage children to share reactions and help them think about specific aspects of the story, e.g. I wonder how that little boy felt when he lost his cat?

- *Hiding the pictures*: this is best carried out in a small group with older nursery and reception age children. The adult first reads the story without revealing the pictures but asks the children to think about the characters and describe or draw them. The children's descriptions and pictures can then be compared with the book illustrations.

- *Using speech bubbles*: this helps older children to empathise with the character. The story must encourage children to create their own dialogue. Photocopy and enlarge the pages of the story that encourage speech – draw a speech bubble coming out of the mouth of the character. The children can then discuss what they think the character is saying and the adult can scribe it in the speech bubble.

- *Drawing pictures*: children are asked to draw their favourite part of the story. Younger children may only be interested in talking about what they enjoyed; they may also need help to recall different aspects of the story. Older children's drawings will indicate what they think is most important.

- *Using visual aids*: storytelling can also involve the use of props, including puppets, miniature figures, models or figures on a magnetic board. If the adult initially demonstrates their use, children will enjoy using these to accompany the story.

Practitioners will all have a core of favourite 'situation' books which they call on as a resource to help children at critical times in their lives. These books are best read with a small group, creating an atmosphere of intimacy. Children' body language and comments will signal if the story has struck a cord as in these few examples:

1. *Sophie and the New Baby* by Catherine and Lawrence

Anholt (3). Sophie is very excited when she is told that there is to be a new baby in the family, but when the baby is born things are different. It takes time for Sophie to grow to love the baby and to enjoy being a big sister.

The story leads naturally into talk about how children feel about their position in family relationships. Bruno had recently had a new sister and was reluctant to leave his mum every morning to come to the nursery. Despite encouraging questions from staff, Bruno refused to talk about his new baby sister. Bruno listened to the story of Sophie carefully and without comment. He then chose to paint and announced that this was a picture for his new sister and he was going to take it home for her.

2. *Once There Were Giants* by Martin Waddell (4). At the start of the story there is a family gathering around a new baby. The story follows the child as she grows, with the adult 'giants' shown on each page. The story ends almost as it started, but this time the baby has become one of the 'giants'; the new baby in the picture is her child. The story helps four- and five-year-olds deal with change and a sense of belonging in a family.

Five-year-old Iram listened to the story on three occasions, entranced but without commenting. One morning he picked up the book and commented, 'I know about that book now. It's the way you start to grow and then it starts all over again.'

3. *Badger's Parting Gift* by Susan Varley (5). The animals grieve when old badger dies. However, they find that their friend has left them some wonderful gifts of skills that he taught them – these will always remain. They celebrate these in memory of their friend. A gentle and positive introduction to bereavement. Given an opportunity, children are often keen to share their experiences of death.

Daniel's granny had always lived with him; now she was very ill and in pain. Daniel had visited her in hospital but had not mentioned it at school. After listening to Badger's final painless and joyful journey down the long tunnel, Daniel turned to his teacher and said quietly and confidently, 'My gran's going to be like that.'

STORYTELLING

Some believe that storytelling is the oldest profession; certainly there is a renewal of interest in this art and storytellers are springing up over the country. Long before books, stories were told to young children as a way of introducing them to the world; it is easier to remember a story than rational explanations of events. The power of storytelling is immense: there is close contact between the teller and the audience, and a warm bond can be established. Children have no visual distractions; rather than providing ready-made images it encourages them to make pictures in their heads, to visualise and imagine. Stories offer children phrases and words that literally 'catch' the ear and these they store to use later in their own stories and play. In stories where there are no right or wrong interpretations, children make their own moral judgements. Although most issues lend themselves to a story, traditional tales and fables contain particular treasure for personal development, gathered from the wisdom of many generations.

While all practitioners accept that reading stories to children is part of their job, some are less confident in telling stories. And yet everyone has the potential to become a compelling storyteller. Some of the important ingredients are to:

- create atmosphere: put on a story cloak, long gloves or hat to denote that you are the storyteller; sit on a special chair, draw children around you and invite them to sit on a special story floor covering

- develop a recognised story starter: 'Are you ready for a story? Are your ears open to listen? Well, here we go.'

- build in repetition: the more that children get to know key phrases in a story, the more they can participate and maintain their enjoyment and concentration

- build in sound effects: use your voice to the full – raise it, deepen it and use a whisper for good effect. Use one or two untuned percussion instruments to create different noises

- inspire: children, particularly the older ones, are not inspired by the bland and cosy but sometimes by what is a little disturbing. Once the group has got used to the conventions of storytelling and are well settled into the class you may judge that it is time to be a little more robust with stories; a little gratuitous fear can challenge thinking to the full. 'Don't go down into the woods today Grandad' warned Peter, 'there may be a wolf there … '. This enthralling introduction to *Peter and the Wolf* immediately draws children into the story

- build in a predictable ending to denote that story time is over: 'and now my story is ended'.

Although storytellers will have a repertoire of tales which they know back to front, stories can also be impromptu and tailor-made to meet a particular need. Skilled practitioners turn daily events into stories. Through observing children closely, staff will quickly identify what concerns them. Observations will reveal issues about children making and breaking friendships, feeling insecure about new situations or savouring pleasurable experiences. It may be insensitive and unhelpful to intervene at the time or even to refer directly to the observed behaviour, but a story can effectively pick up on the issue. Without a written story line to follow the 'invented' story can be more easily adapted to meet children's particular interests and may be personalised, 'This is a story for Ahmed because it is his birthday'. Any child will warm to this gift. Stories which start 'When I was little … ' never fail to interest children. They are fascinated to learn that loved adults once experienced the dilemmas, joys and anxieties that they are faced with. The power of these stories again stresses the important model offered by the adult.

CHILDREN'S STORIES AND FANTASY PLAY

We all have a story to tell but young children slip into stories like fish into water. With increasing use of language children start to place their world into an understandable framework by using social scripts to describe daily events that they experience. This is the beginning of storying. While three-year-old Emily was with her childminder she had watched a video of Mickey Mouse with immense enjoyment. She was also aware that when she was at the childminder's her mother had been having driving lessons and had very recently passed her driving test. Emma lived by the coast where she often watched a Punch and Judy show with her mother during the summer months. Emma skilfully drew on all of these experiences as she portrayed a future scenario for herself.

> When I'm big I'm going to have a Mickey Mouse car and Mickey Mouse sunglasses and a Mickey Mouse lipstick. You can come in my car and sit in the front, but you must do up your seat belt. But first I must have driving lessons, lots and lots – to pass my test. We shall go … go to Punch and Judy. I like Mr Punch, but not the devil, he frightens me.

Scripts drawn from children's own experiences become embellished by stories they have heard and TV programmes and videos they have seen. They put these ideas into their script, experimenting with characters, settings and events. Young children's feet are not chained to the ground by common sense and their imaginations roam into far flung places. Although scripts are a form of story, they are essentially timeless accounts of personal experience; this is in contrast to stories which are told in the past tense, involve specific characters and have some sort of a beginning and end. Initially young children find this type of storytelling difficult and their stories will be relatively undeveloped. However, if they have plenty of adult models and learn that storytelling is a way of sharing things that are in their heads, children's stories will, over time, become more detailed and sequenced. Children's own stories are a valuable means of tuning in to their beliefs and concerns as Vivian Paley the eminent nursery teacher and author found. Vivian had always made storytelling a regular part of her programme, but initially had little success with children sharing their stories. One day when Wally had spent a session in the 'time out' chair because he was always in trouble, Vivian, hoping to interest him, asked if he would like to write a story. When Wally protested that he could not write yet, Vivian offered to write the story down for him. Wally told her a story about a trouble-making dinosaur that ransacked a city and was put in jail. The story ended happily as the dinosaur promised to be good and when he was released from jail his mother was waiting for him (6).

Vivian Paley soon built her practice around storytelling and drama with young children. Throughout her teaching career she has been alert to the 'plots' that emerge from children's play. By highlighting these stories, offering to write them down and encouraging children to re-enact them, Vivian Paley enabled her children to communicate what was important to them. For her, drama has been an essential tool in examining the social and emotional worlds that are the foundations of learning (7). Children will rehearse their scripts and later their stories in dramatic play by themselves or with others, when the play becomes socio-dramatic. Through their play children use what they know or are interested in (their schema) and adapt or elaborate upon this information. Again the important factor is that the child is in charge of what happens. Erikson emphasises that socio-dramatic play helps children to cope with big issues in life such as disappointment, loneliness and anger (8).

Young children need regular and frequent opportunities to play, both for sheer pleasure and for more serious reasons as suggested by Singer and

Singer: 'Imaginative play is fun, but in the midst of the joys of making believe, children may also be preparing for the reality of more effective lives' (9). Practitioners take account of both these aspects when they provide a context for play which gives plenty of scope for children's own initiatives.

Mary Jane Drummond describes children's imaginative play as 'allowing them to pass through invisible doorways into alternative worlds' (10). Nevertheless, while most children are natural players, some find it more difficult to 'pretend' and enter the world of fantasy. In these cases the adult has to take a more central role and find a way of enabling all to enter through the doorways. Children can be encouraged to build stories and recognise that even their simplest recount can be developed creatively. Sometimes it is helpful to provide them with tangible objects as story props. These are presented in story bags, boxes or attractively wrapped parcels. Children, in turn, pull an object out of a container or discover it in each layer of parcel wrapping. With help they knit the items into a story. The adult helps to link the story together, but the most important aspect is not the outcome but the experience of being imaginative together. Vivian Paley suggests that Lev Vygotsky's assertion that, in play a child stands taller than himself, above his age and normal behaviour, can also apply to practitioners as they listen and observe children and try to make sense of their play and storytelling (11) (See Chapter 1).

All practitioners recognise that children need play but the issue of super-hero play which occurs with boys taxes many staff. In some settings weapon and war play is banned usually because of the fear that such play encourages violence and aggression. In reality children continue their play and will use weapons surreptitiously. In one Camden nursery practitioners recognised that encouraging children to be deceitful was not good practice; moreover the ban on weapon play was to ignore and override what was important for children. When the nursery made a conscious decision to accept the play they were surprised to find that the level of aggression was reduced, interest in violent play lessened and the group ethos was more relaxed (12). The case study from Tachbrook Nursery (Chapter 5) offers an impressive example of how children can grow personally when their super-hero play is built on and supported.

Paley sums up beautifully the protection that pretending affords. 'Fantasy of course is the first line of defense against every sort of fear and in fantasy play the children discover the value of peer support as they dare to face and put the beanstalk to the test' (13).

YOURSELVES

Throughout this book the influence of modelling has been stressed. Young children are affected so strongly by the way in which practitioners behave, not only what they say or do – these are the outward signs; they also tune into the way in which adults close to them think and feel. In fostering young children's personal, social and emotional development staff need to invest more of themselves than in any other aspect of work.

This final section is directed at the nature of the work and the qualities required to succeed as a high-quality practitioner.

SELF-REFLECTION

We all have our beliefs, values and attitudes which are based on our own experiences and which have served us well enough in our lives. When working with children and young families from a variety of backgrounds and cultures, these beliefs and assumptions may be shaken. Parents and carers may have very different ways of conducting their lives which are outside the experience of an early years practitioner. Children may not behave as they expect or respond to the practitioner's overtures. Colleagues may have different views about ways of caring for and educating children. All this can be discomforting, shake self-confidence and practitioners can become defensive. To avoid these negative feelings staff need to be prepared to be open-minded, re-examine what they believe, learn from others and sometimes adapt attitudes in the light of what they have learned. Once they are brave enough to reflect and learn from experience, practitioners can see how this helps them to grow professionally when they broaden, clarify and strengthen the underpinning for their work.

FLEXIBILITY

One of the joys of working with young children and their families is that it is dynamic. Edgington sums up the work as 'unpredictable and the best laid plans have a habit of going entirely awry'. She also points out that if control and predictability are what makes you feel comfortable it is likely that such an adult will find working in the early years threatening (14). Practitioners need to have clear planned intentions for what they offer but must be prepared to adapt, or even abandon, plans in order to follow children's thinking and go with the tide of their motivation.

EMOTIONAL MATURITY

Involvement with young families and vulnerable children can mean sometimes dealing with powerful and harrowing issues such as family break-up and child abuse. Natural responses are to feel disturbed, upset, angry and frustrated. It is not easy to handle these emotions but practitioners need to learn the importance of remaining outwardly calm and in control, being able to cope with complexity.

EMPATHY

Goleman describes empathy as our 'social radar' (15). Effective practitioners who have this are able to see into a child's world and, when permitted, enter it. They tune into the dilemmas experienced by families and parents are aware that their feelings are acknowledged and respected. An empathetic response cannot in itself solve problems but it can help a person to feel that they are not alone. Goleman suggests that highly developed empathy goes even further than this by recognising the issues or concerns that lie behind another's feelings. When this happens it becomes possible for practitioners to offer families more tangible support.

OPTIMISM

Practitioners work with children who have had different starts in life and who come into a setting at different stages of development. The exciting thing is that, although we can see what a child achieves today, we can never be sure of the potential she has for tomorrow. This must be a cause for optimism. Practitioners know that their work can make a difference. They understand that, regardless of children's different abilities, given the right climate (described in this book) their personal growth will flourish and this helps progress in all other aspects of their lives.

COMMUNICATION

The need for practitioners to form close relationships with young children is most powerfully demonstrated in the role of the key person (see Chapter 1). Elinor Goldschmied and Sonia Jackson draw a parallel with our own needs for close and intimate contacts

> Why should it be worth the time and trouble to introduce a key person system in a nursery where this has not been the practice? ... thinking of our own relationships as adults may give us some answers.
>
> Most of us have, or would like to have, a special relationship with some person on whom we can rely, a relationship that is significant and precious to us. If we are parted from that person we have ways of preserving continuity even through long separations. We use telephone, letters, photographs, recollections, dreams and fantasies to keep alive the comfort, which we derive from such human relationships. When we lose them, we experience sadness and often deep feelings of despair. If we look back we may recall important people in our early lives who, though they are not there in person, give continuity and significance to how we conduct our present lives (16).

The ability to read young children's behaviour and to communicate with them is at the basis of successful practice. It is expressed so well in Colin Tevarthen's description of being able to 'dance with the children' (17). This implies harmony, recognising the steps that the child is taking, being able to anticipate the next move and adapting ones response accordingly.

Communication, of course, is so much more than talking or writing. Very young children are not concerned so much with words as with action. They represent and communicate their experiences through their bodies (Chapters 5 and 9) and the experienced practitioner will tune into these expressions. Sign language gives children with speech and language difficulties access to communication. Where all adults and children are able to sign, the setting becomes more inclusive. And non-verbal communication does not stop once we can talk. Adults well know that the strong emotions of love and cold anger can be expressed clearly without words. Young children also understand the messages we give them through expression and gesture. Scot's mum abruptly left the family home at the weekend following a blazing row with her partner. Scott arrived at the nursery on Monday subdued and listless. The teacher felt that words would not be helpful at this stage; instead she kept close contact with Scot throughout the session through smiles and eye contact in group times; when going outside she volunteered her hand to Scot who (unusual for him) grasped it and continued to hold it, refusing offers from others to play with them. The next day, Scot's auntie thanked the teacher for her care and attention. Scott had apparently told her that, 'my teacher knows I'm sad and she said she loves me'.

Working with young children is often hard and unremitting; it requires huge physical and emotional energy, intellectual endeavour and it can easily lead to burnout. This job is not for the faint-hearted. And yet the commitment, creativity and passion tangible in good practitioners is there because they have the privilege of sharing the world of childhood and accompanying children in their early stages of growing up.

REFERENCES

1. Nutbrown, C. (1994) *Threads of Thinking*. London: Paul Chapman, p. 93.
2. The Development Education Centre Birmingham (1991) *Start with a Story: Supporting Young Children's Exploration of Issues*. Gillett Centre, 998 Bristol Road, Selly Oak, Birmingham B29 6LE.
3. Anholt, C. and Anholt, L. (1995) *Sophie and the New Baby*. London: Orchard Books.
4. Waddell, M. (1989) *Once There Were Giants*. London: Walker Books.
5. Varley, S. (1998) *Badger's Parting Gift*. London: Picture Lions.

6. Paley, V. (1981) *Wally's Stories*. Cambridge, MA, and London: Harvard University Press.
7. Paley, V. (2004) A *Child's Work*. Chicago, IL: University of Chicago Press.
8. Erikson, E. (1965) *Childhood and Society*. Harmondsworth: Penguin Books.
9. Singer, D. and Singer, J. (1990) *The House of Make Believe*. Cambridge, MA: Harvard University Press, p. 152.
10. Drummond, M.J. (1999) Another way of seeing: perceptions of play in a Steiner kindergarten, in L. Abbott and H. Moylett (eds), *Early Education Transformed*, London: Falmer Press, p. 59.
11. Paley, V. (2004) op. cit. (note 7) p. 82.
12. Holland, P. (2003) War, weapon and superhero play: a challenge to zero tolerance. Summary of a paper presented at Tower hamlets Early Years Conference, 6 June.
13. Paley, V. (1990) *The Boy Who Would be a Helicoptor*. Chicago, IL: University of Chicago Press, p. 162.
14. Edgington, M. (2004) *The Foundation Stage Teacher in Action*. London: Paul Chapman, p. 4.
15. Goleman, D. (1998) *Working with Emotional Intelligence*. London: Bloomsbury, p. 133.
16. Goldschmied, E. and Jackson, S. (1994) *People under Three: Young Children in Day Care*. London: Routledge.
17. Trevarthen, C. (1992) An infant's motives for thinking and speaking, in A.H. Wold (ed.), *The Dialogical Alternative*, Oxford: Oxford University Press.

INDEX